RUSSIA WITHOUT STALIN:
The Emerging Pattern

Also by Edward Crankshaw:

RUSSIA AND THE RUSSIANS
CRACKS IN THE KREMLIN WALL
GESTAPO: INSTRUMENT OF TYRANNY

RUSSIA
WITHOUT STALIN:

The Emerging Pattern

Edward Crankshaw

NEW YORK · THE VIKING PRESS · 1956

ACKNOWLEDGMENTS

I should like to thank the editors of *The Observer*, the *Atlantic Monthly*, and the *Virginia Quarterly Review* for permission to incorporate certain passages which have already appeared in their pages.

E.C.

CONTENTS

RUSSIA WITHOUT STALIN:

The Emerging Pattern

INTRODUCTION:
THE LEGACY OF STALIN

THIS book was started in the last months of 1955 after my first visit to the Soviet Union in a number of years. The greater part of it was written before the critical Congress of the Communist Party of the Soviet Union (the Twentieth Party Congress), which took place in February 1956. In the later chapters I was able to take account of the published reports of the speeches at that Congress. The whole book was finished, however, before the world was told about Khrushchev's remarkable denunciation of Stalin in secret session on the last day of the Congress. I have not thought it necessary to add an account of this occasion. It was a logical, though curiously dramatic, development of certain trends examined in the following pages. I do not wish to alter anything I have written in the light of it, and it seems to me to confirm the general argument of this book quite decisively. The most interesting aspect of the whole affair is the effect on the youth of the Soviet Union. For the young brought up to believe all their lives in Stalin as the great, the infallible teacher and leader, the shock must have been profound and at the same time complex in its effects. Those effects have not yet had time to show.

When Stalin died—mysteriously, as he had lived—on the night of March 5, 1953, he left behind him no will or testament that was ever published. He left behind him a group of men, his closest colleagues, whose working lives had been spent in the shadow of his genius. This group had to sort itself out into some sort of order and at the same time apply itself intelligently and effectively to the complex and daunting problems involved in governing a society created by an autocrat and until then held together and run by him on arbitrary lines. Their task was all

1

the more difficult because during the last years of his life the dictator had been losing his grip. In the weeks before his death the machinery of state had run wild; and with the indictment of the unfortunate Kremlin doctors and the "exposure" of a standing conspiracy involving high personages unnamed, the Soviet Union had been allowed to drift to the very brink of a new Terror, which seemed about to repeat the excesses of the monstrous purges of the middle thirties.

Generations may pass before the world knows the true circumstances of Stalin's death, or what lay behind the "doctors' plot." Familiarity with Russian history suggests a dozen possibilities. For example, it would not be in the least surprising to learn that the mounting hysteria of those last weeks represented the convulsive efforts of the ailing tyrant to reassert himself and crush the pretensions of ambitious or dissenting colleagues; or that, to forestall this action, some of these colleagues took it upon themselves to hasten their master's end. We do not know. But speculation of that kind is in order and, indeed, inevitable. Without looking to Tsarist history for precedents, which abound, we have only to reflect on the formal and solemn charges brought so short a time before against the Kremlin doctors (still awaiting trial when Stalin died), who were accused of murdering Zhdanov and Shcherbakov and of plotting to murder a representative section of the Soviet higher command—at whose instigation it was never revealed, because Stalin himself was dead before they could be tried. In a country where this sort of thing can happen, everything is possible and the worst is probable.

The times were unsettled indeed, and dangerous, for Stalin's successors, because any new upheaval within the Soviet Union would tend to disrupt internally a society already strained nearly to the limit by the demands of the external cold war. But the group of Stalin's "closest colleagues" faced these problems and, with only one major casualty, came through. They are still faced with many serious problems, including one of extreme stubbornness which could yet ruin their regime. But it is a remarkable achievement for these men to have moved as far as they have, and it is not to be underrated. It is not as though they had unlimited freedom of action to adapt themselves to changing facts of life. Inhibited by the inertia of Soviet society on the one hand, and, on the other, by the ideological chains which they themselves have helped to forge, they have little room for manœuvre. Yet beneath their rule the Soviet Union not only is recovering from the paralysis that crept over so many aspects of life during Stalin's last years, but is also making its weight felt in the world at large with a new subtlety and confidence and in a manner that calls for a more alert and flexible response on the part of the West than the statesmen of the West seem able to command.

This new situation, as it unfolds, is an enthralling study. And although there are huge gaps in our knowledge of what is going on, the post-Stalin government has now been in existence long enough to make worth while an attempt to sort out the impressions of its activity and aims accumulated over three years, and to relate these impressions to life in the Soviet Union today. It is impossible to think usefully about Soviet foreign policy, about the conscious impact of the Soviet Union on the rest of the world, without knowing something about Soviet domestic policy. And it is impossible to appreciate Soviet domestic policy without a picture of life in the Soviet Union and some understanding of the problems to be solved by any Russian government of a dynamic nature.

1. RETURN TO MOSCOW

AT FIRST sight it seemed that nothing had changed at all. My last sight of Moscow had been on the eve of May Day in 1947; it was now September 1955, and the city seemed just the same. I might never have been away. I knew in fact that there had been a great deal of change. Forbidden to enter the country, I had had the task of following from week to week, from year to year, in the closest possible detail, everything that could be discovered of what was going on inside it. This has been an absorbing study, even at its dreariest, when the whole system seemed to be running down under the dead weight of a sick dictator. There had been impressive material advances during Stalin's last years, though gained at very great cost; and I knew that under his successors there had been a change in the moral atmosphere. But this second-hand knowledge was not strong enough to stand against the first impression of the city I knew so well, when all the old, familiar sights and sounds and smells massed together to produce the image of an unhappy past quite at odds with the real promise of the present. Certainly the immense, nondescript crowds trailing forever through the streets of central Moscow were better dressed than they had been; they were better fed; shop windows were better stocked, and there were far more of them; battered woodwork had been repainted; the streets were better lighted; there was a great deal of new building, the sites often marked by a thicket of cranes; and the city's insignificant sky-line was now punctuated and dramatized in a pleasing manner by the looming, pyramidal shapes of the new sky-scrapers; there was far more motor traffic, including scores of grey taxi-cabs with a chequerboard pattern on their sides. Life was clearly better, fuller, richer by all material standards. And so it should have been!

5

Eight years had gone by, and in 1947 things had been very bad indeed. New clothing was virtually nonexistent. Food was so short that it was a common thing to find men with two full-time jobs to supplement inadequate rations with costly purchases on the free market, where the peasants made rouble fortunes, soon to be swept away by the great devaluation. Stalin's plans for postwar reconstruction had been disastrously upset by the drought of 1946, the worst since 1891, the year of Tolstoy's "Hunger." There was famine in the Ukraine, and Kiev was a forbidden city. The general mood of a driven, exhausted people, denied the respite and the rewards they believed they had paid for with their sacrifices in the war, was of black anger and despair. They were being told that there was grave danger of another war and they must be ready to face it. They were not told that Stalin had condemned them to yet another indefinite term of hard labour on short rations so that he might defy the West instead of trying to work with it, so that he might exploit the chaos of postwar Europe in the interests of militant Communism—or the expanding Soviet Empire. They were told, simply, that the West was preparing to attack, and they were inclined to think that if this was really so, then all their sacrifice had been in vain and life was not worth living.

Since 1947 the Soviet Union had come a long way. It had made good the destruction of the war and gone on to develop its heavy industry, one of the wonders of the world, to a point far in advance of the prewar achievement. It had embarked on immense schemes for capital construction. It had even begun to pay serious attention to the problems of food production. The standard of living, so cruelly depressed, was rising, although the production of consumer goods was still sacrificed to the demands of heavy industry. As for building, although the housing situation remained a major scandal, even by Soviet standards, it was clear from all reports that the Soviet Union had entered one of those periods of intoxicating building activity which in many other countries have coincided with the critical phase of an industrial revolution. The Russians, in a word, were on the upswing; and yet, at first sight, they looked depressingly as they had looked in the bad years after the war.

Perhaps I was unfortunate in my approach. In Moscow it was
dark, raining, and late. But Russia had really begun some hours
before, at Helsinki airport, with the change to the Soviet Aeroflot
plane. The waiting room at Helsinki, gay and light and simple,
was crowded with as unprepossessing a group of Soviet citizens as
I had ever seen. Grubby, down at heel, and dressed like the survivors of a shipwreck, they defeated curiosity. Into the sharp and
bracing atmosphere of Finland, with its self-respecting manners
and its almost reckless independence of mind, they brought the
miasma, which seemed to cling to their very clothes, of the press-
gang. I don't know who they were; I had no desire to know. It
was impossible to contemplate these figures and to reflect that I
was flying into the land where they would be at home and unre-
markable without a feeling of extreme depression. And the depression, once induced, persisted. It was all much too much like
old times.

I find it hard to understand how anybody can escape being depressed at his first sight of the Soviet Union. Perhaps it is because,
ignorant of Russia, the visiting tourist, or delegate, expects too
little—though, if this is so, goodness knows what sort of picture
he has in his mind. Perhaps it is because, conversely, being deeply
attached to the Russians, loving them, knowing what they are
capable of, having lived with them through the most terrible
period in their history (though not sharing their suffering), I expect too much. The exterior they present, collectively, to the
outer world is not inspiriting and in no way mirrors the infinite
variety and vividness of their private lives. And yet short-term
visitors who know nothing at all of private life in the Soviet
Union, of the elaborate and complex network of interests and
enthusiasms, loves and hates, that lies beneath the drab surface,
come back with glowing rapture over, precisely, that surface. One
can only conclude that they did not expect to find ordinary human beings, and one wonders why, because Russia today is one
of the best documented countries in the world, and if there is one
thing that emerges from every book written about Russia from
the inside (except those written by that peculiar sub-species of
economist which really believes that impersonal statistics have a
meaning) it is that the Russians are the most human beings in

the world. Perhaps visitors to the Soviet Union never read.

I myself expected a good deal. I had seen with my own eyes the sort of effort the Russians had put into the business of winning the war, once they had all agreed that it was important to win it; and I knew that they had been putting much the same sort of effort, though less willingly, into rebuilding their country after the war. They were now citizens of a great industrial power, and although their economy was patchy in the extreme, in chosen directions they were showing the way to the rest of the world. Their steel industry, for example, had increased its production from nine million tons in 1945 (it had been eighteen million in 1940, before the Germans smashed up the Ukraine) to about fifty million tons in 1955—or nearly three times the British output, though still less than half the American. The Soviet Union has two hundred million citizens, compared with Britain's fifty million and America's one hundred sixty million, so the output of steel per head still lagged behind Western standards. And, of course, the Western output represents an annual increase on a steady level of high production maintained for many years, whereas the Soviet output represents the initial conquests of a land starved of steel. But all in all it is an outstanding performance; one should expect a great deal of a land producing so much steel, often by methods of outstanding efficiency, and showing itself capable of turning the products of its steel mills and other metallurgical enterprises into jet aircraft and warships and submarines as advanced as any in the world, to say nothing of machinery of all kinds, canals, dams, and such homely showpieces as the Moscow subway. And yet the first thought on contemplating the public face of the creators of this economy was to wonder how on earth they did it.

The second thought, clouded with faint exasperation, was that since, in spite of all appearances, they had in fact done it, they ought in that case to be able to do better for themselves. It was no answer to say that their rulers, for a time reinforced by the Germans, had for a quarter of a century deprived them of every opportunity of doing better for themselves, by starving them of all the amenities of life except for ice cream, a number of splendid theatres, a subway—and a public amusement park with a parachute jump. They were no longer so starved. Faces once haggard or gaunt were now sleek. There was nowhere the pallor of hunger. Clothing and shoes—above all, shoes—were sound, and exhibited a variety indicating some freedom of choice. But the general effect was atrocious by any known standard, and it was plainly uncalled-for to blame the government for the wasteful and horrid abuse of quite passable materials. Once in a while a man, more rarely a girl, would go by who showed what could be done with the available materials, given determination and a little taste. But the general effect was worse than it had been in the bad days when people went in rags and tatters and lent them dignity.

I have often been attacked since returning from Moscow for deploring the squalor of Muscovite fashions. There are more important things, people say, than dress; one should be pleased by the fact that Soviet men and women show a proper consciousness of this. Well, I am not pleased. In any case, the criticism misses the point, for Muscovite women think a great deal about dress, and it gets them nowhere. It is possible to have a utilitarian attitude to dress and still be always neat and sometimes elegant. You can be like the Chinese under Mao Tse-tung, dressing—men and women alike—in dark blue siren suits, or like the girls of Italy in their almost uniform black frocks. The Muscovites do not do this. They think a lot about dress and look like rag bags. I see no virtue in this. It is a new Philistinism, a sad descent from the neat head-scarf, the apron, the bare legs or the grey woollen stockings of the country peasant. It is the blowsy genteel, the lower-middle-class mentality *in excelsis*. It may be Socialism on the way to Communism; but what it looks like is the now middle-aged children of the proletariat on the way to Laburnum Villas.

This is unfair; but I am offering an impression, not a judgment. Also, Russia had been unfair to me: in those first hours of what should have been carefree reunion, she had tried my affection too hard. The Soviet Union, as usual, in trivial things as well as great, had failed to rise to the occasion. At Helsinki airport she had paraded that seedy collection of Soviet citizens

with a "take it or leave it" air. The waiting airplane turned out
to be the shabbiest at Aeroflot's disposal. The stewardess, a pasty-
faced and sullen slattern, might have come from straight behind
the counter in a British railway-station buffet. The pilot, evidently
the champion fuel-saver of the Soviet Union, showed the utmost
reluctance to open the throttle enough to get the machine off the
ground, and the journey, all the way to Moscow, was much too
like those endlessly repeated wartime journeys, with the aircraft
hedge-hopping to keep out of range of German radar and out of
sight of German fighters. (On the other hand, the pilot had eyesight second to none; the way in which he threaded a passage
through the towers and pylons on the outskirts of Moscow, in
pitch-darkness, was superb: never once, when banking suddenly
to avoid an obstacle, did he turn the machine on its back, and
when he made his landing the first part of the airplane to touch
the ground was, amazingly, one of the wheels.)

At Moscow airport it was pouring rain. A pleasant young
woman from Intourist checked my name on a list and together
we made our way to the waiting room for foreign delegations.
What delegation did I belong to? It was the first time I had heard
the question that was soon to sicken me—as the sight of the delegations themselves came to sicken me: clueless and crazily assorted
companies of men in dark suits or sports jackets with flannel
trousers, and women in beige or navy, clutching extravagant bou-
quets and being whisked in and out of government limousines, in
and out of hotel lifts; being sat down to dinner at improbable
hours; waiting dazedly in packs by hotel doors; apprehensively
sorting through jumbled piles of luggage; lining up to hear where
they would madly rush to next and trying to follow the stiff, uneasy little speeches of inexpert interpreters. "What delegation do
you belong to?" And the look of bewilderment, then pain, then
final, resolute rejection coming over the features of the head man
when I said I did not belong to any delegation: I was on my own.

But this first time I was not rejected. I was positively welcomed.
The young woman was worried. She had lost two of her flock
between the airplane and the waiting room, which were separated
from each other by only twenty yards of asphalt: a mother and son.
Had I seen a mother, English, travelling from Leningrad with a

little boy? I said there had been no little boys on that plane. But, she persisted in sudden despair, I must be mistaken. "Leningrad sent a telegram. Look, here are the names! One room at the Hotel National for Mrs. X and son."

I looked at the names. They belonged to two English travellers, whose acquaintance I had already made—a charming and elegant mother allowing herself to be shown round Soviet Russia by a completely grown-up son. It took about ten minutes to convince the young woman that it was inaccurate to call Mr. X a little boy.

There followed a five-minute interval for total despair while she digested the fact that the Soviet Union had committed a *faux pas* in inviting the wife of a distinguished professor of international law to share a double bed with her twenty-five-year-old son. Suddenly the despair plunged to a new, a deeper note. "But we still have to find them! Oh, where can I look? Their car is waiting. We must find them an extra room. What if they have wandered off in the darkness and lost themselves in the countryside?"

We were twenty miles from the city. I explained that this was improbable. The English, I said, when lost, tend to stay put until found. Furthermore, when abroad they are not easily parted from their luggage. Since I knew them, hadn't I better go with her to find them?

Joy—then cankering doubt, deepening swiftly to further despair. "But where can we look? It is dark. Vnukovo airport is large, the largest in the Soviet Union, possibly in the world. Several square miles. I lose count of how many. And in this inky night—"

I said it was unlikely that the missing pair had covered many square miles. They had alighted outside the main doorway. They had probably gone straight into the main waiting room. Or the baggage room. Or the buffet? Was there a buffet?

"No, there is no buffet. There is a kiosk where you can buy soft drinks. Even chocolate. But it is closed."

Well then, the main waiting room.

Interval for consideration from all sides. Then, reluctantly, yes, it was possible . . .

But they were not in the main waiting room. This lofty, pillared, vaulted hall, the pride of the Soviet airport architecture, combined the decorative felicities of the waiting room at Euston Station and the hall of the National Liberal Club with the spaciousness of York Minster. The floor was pure Russia: my first true glimpse of Russia for over eight years. Everywhere on the benches were rows and piles of somnolent or sleeping peasants with bundles as large as themselves. Standing about in the aisles were a few Army officers, one or two sailors, and a sprinkling of dark-coated officials with briefcases. I said, "No, they are not here after all."

"But how can you tell? We must look!"

I said I had good eyesight and knew how they were dressed, which was more than she knew. I did not attempt to explain that it was unnecessary to peer beneath the head-shawl of every withered or apple-cheeked peasant woman to find out whether it concealed the elegant wife of a Professor of International Law. So round we went, and again and again came the plaintive question to anyone who looked awake: "Have you seen a foreign lady with a little boy?"

We found them in the end. After my young woman had inconsequently lost all interest and started chattering happily about other things—just as I myself was beginning to get a little worried—we ran them to earth in the baggage room. The young woman by that time was so busy telling me about her university career that for a time she paid them no attention.

So that was that, and because the Intourist girl had been pleasing and intelligent, because it was comforting to be once more among pleasing and intelligent people who could not keep a practical idea in their heads for two minutes at a time, because the authorities still did not mind peasants' sleeping on the floors and benches in the great hall of their showpiece airport, I had worked through the first shock of muddle and untidiness and was beginning to feel acclimatized.

But a heavier attack was to come.

It was just midnight. It was still raining. I was introduced to my car, not one of the shining limousines for delegations, but a rather grubby little Victory car. The chauffeur, to all appearances, was the sort of creature who, I had allowed myself to hope, had been left behind in the race for steel. Perhaps he had been, which was why he was an Intourist chauffeur. He was down at heel and he was surly—at least he seemed to be surly. He did not like my luggage, which was really very little. He had to break off a vociferous row with a colleague; but he managed to continue the row, in *l'esprit d'escalier,* for a mile or two down the road, lurching violently from side to side with every satisfactory retort. Then he lapsed into black silence, accepted a cigarette as his right, grasped the steering wheel firmly, decelerated, and proceeded to drive at a steady eighteen miles an hour. Coming through the airport gates, and making a couple of right-angle turns, I had been apprehensive: five miles an hour was fast enough for those turns, but we took them at twenty-five. Now, ahead of us, we had a dead straight road, the Mozhaisk Chaussée, wide and glistening in the rain, for another fifteen miles, slightly undulating. We held to our eighteen miles an hour. Cars swept by, including one with the lost English tourists, the mother and the "little boy." Occasionally we overtook a truck, hung behind for half a mile or so, until the headlights of another vehicle, coming toward us, were close enough to make the game worth while, and then started to pass, drawing over to the other side of the very wide road, decelerating as we drew level, and proceeding meticulously abreast until forced back suddenly by the oncoming vehicle. While this was going on, all vehicles on the road engaged in that remarkable practice, common to East Europe and the Balkans, of switching headlights on and off until the other party is quite dazzled, then switching everything off and proceeding through the night until, after the final approach in total darkness, all lights are switched on for the great crisis of passing.

We were not only going very slowly; we were also engaging in the traditional Soviet game of fuel saving. This consists in cutting out the engine to coast down the first incline, then tottering to a standstill half-way up the next slope, then changing into first gear, revving up triumphantly with a sudden glorious expenditure of fuel, and starting to coast again after the top of the hill is reached.

I pulled myself together and asked the driver why he was going so slowly. Was he about to run out of benzine? No, he had plenty. But it was a new engine; he was breaking it in. Was it necessary to send a car that had to be broken in, at dead of night on a straight road to the airport? Were there no others? No reply. Then—after a time, and with all diffidence—did these long coasting glides, with the engine switched off, materially assist in breaking the engine in? No reply. I reflected that, though I was hungry and tired and in need of a drink, this stately progress was an improvement on a ghastly drive I had once suffered in an enormous Zis; the driver of that machine had accelerated, with immense verve, to ninety miles an hour, then cut out everything, until after three miles we came to a standstill; then repeated the process, to infinity, for seventy miles. And as I sat being thankful for small mercies there suddenly soared up, over the trees that crowned a gentle rise, an enchanting vision in red and white lights, like an elaborate set-piece in a fireworks display, filling the sky. It was the new University, built since my time, soaring unbelievably from the very point on the Sparrow Hills where Napoleon had stood to gaze out over the glittering domes of Moscow. It was a point the Germans never reached.

The journey was not over. Near the outskirts of the city the driver wavered, then stopped, then, without a word, threw open the door, leaped out, and engaged in heated conversation with a man on the pavement. This went on for three minutes, with much pointing and gesticulation. Then the driver came back, started his engine without a word, and drove slowly to the next corner, where precisely the same thing happened. I said nothing; the driver said nothing. He went through the same procedure twice more. Then we came to a crossroads with a signboard. Still without a word, the driver stopped, switched off the engine, and went, at a trot, up to the board. Could he read? This time he returned, swung the car round, and proceeded in a direction I knew to be wrong.

"Is it possible," I asked with the gentleness of controlled apprehension, "that we are in unfamiliar surroundings?"

He actually spoke. "The roads and the signs are new," he said.

"The signs perhaps. But the roads? There are only two, and they seem to me much as they always were. I remember them putting up barricades just here in October nineteen-forty-one."

No answer. Another stop. Another confrontation. Much head-

shaking, and the first signs of emotion on the driver's face as he returned. The emotion was, of course, despair. But still no word. The
lights of the stupendous, sky-scraping University building now
hung against the darkness high above. We swung out of the major
road and into a little street that really was new. Its function,
clearly, was to connect various buildings on the University site.
We turned a few corners at random and came to a standstill in
the shadow of a concrete-mixer.

The driver sat looking ahead at an expanse of rubble, the
foundations of a new building. After a pause for mature reflection, he muttered, "Difficult," then, more clearly, "Very difficult.
What can we do?"

Determined not to stampede him with any sudden proposal, I
replied conversationally, "You have lived in Moscow for long?"

"Ten years."

"You were not born here?"

"No, I was born at Rostov."

"A very fine city."

"A very fine city, but not so fine as Moscow."

"Not so big."

"Smaller."

"We should be looking for the Kaluge Chaussée, it seems to
me. But if you, after ten years, cannot find it—"

"Until last week I drove a tram. Never mind, we shall have to
wait until somebody comes and then ask again. It is late. It is
possible that nobody will come."

"It is very late. Nevertheless, I think I know the way to the
centre from here."

"But you are a foreigner?"

"Indeed, yes. I am an Englishman."

"Then how can you know the way?"

I told him that I had lived in Moscow for quite a long time,
during the war and afterward. I told him that, although my
knowledge of Moscow was infinitely less than his own, I had,
nevertheless, many times visited Vnukovo airport and was familiar with the remarkably uncomplicated route between it and the
city centre.

He listened attentively (it was an hour past midnight, and,

although it was September, I thought I could see the first pale-
ness of dawn), thought a little, and then exclaimed, "It is impossible!"

"Karl Marx had a saying," I replied, " 'There is no such thing
as the impossible.' "

"Karl Marx!" he said.

"Perhaps it was Lenin?"

"Listen!" he exclaimed. "I have had an idea. We have taken
the wrong direction. Let us see!"

In the end we got there. From time to time, feebly, I would
suggest keeping to the main road, which led straight to Red
Square, in an attempt, mild, benign, and ineffectual, to counter-
act a tendency to explore the outer suburbs. But there was no
more conversation, though sometimes now a tolerant smile, as he
got back into the driving seat after the last encounter with a
passer-by. We approached the Kremlin, splendid under its red
stars, in sullen silence. It did not mean a thing. This, I was
thinking, is where I came in. I have been here before. Why have
I come again? Then, after creeping like a snail over the wide
spaces of the deserted Kammeny Bridge, we suddenly accelerated
sharply and tore at fifty miles an hour, regardless of fuel or possible arrest or anything else at all, round the dreamlike zig-zags
of the Moscow one-way system across the vast expanses round the
Kremlin, and skidded to a stop under the last traffic lights.

The driver, within sight of home, turned and beamed. "English?" he said.

"Yes, English."

"But you speak very good Russian."

"Not good enough," I said.

"Oh, but very good. One would think you might have visited
Moscow before?"

"But indeed I have," I said.

"Moscow is a beautiful city. Is London also a beautiful city?"

"Very," I said.

The traffic lights turned green. We stayed where we were.
There were still a few cars about in the centre; one, behind us,
honked impetuously, then remembered such noise was forbidden
at night, and stopped.

"You learned Russian here? You speak it so well!"

"Yes, here," I said. "In Moscow. During the war. A beautiful language."

The lights turned back to red. He suddenly let in the clutch, accelerated, then stopped with a bang.

"Lights red," he explained. "Must stop. . . . You have traffic lights in London?"

"Yes, we have traffic lights."

"There are many people in London?"

"Yes, very many."

"But not as many as Moscow?"

"More," I said, as the lights turned green. "Several millions more."

"Is it possible? . . . You have a Metro in London?"

"Yes," I said. "It also is bigger than yours. There are more stations. It is longer. But yours is much more beautiful and will be bigger one day."

"That I can believe," he replied. "Now it says 'go,' " he exclaimed, as the lights turned red. We went.

Outside the hotel, I offered him another cigarette.

"English cigarettes? Very good!"

I told him to take several, to take the box—one of those pleasant aluminum boxes made by Hedges and Butler for the airlines.

His eyes lit up, and he stroked it with sudden delight. "It is an important day for me when I meet an Englishman," he said. "I shall take this home to my wife and keep it as a souvenir of a very happy evening." And then: "Tomorrow you will wake in Moscow. I can tell you, it will be a wonderful thing to see Moscow for the first time."

I had indeed come home.

2. REFUSALS AND ACCEPTANCES

IT IS not, of course, all like that. For example, the English tourists on that airplane had been whisked away in the Zis limousine that passed us at high speed on the road, and, by the time my own driver had exhausted inspiration and come to a standstill by the concrete-mixer on the University site, were safely in bed, mother and son triumphantly separate. With them the organization had worked, apart from the little incident of getting lost. It often works. But equally often it does not, and perhaps it was a good thing that it had not worked with me; otherwise I might have decided that after eight years the Russians had at last been dragooned into efficiency, and I might have drawn some faulty conclusions. Just walking round the place, I found a great deal of efficiency to admire and visible signs, in the way of motor cars, cranes, bull-dozers, giant buildings of all kinds, and television sets, of many centres of efficiency scattered over the great plain. But the Intourist girl, a graduate in law, who never thought of looking in the baggage room at the airport for lost passengers, and the chauffeur who did not know the main way into Moscow and could only reject the idea that a foreigner might know better—the chauffeur who also, quite simply, did not know how to drive—these are never far away. And behind the chauffeur stands the manager who details an ex-tram-driver who has never been to Vnukovo airport to meet a foreigner in the middle of the night; and behind the manager the organization which, responsible for the shop window of the Soviet Union, cannot assemble an adequate staff. And so it goes, all down the line.

And what it comes to is this: that with all its fabulous material resources the Soviet Union is still desperately short of one thing: skilled man-power, or, in English, people. And this with a population of two hundred million. The educated and the intelligent still grow very thinly on the ground. And the great, the ceaseless struggle of the government is the fight against my Intourist chauffeur and everything he represents. There the government has my sympathy. But it has another fight on its hands as well— against the inconsequence and unpracticalness of the Russian nature, which manifests itself in the most intelligent. And there I do not sympathize at all. Only those who make a god of efficiency could possibly sympathize with any attempt to make the Russians efficient, as well as intelligent. The combination of fecklessness and stupidity is certainly dire; but the combination of fecklessness and intelligence is the most attractive thing in the world. The government seeks to stamp it out. And, of course, fecklessness does not go with the grim attempt to catch up industrially with the United States in a given number of years; the planners must be driven almost to drink when they find month after month, year after year, the same model factories operating in the same lunatic rhythm—starting each month slowly, then accelerating wildly in the last week to catch up with the plan, then relapsing again, and so on to infinity. But this sort of inefficiency is inseparable from the most precious thing in the Russian character—the capacity to live, vividly and intensely, in the present, seeing the future only as a dream.

I would rather not talk of the Russians at all in terms of efficiency; but the government insists on it. Nothing could be more vulgar than to speak of a country in terms of motor cars and machines and the material possessions of the twentieth century; but the government insists on it. The government insists that the Soviet Union shall be measured not by the special and wonderful qualities of its people but by its material progress. And for thirty years it has sacrificed everything to this material progress—everything except one basic idea, the Communist idea, which, paradoxically, has often worked against material progress.

One is not at first, on revisiting, very conscious of the Communist idea. One is conscious, rather, of being in the centre of the dizzily complex structure of a modern society, composed of millions of individuals, not ants, each supporting himself by his own special skill, each living his own private life and, as in any other country, preoccupied almost wholly with his own special and

personal interests. And, indeed, the private lives of Russians are
fuller and more personal than those of any other people in the
world. Just as it is roughly true to say that in the Soviet Union
the planned society has been called into being not because the
Russians take readily to planning but because they are constitu-
tionally incapable of planning, so it is roughly true to say that
the incessant hectoring of the people by the Party is designed not
to canalize their political thinking but to inject into the most
a-political people in the world some kind of political consciousness against their will: a political consciousness, naturally, of the
kind desired by the government itself.

We shall have more to say about politics later on. But it is
necessary to establish at once that for the ordinary Russian citizen politics means next to nothing. Russians have, I think, always been like this. And while this indifference has obvious advantages, one disadvantage is that the many find themselves extremely vulnerable to the few who think politically. Whether
the government is wholly wise in trying to instil a political consciousness into the millions is open to doubt. The whole question
of conditioning, when it concerns the human mind, is open to
a great deal of doubt, as anyone who has lived in the Soviet Union
for any length of time discovers for himself. There are now some
nineteen million members of the Komsomol, the League of Communist Youth. They are being taught to think politically, and it
would not surprise me in the least to discover that many of these
are in fact beginning to think dangerously. Most of them, of
course, in spite of every exhortation, are not thinking at all; the
Communists have made politics so dull that it has come to stand
for total boredom.

It should not be necessary to make this point, but there are
still so many in the West who think of Soviet Russia as a country
with a high level of political consciousness that the obvious contrary has to be stressed at the outset of any consideration of these
people. We suffer from this delusion, I suppose, because the
leaders insist all the time on ideological preoccupations, and because the great political trials have given the outward impression
of intense political activity. This is because the purges and the
trials affect active Party members, that is to say members of a

small political élite, who stand apart from the rest of the country. The so-called political crimes of the ordinary Soviet citizen are not in any reasonable sense political crimes at all, in nine cases out of ten. Critical remarks about the system or the leadership should best be seen as normal grumbles that have gone a little too far, not as the expression of incipient political revolt. Since Stalin's terrible action against the peasants which ended in collectivization and was in effect a series of localized civil wars, there has been no major rebellion on the part of the peasants or the factory workers. But there has been a great deal of smouldering passive resistance to government decrees, constant evasion of statutory obligations, and sometimes, in periods of unusual hardship, physical violence and rioting—in cities, as in Kharkov in 1947, as well as in the countryside and, more latterly, in the labour camps. And never, to my knowledge, has any of this been inspired by a political idea. The passive resistance, the evasions, the outbreaks of violence, could never be seen as growing out of political convictions or an opposition in principle to the system as a whole. They have to be seen as the spontaneous and unthinking rebellion of hard-pressed men and women against immediate and local oppression or unfairness—against, that is to say, particular aspects of the system which happen to affect them, individually or as part of a group, very closely. This is borne out by the reports of countless refugees from the Soviet Union— called nowadays, for some deep reason, "defectors"—who, while reviling the system, have never for a moment considered what might be put in its place and are, in fact, simply objecting to certain excesses of the system. It is borne out by the activities of some of the more politically conscious refugees, whose political ideas are limited to overthrowing the current regime and putting in its place one very like it with themselves in positions of authority. It is borne out by the remarkable behaviour of those Russians who took part in the notorious strikes in the labour camps clustered round the Vorkuta coalfields in the far north: these, of all people, immediate victims of Stalin's tyranny, might be expected to lead the van on political revolt and to be obsessed with the necessity of overthrowing the system that permitted forced labour; but all they wanted was to have their living conditions improved. It is borne out by Russian history, which is a history of innumerable revolts against the immediate pains of oppression, leaving the source of oppression untouched and even uncriticized.

It is the Soviet government that underlines the political importance of all rebellious action by calling it counter-revolutionary and by punishing the offenders for crimes against the state.

In England, from time to time, an individual citizen, driven out of patience by what he takes to be the bureaucratic iniquities of Whitehall, refuses to obey an official order. Sometimes he may even assault the government inspector who arrives to enforce the order. Sometimes he goes so far as to knock down a policeman—for example, when a county council, armed with full legal powers, seeks to dispossess him of a house or small-holding scheduled for "development" in return for what seems to him inadequate compensation. More often than not the nonconformist wins the admiration of his neighbours for having the courage to stand up against "Them." And, if he has to be punished, he is not charged with subversive activity, or treason, or *lèse majesté*. He is charged with common assault or with obstructing the police in the course of their duty, fined or sent to prison for a few weeks, and received back into the bosom of society. Now this unfortunate victim of the mills of bureaucracy, which grind rather smaller than the mills of God, is a being in full revolt against the whole impersonal caste of bureaucrats. But in ninety-nine cases out of a hundred there is no political idea behind his private rebellion; he has no thought at all of starting a movement to overthrow the government, the system. He accepts these as part of the air he breathes. He is in revolt against certain abuses of the system, as applied particularly to him. And, very likely, he will write to the prime minister, or the Queen, petitioning them for justice. Equally, there is no political idea burning in the minds of those who applaud him for his stand.

It is the same in the Soviet Union, but on a hugely magnified scale, because in the Soviet Union every individual every day finds himself in collision with the bureaucracy, with "Them"— or, through his own quick-wittedness, just avoiding collision. In a land where the power of the state is absolute and almost all-pervading, where the demands of the bureaucracy, of "Them," penetrate into almost every kind of activity, the individual is, and must be, in constant rebellion against this or that aspect of the system. And since the system could not survive if such rebellion were allowed to become effective, the government has to punish it not as a passing threat to law and order but as a standing threat to the security of the realm. Thus it is that while the personal rebellion of a British small-holder against his local county council is punished as a minor civil offence, a similar action on the part of a Russian peasant is punished as a counter-revolutionary offence. It is because of this that some people derive the impression of a land seething with suppressed revolt against the system and the government. It is a false impression: the revolt is all against the bureaucrats—the local bureaucrats and the bureaucrats at the centre. There is no thought of storming the Kremlin, which created the bureaucracy. Just as the Tsar was regarded as the protector, the wise father, who, if he knew, would punish the police and the civil service for their harsh and arbitrary methods, so the Soviet leaders in the Kremlin are pictured as the champions of the people against the impersonal machine of government, which is always threatening to get quite out of hand.

This is an idea which the Soviet leaders encourage. In these days the officially inspired campaign against the evils and inertia of the bureaucracy is stronger than ever before. It has two purposes: one is the straightforward and necessary purpose of reducing red tape and idleness and corruption in an administrative machine of such colossal proportions that these things, endemic to all civil services, proliferate on a truly formidable scale; the other, humanly enough, is to divert the rebellious instincts of the people, the anger and the bitterness at injustice, away from the creators of the system, so that the manipulators of the huge and impersonal machine may appear as its foes on the side of the people. There is just enough truth in this impression to make it seem plausible.

At any rate, the people believe it. The people of a country which for seven centuries has known nothing but autocratic rule, carried out first through a feudal nobility, later through a steadily expanding civil service, are bound to look for justice to the only man in the oppressive edifice of government who seems to be disinterested and untouched by the struggle for power and loot—the man at the head of the pyramid, who has no axe to grind—the Tsar. And so they did. It was to this deep tradition that Stalin in his later years owed his strength. And today, in Russia, three years after Stalin's death, one encounters curious little manifestations of unease because Stalin is no longer there. Who of the new leaders, I was asked several times and in almost identical words, is strong enough to control the bureaucracy?

It was not the sort of question one could argue about. To try to answer would have moved the conversation straight on to forbidden ground. For nothing could be more clear than that these simple souls (one or two of them, indeed, not so simple) were oblivious of the implications of that question. Nor did they see that it is precisely the bureaucracy, with its new stratification of castes, with its already formidable vested interests, often in healthy conflict, with its accumulating weight of inertia, its freedom from ideological fanaticism, that acts as a very strong check today on the firebrands of the Party and on the arbitrary despotism of the autocracy in the Kremlin. They did not see that if they wanted to change the system, substituting by slow degrees a more widely based government with room for a variety of interests and points of view, they must do it through the great bureaucratic machine built up by the Party leaders as their instrument, and now almost a power in its own right. They did not see this because it had never crossed their minds that it might be desirable to change the system. This is a fact which too many Western observers ignore. The Soviet masses are against the excesses of the MVD, against the government inspectors, against the tax collectors, against officialdom everywhere. But they are for the Kremlin.

It is easier to understand this if we reflect for a moment on who the Soviet people are.

They are the survivors, and the heirs, of a colossal political upheaval. In fifteen years this upheaval annihilated and swept away the whole natural and widely based leadership of a great empire, except for the membership of a minority revolutionary party and those who, on reflection, decided to accept the highly unpopular dictatorship of that party. In the next five years a further upheaval finished off all those among the survivors who would not submit, or were suspected of not submitting, absolutely to the personal dictatorship of Stalin. That brings us up to 1937. Four years later came the war, which killed off the flower of younger generations that had grown up under the new regime to replace the casualties among their elders.

It is not as though there was ever much stock of natural leadership in Russia; but there was some. In the peculiar situation of the empire in the last years of the Tsarist autocracy—which saw also the first feeble but portentous beginnings of the Russian industrial revolution—there had developed a formidable liberal intelligentsia to set against the reactionary elements of imperial officialdom, an intelligentsia which was often forced into revolutionary attitudes because the facilities for legal opposition were inadequate. By the turn of the century every university student of character and vision was a revolutionary of sorts, though by no means always a Marxist. While the rural masses, the peasants in their tens of millions, muttered and groaned in the traditional Russian manner and thought only in terms of immediate palliatives, the intelligentsia, influenced by Western ideas, looked deeper and saw past the local police chief or provincial governor to the throne itself as the root of all evil. And behind them stood the new urban proletariat with its dawning political consciousness. Thus when, in March 1917, the time came for the Tsar to go—when, that is to say, the illiterate masses themselves came to recognize that the autocracy itself, the system based on Nicholas, was responsible for their misery and the disastrous conduct of the war—there was immediately released a pent-up torrent of ideas, turbulent, exhilarating, which swept away the very foundations of the past and then, expanding, gradually lost its impetus and its volume until, dwindling to nothing, it simply vanished into the arid sands of the Stalinist desert, where the new earthly paradise was already being built by slaves.

Very few of the men of spirit who welcomed the Revolution were Bolsheviks. Most regarded Lenin with extreme suspicion, if not abhorrence. They had helped to make the Revolution, but there was no place for their chaotic and liberal ideas and groping doctrines in the clear-cut policies of Lenin—of the man who proposed to bring salvation to the Russians through the absolute dictatorship of the only party that was both disciplined and guided by an infallible light. They had to go. And, in due course, after Lenin died, many of those who had accepted his personal authority found themselves unprepared to accept the authority of the man who contrived to succeed him. They had to go too, and with them much of the life and colour and hope of the new Russia. And so it went on. For fifteen years the regime waged implacable war against every individual of character and intellect who was not prepared to submit to it absolutely. Generation after generation lost its most brilliant ornaments in this way. But, equally, generation after generation produced more individuals of ability who were prepared to accept in general terms the only regime they knew. They came up from the peasant masses, mostly via industry.

In 1917 eighty per cent of the population of Russia were peasants, mainly illiterate, the children or grandchildren of serfs, engaged in agriculture of an extremely primitive kind. These formed the great reservoir for the citizens of the future. Now nearly half the population work in towns, in the new factories built under the Five-Year Plans. Most, overwhelmingly most, were born in peasant villages, or are the children of peasants migrated to the towns. These are the Soviet masses. The town workers have been absorbed into the system; but the peasants, the collectivization notwithstanding, still stand outside it. Above both stands a new élite, in effect a new governing caste, now impressively large, which has a vested interest in the system: the Party chieftains, the factory managers, the higher civil servants, the Army officers, the Soviet intelligentsia. These, themselves more often than not risen in their own lifetimes from the factory tenement or the peasant hut, have for many years been cut off not only from the West but also from the vital Russian tradition. They have had, painfully and wastefully, to find out things for themselves which they would have absorbed as unconsciously as the air they breathe had they been able to draw on the experience of their predecessors and their Western opposite numbers. Limited as they have been, they have performed wonders. Their task now, having educated themselves, is to turn the great reservoir of backward humanity which is the population of the Soviet Union, the headless masses, into the stuff of a modern industrial society.

This is what the contemporary domestic situation is.

Each country has its own overriding problem, and contemporary history is made by the running efforts to solve the vital problems of the day, often without a clear appreciation of their true nature. Thus the contemporary British situation revolves round two immense and interlocking problems: How is Britain, founded and vastly expanded on the simple arrangement of exporting unlimited manufactured goods in exchange for unlimited cheap food and raw materials in a not very competitive world, to adapt herself, with her unnaturally swollen population, to a contracting world with widespread industrialization and a diminishing surplus of food and raw materials? How, again, are the masses who now, through their trade unions, dominate the country, and who can no longer be freely exploited in the interests of the few, to learn in a short time the sense of responsibility and restraint without which, coupled with hard work, the country will founder? The Soviet problem is very different: How to raise up the peasants and integrate them into the system so that they pull their full weight? How to develop a stable society in a rapidly expanding economy without allowing it to degenerate either into a class society full of inequalities and potential revolutionary situations on the one hand, or, on the other, into a monstrous ant-hill?

There is no place in this book for a discussion of Leninism or for retelling the dark, enthralling story of how Soviet society arrived at the point at which we find it. I have done that elsewhere. There is no place for a discussion of possible alternative systems; the existing system is in full swing and, short of a major catastrophe, no power can stop it from developing and evolving —evolving because nothing can stand still. What we are all concerned with now is the Soviet system as it is, and as it may be expected to evolve. The leaders of the Soviet system are certainly Marxists, and lately, while amending certain basic teachings of Lenin, have been at pains to emphasize their continued faith in the ultimate doom of the bourgeois world and the ultimate triumph of global Communism. Later we shall have to examine just what they believe, and why. But first we must look at the raw material they have to work with. In the last resort the Soviet system is based on people, predominantly Russians. These people do not stand still. They have themselves been partly conditioned by the system, but, at the same time, they themselves are modifying the system by their very existence. It is only when one has some idea of the Russian people as they are that one can begin to appreciate the problems of the Soviet leadership and to understand the deep compelling reasons for many actions which seem on the face of it to be arbitrary and inexplicable.

3. "RELICS OF THE PAST"

NEARLY fifty miles from Moscow, on a little hill, stands the town of Zagorsk. It used to be called Sergiev, after the Monastery of St. Sergius, the Troitsko-Sergievskaya *Lavra,* which was one of the most holy places of Russia—as it still is to this day for those who believe in that sort of holiness. Many do believe, predominantly the old; and Zagorsk remains a place of pilgrimage. The town is nothing except a few broad cobbled streets as wide as Trafalgar Square and a great open place in front of the fortress monastery as wide as a desert. There used to be a famous toy-making industry there, and a handicraft museum; but all that has gone, and only the monastery remains. It is a fairy-tale monastery, a doll's-house fortress, bright with primary colours and enchanted buildings frozen into fantastic shapes. But the walls of the toy watch-towers are thick, and twice withstood the assault of the Polish invaders, who took Moscow four centuries ago. Inside the walls behind the great gates is the Holy Russia of exactly forty years ago—or four hundred years ago—untouched. For many years it was a museum. The monastery bells were silent, and in the metropolitan's apartments and the vestry room, the *riznitsa,* was displayed the most astonishing collection of ecclesiastical art ever to be seen. This is still there. But now the church is back again, and the monastery houses the theological seminary where young men in considerable numbers are trained for the priesthood.

The most spectacular building, embowered in trees, is the Cathedral of the Assumption, crowned with onion domes painted since the war in the sharpest of royal blues, scattered with golden stars. The paint is a little faded now, but when it was fresh the domes with their fretted gilt crosses made a composition of heavenly splendour. These, with the Rastrelli belfry, a sturdily elegant column over three hundred feet high, dominate the town; but they are not the holiest places. As always in Russia, the holy shrines are the insignificant ones. They are the chapel of St. Sergius, with the image of the saint, and the holy-water grotto built into the wall of the Cathedral of the Assumption. It is to these, and to the small, cramped Cathedral of the Trinity, with its superb ikons, that the pilgrims come.*

On a feast day the whole fabulous apparatus is going full blast. The quiet air in the monastery courtyard beneath shady trees is rent and riven by the sound of bells: not the remote, mathematical meditations of the English countryside; not the calm, contemplative melodiousness of Italy; not the elaborate, sliding intricacies that float across the polders of the Low Countries; not anything at all that we in the West understand by church bells, but rather a barbaric frenzy, with maddeningly reiterated rhythms and syncopations in a maddeningly repetitive counterpoint. Wandering into the middle of this one fine September Sunday, with the lime trees and the birches gleaming gold, I found myself in equatorial Africa. These bells were drums, endlessly beating out the terrifying simplicities of an unknown superstition. You can hear them exactly, any time you like, in a gramophone recording of the Coronation Scene of Moussorgsky's *Boris Godunov*. Boris was not crowned at Zagorsk; he was crowned in the Moscow Kremlin. But he lies buried at Zagorsk, and over his monolithic tombstone, which stands in the open beneath the trees outside the Cathedral walls, there stream out incessantly the very sounds that have immortalized his sombre tragedy. Moussorgsky's tremendous, solemnly spaced chords, violent to the point of brutality, reproduce exactly the brazen assault of the great tenor bell; his violins, with their endlessly overlapping circles of shrill reiteration, are a jangle of toy bells —a flock of frightened starlings crossing and recrossing the great sound-waves of a Chinese gong.

There is no frenzy about the bell-ringers. When the morning service is over a greasy-looking priest comes out onto the terrace

---

* The Russian conception of a cathedral is different from ours. Inside the walls of the Moscow Kremlin, for example, there are several cathedrals, which are, in effect, self-contained oratories, or chapels.

of the baroque refectory and makes a highly secular sign to his bearded mate (there is no other word for him) high in the Rastrelli tower, who turns to the bell-ringers to tell them to knock off, which they do in midpeal, so that the silence in its suddenness itself has a quality of violence. But the business of praising God goes on. In the St. Sergius chapel, under the holy ikons, there is a sweating press of men and women, mainly women, mainly old, queuing to kiss the toe of the saint. In a dark corner by the image of the saint a youngish priest of extreme greasiness gabbles away at the Holy Office, paying no attention to the old women who seize the hem of his habit and kiss it. Little groups of women suddenly, two or three at a time, set up a new chant, which, swelling, floats above the dark and noisome scene like a visitation from another world, such is the purity of line achieved by their quavering voices. God is in that pit, in the stink, the sweet music, the groaning genuflexions; and, outside, people waiting their turn cross themselves incessantly, flinging their arms wide in the broad Russian manner, and bowing almost to the ground.

Not far off is the holy spring, and here the crush is even greater as old women with china vases, cracked tumblers, chipped enamelled mugs, green glass beer bottles clutched in their hands push and struggle to reach the holy spring in its grotto, and then fight their way out, tremulously folding the mugs and bottles in their shawls to shield the precious fluid, as they mingle with the tourists in the monastery courtyard. For Zagorsk is a three-star tourist attraction as well as a place of holy pilgrimage. On that Sunday in September there were five charming Komsomolkas, young girls of seventeen belonging to the League of Communist Youth, wearing the discreet little badges of Moscow University. They had come out dressed neatly in their Sunday best—hatless, with unobtrusive black frocks—and I shall never forget the expression on their faces as they stood watching the pandemonium of religious frenzy, or black superstition, in St. Sergius's chapel. Clean-limbed, slender, with fair gleaming hair carefully brushed back from the high, arched foreheads, they gazed in stupefaction at something they had never before imagined, or could now believe to be possible. They did not sneer or giggle;

they simply gazed wide-eyed. And I am sure that when they went back to Moscow on the crowded electric train each and every one of them was full of a solemn sense of rededication to the cause—to the heart-breaking task of making the Soviet Union a model to the world and of rooting out "survivals of the past."

The other tourists were not bothering. They had come to see the churches and the treasures and to picnic in the open air on what was to be the last fine Sunday of the year. They spread themselves on the benches and the low stone walls in cheerful family parties and addressed themselves to bread and sausage and fizzy drinks of garish colours. They were entertained by everything they saw and heard: the bells; the monks, standing and conversing among themselves, aloof in the Orthodox manner from the people seeking God; the peasant women with their rags and bundles; the pilgrims; the pigeons. And to complete the picture, in the middle of this scene of bourgeois relaxation stood the traditional Russian Idiot: a young man with a beard and a bundle, fine features and long hair, stretching out his arms to all the sights, crossing himself, turning to babble and beam at anyone who came near him, still touching by his presence the hearts of the new products of the Soviet age: the Holy Fool.

Zagorsk has television now. Every roof-top sprouts a crop of masts, one almost for each room. And into the old-fashioned houses of this empty country town come, every night, living images of the outside world, of the might and glory of the Soviet Union, its mechanical skills, its vigour and zest, its highly developed arts. But the mad bells still ring out over the tomb of the tragic Tsar. And the Holy Fool, beaming and babbling, still draws the suburban stalwarts of the Five-Year Plans to the deep magic of the goodness of total silliness.

Zagorsk, if you like, is a showplace: such a showplace that the government has caused what used to be a terrible, pot-holed, rutted country road to be remade into one of the finest roads in Russia so that foreign delegations may be conveyed there swiftly and in comfort—not, as a rule, on feast days. But it is far from being alone. I remember one day stumbling on a small church in an outer suburb, where there were no made-up roads and the ruts were two feet deep. For all I knew the church was closed, or used as a granary, or a village club room. But the doors were open and I went up the long flight of steps under their canopy to see what was inside. Coming from the sunlight into the dark interior, I could see nothing for a moment. I could only hear a wild wailing, like a sound at a wake. And, indeed, it was a wake. There, on a bier, rested a coffin, and round the coffin were a number of men and women, kneeling or prostrate, groaning and wailing, and banging their heads on the stone floor. I tried to slip away silently, but I had been seen. Three women with candles made a rush at me, and I wondered how to apologize. But I was not required to apologize. In that cavernous doorway they fell on me with rapture, catching hold of my coat, stroking my sleeves, all but embracing me and falling on their knees. One was old, but the other two were in early middle age, and one of these seemed to be in charge. "Glory to God! A stranger has come!" she exclaimed. "To the stranger, welcome!" the others responded. And by now the kneeling peasants had got up from their knees, except for one very old woman who remained prostrate; and all crowded round, exclaiming in chorus, "Welcome to the stranger," the women crossing themselves and bowing, the men bowing almost to the ground.

I said I was sorry to have interrupted them at such a grievous time. "It is our honour and glory by the mercy of the Holy Mother to receive you," said the woman with the candle. "Now you must stay. Now you must see. Sir, here lies our beloved Ivan Serafimovich, lately dead." And, turning to the others: "Make way for the stranger who has come to look on Ivan Serafimovich!" The mourners made a lane, without a murmur, and bowed again. At the end of the lane stood the coffin, swathed in scarlet bunting, and in the coffin, open to the air, lay a little waxen old man, his head and shoulders outlined by elaborately pleated white paper like an Elizabethan ruff, or a pie frill. I contemplated the dead man and crossed myself, but without the broad Russian abandon. The mourners held their breath and did the same. Then suddenly the old, old woman leaped up from the floor and seized my hand and kissed it. "The

wife of Ivan Serafimovich," said the woman with the candle.
"Babushka beloved, the stranger has come to bless Ivan Serafimovich with his kiss."

"Ai, ai," moaned the mourners, in an orgy of crossing. "Glory
be to God and infinite the mercy of the Holy Mother."

There was nothing for it. I kissed the dead man on the forehead. The old widow embraced me and I kissed her too. And
then I found myself walking back into the sunlight through
the lane, which had re-formed and I was showered with cries
of awe, wonder, and delight. Ten minutes later I was on the
trolley-bus, heading for the city centre.

I suppose this sort of thing would be taken by some as an
example of the deathless power of Christianity, by others as a
proof that the Soviet government lives up to its professions of
religious freedom. It seems to me neither. Anybody who cares
to call these things evidences of the Christian faith is welcome
to do so; but it is the last thing that would occur to me. As for
religious freedom in the Soviet Union, while making a great show
of this to the outside world the government conducts at home a
campaign of militant atheism, combined with frantic propaganda
to raise the moral tone of Soviet society. The first seems to me
deplorable; the second, in the context of Zagorsk, has my
sympathy. Few things strike me as more odd than the concern
shown by cultured and delicate-minded Christians in the West
for the survival of the dark superstitions of the Russian faithful
and the sleek, cynical opportunism of the Russian Orthodox
priesthood. I am one of the few articulate members of my own
generation never to have been a Communist, or, as far as I can
make out, anything like one; but just as I felt much closer to the
five young Komsomolkas—priggish no doubt, charming certainly
—looking down their pretty noses at the old women of Zagorsk
than to the high priests of that establishment, so I find myself
closer to those Soviet Communists who are trying to make the
Soviet Union work than to the editorial-writers of the West who
have come to equate Christianity, in spite of its origins, with
what they like to call Western Values and thus exalt the mumbo-
jumbo at Zagorsk, and elsewhere, to the role of a shining liberal

or spiritual bulwark against the forces of darkness which deal in
better drains.

I could supply many more little scenes from life to show the
old Russian close beneath the Soviet skin: the very powerful old
Russian, who stands forever in the way of those who, however
wrongly or misguidedly, want to create a better sort of Russian.
But I know from experience how such travellers' tales from the
Soviet Union, unless they fit in more or less exactly with existing
preconceptions, whether favourable or adverse, are quite firmly
disbelieved—and not always politely. So I shall supplement my
own tales with some anecdotes taken in the last year or so from
the Soviet press. And these, every bit as much as Zagorsk, give
a vivid idea of the sort of thing that any dynamic government
in Russia, of whatever political colour, must find itself up
against. We in the West are so used to governments' appearing
to lag behind the people that it is hard for us to conceive a state
of affairs in which, as in Russia from time immemorial, all
positive advances are forced upon the people from above. The
history of Russia flames and flickers with peasant revolts large
and small; but invariably these have been the convulsive up-
risings of men driven desperate by oppression or privation, and
have died down as hopelessly as they began—because they lacked
a political idea. The first attempted political revolution was
conducted not by the downtrodden but by enlightened Army
officers, the Decembrists, in 1825. It was not until the abortive
revolution of 1905 that politics, as we understand them, played
any part in a popular rebellion. It was not until March 1917
that the people succeeded in capturing power from a by then
hated autocracy; but even then they did not know what to do
with their power, thinking as they did only in terms of bread,
peace, and land for themselves. So that seven months later Lenin,
who had played no part in the March Revolution, was able to
take the power from them and establish the dictatorship of his
tiny party of devoted Bolsheviks. Ivan the Terrible with his
Unification, Peter the Great with his Westernization, Catherine
the Great with her Enlightenment, Alexander II with his aboli-
tion of serfdom, Lenin with his total destruction of the old

system, Stalin with his industrial revolution—it has been the same story for five hundred years: the story of absolute rulers forcing the masses forward, for good or ill, and through an infinity of tears.

We have glimpsed some of the masses at Zagorsk and at a village funeral. But they are everywhere. And although one of the really stupendous achievements of the Soviet regime has been to teach the millions to read and write (to what end?), the antique Russian peasant is never far away. I suppose most people from Western countries think of the collectivized agriculture of the Soviet Union in terms of tractors and giant machinery, milking machines and silos. And, indeed, there are many collective and state farms that are models of their kind. But most are not. And it is far more to the point to think of the *kolkhoz* in terms of the traditional village of the Russian plain: the immensely wide village street, unmetalled, and made wide so that during the autumn rains and the spring thaw new tracks can be made by wheeled vehicles when the first track is rutted axle-deep; the wooden cottages with tiny fretwork windows and sheet-iron roofs, each standing behind wooden palings in its own long and narrow plot; the sparse poplars; the church, now often desecrated, washed prettily in pink or ochre or pale blue, its onion dome surmounted by a fretted, gilded cross.

All these are old. They formed the pattern of the village in the days of the serfs, still less than a century ago. The serfs were liberated and left with too little land to sustain them, and there was hunger in the villages. The pattern remained the same in 1917 when Lenin told the peasants to seize the land from the great estates, which they then worked for themselves, the more able and the more ambitious peasants going ahead rapidly and accumulating land and stock and hirelings. It remained the same twelve years later when Stalin launched his frontal attack on the *kulaks* and dispossessed them in the course of a struggle that was in effect a series of localized civil wars. Then the land split up among the peasants from the great estates was pooled again, and run as a great series of cooperatives by individual villages. But although the pattern of work was different, and although individuals in their hundreds of thousands had been killed or deported or had starved to death, and although in the course of the struggle the peasants slaughtered their cattle and their horses and burned their crops, rather than let them fall into the hands of the state, when it was all over the eternal village remained. The only difference was that the individual holdings were now amalgamated into a collective; livestock was held in common; the villagers were mobilized into work gangs under a chairman; and the state had first claim on their produce. There was one other difference: the most able peasants, the kulaks, with their independent, forceful, frequently grasping ways, had vanished, so that the land was farmed less well.

And, indeed, a decade after the collectivization, at the moment when the Germans came and laid waste everything they saw, the land of Russia was still producing less—in the way of livestock a great deal less—than it had produced before the collectivization had been carried out. Through all this the village remained essentially unchanged as a social and economic unit; the peasants still gave to their private plots more attention than they gave to the communal fields; and the mechanics and tractor drivers of the MTS depots, established not only to make the best use of the new machinery as it became available, but also to infiltrate alien watch dogs into the life of the collectives, themselves became absorbed into that life. The village went on. When it is realized that there are still villages in the Soviet Union several hundred miles from the nearest railway station, fifty miles from the nearest main road (and by main road I do not mean the brand-new concrete highways built by German prisoners of war, which have transformed the life of Western Russia, but the old unmetalled roads, built for sledges in winter and horse transport in summer, impassable because of mud for weeks on end in spring and autumn)—when one realizes this, it is clear that village life must change slowly indeed.

There are periods each year when it is impossible to move between two great towns such as Kuibyshev and Kazan, both on the Volga, except by air. Tens of thousands of villages, or settlements, are cut off from all communication with the outside world during these periods. There are collective farms and state farms all along the great highways; one sees them as one passes, one is shown over them, one can visualize the conditions of life on them. But ranging away into the almost infinite distance are others which nobody sees, unless by accident such as a forced landing in an airplane or a forced and unimaginable detour by car. Thus there are almost totally isolated villages within sixty miles of Moscow or Kiev. These must have television now. But there are many more, a hundred miles away, which have no television. When trying to visualize village life in the Soviet Union one must think not of farms near main roads and railways, but of those which never see a stranger. Life here is primitive indeed.

Zhirnovo is a village in the district of Shabalinsk; one day a correspondent of the Moscow *Literary Gazette* found himself visiting it, riding on a truck straight into a scene from medieval Russia—except that there were bicycles and silk dresses. He described at great length what he saw, which was a saint's-day celebration. Everyone for miles around was coming in to celebrate St. Tikhon, and all work stopped.

"Who was this Tikhon?" the Moscow journalist demanded.

"They say he was a holy man in the old days. There was a chapel called after him. The chapel disappeared a long time ago, and you won't find an ikon in every house today. But they celebrate his feast day all the same."

And so they did. "The nearer we got to Zhirnovo the more people we overtook," the journalist reported. "They streamed along that road: old people with bundles and baskets, loaded with bottles and food; young girls in silk dresses walking barefoot and carefully carrying their best shoes; young men on bicycles weaving their way through the crowd."

At Zhirnovo he found a deserted village. The actual celebrations were taking place a little distance away. The kolkhoz was abandoned. Even the management was missing. Almost the only person about was the director of the village co-operative, and he was loading up a three-ton lorry with crates of vodka to sell to the revellers. When the journalist asked how long the party would last he was told that normally it went on for three days, sometimes a whole week: the hay-making had to wait. So he went to see for himself.

What he found was an orgy. Every house and hut was bursting at the seams with peasants getting drunk on vodka and home brew. There were dancing and singing and brawling in the village street. "Anyone who fell down was promptly dragged off to the fence, where they poured cold water over him and left him lying until he came to. And then he would start in again on the vodka and home brew with new zest." The drink was being sold by the manager of the village co-operative, who was also a local Party secretary; the local Party members were out in strength. The kolkhoz cattle stayed shut up in the byres: "There was nobody to water them or lead them out to pasture. They languished, unfed, in unswept stalls. . . . For three days they drank, fought, and idled. Some did not even know who the feast day was for, or why it was being celebrated. Tikhon had simply become an excuse for a drunken orgy. But nobody tried to keep these people from unrestrained, insensate drunkenness. There was nothing to stop their behaving as they did."

Literary Gazette was very indignant about this aspect of affairs. How can we ever expect to raise the tone of village life if the Party officials themselves, the kolkhoz managers, treat this sort of orgy as part of the natural order of things, and even join in it themselves? "Instead of fighting against such survivals, against religious prejudice, the Communists of the Michurin kolkhoz themselves supported them! Furthermore, the fact that a feast was being prepared was known not only to the local Party organization. It was known to the Party committee of Shabalinsk District, to the District Department of Culture, to the District Branch of the Society for the Dissemination of Political and Scientific Knowledge. Even the provincial administration knew all about it. They all knew. But they all treated it as something inevitable and natural about which nothing can be done."

A village festival in honour of a forgotten saint—it might have happened anywhere; but it happened in the Soviet Union, where there are no saints, no superstitions, no anti-social habits. And it was reported at extreme length in a Moscow journal on July 24, 1954. These are the people who are supposed to have been conditioned to a total acceptance of the Communist way of life— not simply the resisters, conscious or unconscious; not simply the unthinking masses. The local Party leaders themselves took part in those goings on, individuals belonging to the eight million shock troops of the Communist millennium.

Holy Russia is also to be found in the great cities. It is not necessary to go all the way to Zhirnovo in Shabalinsk District. Tushino is a suburb of Moscow, celebrated as the site of Moscow's main military airport, where, each year, the grand display of the Soviet Air Force takes place. It stands, one would have said, for everything up to date in the Soviet Union. And so, up to a point, it does. But it also stands for something else. In May of last year the paper *Moscow Pravda* (not the internationally known *Pravda,* but a local paper) published an account of a miracle woman, "the healer of Tushino," Babushka Martynova, who has an able-bodied assistant known as Aleshka the Stoker. There in a cottage on Zakharkov Street, Granny Martynova's miracles are performed daily; and *Moscow Pravda* showed particular indignation because the pilgrims to her house included not only illiterate peasants and unskilled workers but also representatives of the new Soviet élite. Some of them were mentioned by name: a well-known musical-comedy actor; the foreman of the technical control department of the "Hammer and Sickle" factory, one of Moscow's prides; a chief technician of the Moscow transformer factory. This is what happens—a scene that might be taken straight from a Russian satirist of the nineteenth century:

Against the wall of Granny Martynova's pigsty a patient queue waits in silence. All are men, except for one woman who is "youngish, smartly dressed, with a brightly coloured head-shawl, and who has come on her husband's behalf. Granny will not heal women. The queue, with its strange mixture of primitives and intellectuals, is marshalled by Aleshka the Stoker, brawny and tough, who also acts as master of ceremonies."

He lets in six at a time. "The old man with a goatee, the man in the green hat, a heavy, fat man with three chins, and the others who had entered the hut saw a very old woman sitting in the corner. Beside her there stood an ordinary tub full of water, and a mug. Aleshka the Stoker went up to the old woman and shouted into her ear: 'Now, Babushka, up with you!' The old woman rose importantly from her seat, touched the tub with a shaky hand, bent right over it, and soundlessly moved her lips. Somebody coughed. 'Sh-sh! Quiet!' hissed Aleshka the Stoker. 'Granny is putting a spell on the water!' "

And one after another the "pilgrims" go up to receive Granny's healing touch and a mugful of water from the washtub, ladled out by Aleshka—ordinary well water, the Moscow newspaper declared, "put under a spell by Granny Martynova, and guaranteed by her as 'a universal specific against cancer, heart disease, stomach ulcers, neurasthenia, rheumatism—in a word, against any disease.' "

For every mugful Granny Martynova demands, and gets, a ten-rouble note.

I could quote numerous examples of this kind of thing from the Soviet press of the last year or two. Under Stalin such things were not mentioned, but they existed. And they are widespread and strong enough to make it necessary for the new government, after decades of dwelling on the universality of the new enlightenment, to admit them and bring them into the open. There was the story of the village ghost, reported in *Komsomolskaya Pravda* in March 1954, which terrorized the village of Ivanovka, in the heart of the great plain, until it was attacked and unmasked by some intrepid young Komsomols. At almost the same time, and reported in the same paper, the neighbouring village of Yurmanka was found to have a miracle-working ikon. It was an ikon that materialized out of nothing. Old women are always reporting such things, but what made this case particularly bad was that the miracle was observed and reported by two young Komsomolkas, who had no business to be in church at all (they can be expelled from the Komsomol for attending a religious service), and who completely disgraced their generation by being ready to believe in miracles. It was not only they who believed. Soon the two neighbouring villages were in a turmoil, and from all over the district people came to gape. The old peasant woman who had been the first to have the miracle vouchsafed to her "collected one-and-a-half buckets full of nickels and coppers" from those who came to stare and pray.

In the same article the writer had something to say about the goings on in the Province of Ulyanovsk, the home ground of Lenin, and now called after him instead of by its old name, Simbirsk. This province alone, according to *Komsomolskaya Pravda,* boasts a holy mountain and no less than three holy springs. Believers crowd to them from miles around to be cured, "even young people," and all under the eyes of the local Party officials. In the same province, school children are still allowed "to dress up in cassocks, read the lessons, sing in the church choir, and serve for the priests."

"Over the sea, over the ocean, on the island of Buyan, lies the stone named Alatyr, and on this stone sit three old men; there go to meet them the twelve sister-fevers—the shivering one and the trembling one, the wheezing one and the burning one . . ."

That is part of a wise woman's spell for turning spring water into magic water. It might be found anywhere; but in fact it is used in the Soviet Union. It is this kind of thing that the Communist Party feels it necessary to fight against, and it makes a long and bitter struggle—this, and the priestly performances at Zagorsk and among the mummified monks in their rich brocades under the Pechorsky Monastery at Kiev, and the drunken orgies on saints' days. It is this sort of thing that one must bear in mind always when reading accounts of the drive against religion and superstition, against "survivals of the past." The dark peasants of Chekhov and Turgenev are still very much a force in Soviet Russia, and their spirit is not far below the surface in many representatives of the Communist élite. To achieve a reasonable and enlightened attitude toward life the Russians had farther to go than any other people of Europe when Lenin pitched them into the twentieth century. To catch up with the rest of us, and in some respects to overtake us, the pace has had to be killing. And so you get an effect of extreme patchiness—as when one sees the chief technician of a modern factory paying ten roubles for a mugful of magic water, as when one sees atomic-power plants being produced in a country which has the utmost difficulty in installing elementary plumbing.

4. MORAL REARMAMENT
WITHOUT GOD

THE Communist Party of the Soviet Union stands for global revolution abroad, for a dictatorial system of government at home. That much we all know. But, no less importantly, to the best elements in the Soviet Union it stands for something else, for a species of moral rearmament—moral rearmament without God or Doctor Buchman. That is why the good Communist in Russia simply does not know what we mean when we equate the Communist Party with subversion and conspiracy.

Elsewhere I have written more than enough about the conspiratorial aspects of Leninism, about the unscrupulous use made by Stalin of the Communist idea in the interests of Soviet expansionism, about the cold war. It will be necessary later on in this book to return briefly to these questions. But what we are concerned with now is what the ordinary Russian means by Communism, the ordinary Russian interested neither in winning personal power at home nor in organizing subversion and revolt abroad. What he means by Communism, and what Communism means to him, is something very different from what most of us imagine.

Communism means, of course, different things to different Russians. To the old women at Zagorsk it means anti-Christ, but these old women do not play an active role in the country, though their negative strength must not, as I have tried to show, be underrated—and is not underrated by the government. To countless Soviet citizens in middle age, scattered thickly all over the vast surface of the Union, it means disillusionment; but for the most part these are not prepared to stand in the way of younger men and women who, in new times, make a better job of things—though they may observe the enthusiasm of the

43

young with an ironical, or mocking, or sometimes bitter eye. For the overwhelming majority of citizens of all ages it means, simply, the machinery of state—the only machinery of the only state they know, neither good nor bad, but inescapable. But to the men and women who want to do things, who have ideals and are ready to make sacrifices for them, it is the giver of life: it stands for science and enlightenment and progress in a country that believes in science and enlightenment and progress, as far as its best elements are concerned, no less absolutely and fervently than their Western cousins once believed in these things only fifty years ago.

And they have cause, let there be no mistake about that.

The last terrible upheavals inside the Soviet Union, the terrible purges carried out by Stalin through his policemen Yagoda and Yezhov, were over and done with by 1938. That was the year in which the six young Komsomolkas at Zagorsk were born. They stood by the tomb of Boris Godunov, looking down their noses at the indignities of the past, with all the future in front of them, and with no memory at all of the convulsions that barely twenty years ago made a shambles of the Soviet intelligentsia, caused the intelligentsia of the West to break with Communism, and confirmed all those who were sceptical of or hostile to the "great experiment" in their worst suppositions. These youngsters, who mean a great deal more to the Soviet Union than foreign opinion can ever mean, have no memory of these horrors. In Russia today, to have any clear memory of that terror, which obliterated all opposition, real and potential, to Stalin, which wiped out the old guard of idealists—because idealists are dangerous to an autocrat—which decimated the armed forces, because the Army was the only possible breeding ground for organized revolt, which demoralized a great nation and turned it for a time into a defeatist rabble—to remember this at all clearly the Russian of today has to be well over thirty; to be scarred by it indelibly he must be nearer fifty; and Russia is a country of the young.

Venyamin Kaverin in his remarkable novel about the life and work of a Soviet woman doctor and medical researcher, *An Open Book,* follows his heroine from her pre-revolutionary early childhood until the eve of the Nazi attack upon Russia and relates it in many particulars to the national events of her time. He gives, perhaps better than any other Soviet writer, the attitude and state of mind of a dedicated Party member—not a career Communist, but a professional worker whose life is guided by the Party and receives its sanction from it. He creates an illusion of actuality, of the life of a gifted individual being lived against a background of intense political upheaval and striving, without, however, so much as mentioning the great purges of the thirties which affected every Party member deeply in his personal life and caused the ruin of hundreds of thousands. Kaverin does not mention the terrible strife of the collectivization, and the famine, which nearly brought the system to an end and which, in later years, Stalin was to acknowledge as having been a time more difficult and terrible than the war itself.

It is a remarkable performance; and it is all the more remarkable in that Kaverin has not totally ignored the existence of an opposition. From time to time in his pages the reader encounters individuals who hate the regime and all it stands for and try to obstruct its development. These are not caricatures of men; they are quite plausible. At one and the same time they have more power than, as individuals, they ever had in life, and are less effective than ever they were in life. They are shown as obscurantists rather than as evil men, as unhappy relics of the past rather than as men with a belief in a different future; and in their resistance and their plottings they are very cleverly presented not as opponents of the regime as such but as personal opponents of the life-bringing heroine, the doctor and microbiologist, Tanya Vlasenkova, with whose progress the sympathy of the reader is completely engaged. "Oh yes, there was an opposition. There was a man called Trotsky, a traitor to his country. There was another called Bukharin, who tried to sell the Soviet Union to the Germans. There were industrialists, and factory workers too, who hated Communism so much that they sabotaged their own machines. There were peasants, hard-faced, grasping kulaks, who killed their cattle and burned their crops in a wild attempt to ruin the Soviets so that capitalism could return. Yes, there was indeed an opposition. But now it has been smashed, smashed forever; and although there are still people who are afraid of the future and cling to the past, people still possessed by the dark, antique, capitalist mentality, at the cost of eternal vigilance these can be kept at arm's length and rendered ineffective." That is how the more serious minded of the younger generation see the "opposition." It is a sobering thought.

And now, as a scapegoat for all recent ills, they have Beria, "that man," the dread chief of the Security Police, and for years one of Stalin's closest colleagues, who is alleged, and by many believed, to have plotted against the Politburo and to have been personally responsible for all the judicial crimes and perversions of justice over many years.

There has been running in Moscow a play by the Ukrainian dramatist, Alexander Korneichuk, which was first published at the end of 1954, a month before Beria's execution. Korneichuk is a prominent Party man as well as a writer, and more than once in the past his talent, which is considerable, has been used by the Party to bring home to a large public an important change of policy. He was, for example, the author of the wartime play, *Front*, which, in 1942, told the Soviet people that Stalin was making a clean sweep of the veteran "civil war" generals and replacing them with a new generation of tough leaders, often promoted above the heads of their seniors, schooled in mobile warfare and able to cope with the pace of the blitzkrieg which had torn to ribbons the old-fashioned defensive dispositions of the grand old men of the Red Army, the Büdennys and the Timoshenkos (including Stalin himself—though this was not mentioned). I can well remember the deep excitement at the first performances of that play, which dramatized the conflict between a splendid old general of the old style and his up-and-coming subordinate, intolerant, harsh, insufferable—but deadly in action. It was a sweeping away of the cobwebs. At the same time it explained the terrifying failures of the first six months and promised future success.

And so, toward the end of 1954, while Beria was still in prison, Korneichuk was required to write a play that, among other things, would explain the excesses and abominations of the

Security Police in the recent past and at the same time show that these were over and done with forever.

The play is called *Wings*. It is not basically about the Secret Police. The main theme has to do with letting fresh air into the bureaucracy as a whole, with particular reference to industry and agriculture; it is an attack on the chair-borne agronomists and industrial consultants, who, afraid to get mud on their boots, proliferate in the ministerial offices and sit on the necks of the men in the fields and the factories who are trying to get on with the job. But the hero, Romodan, has a private life as well as a public one. He has a wife, Anna, and a daughter, Lida. They have long been separated, but in the course of the action they meet again. Anna has only recently come back from prison; she had been sentenced on a false charge of collaboration with the Germans during the war. Romodan knew all about this at the time. Anna knew that he knew, and thought he had not lifted a finger to save her. Now they are talking:

Romodan: But why didn't you answer a single one of my letters? Why did you refuse to take money? After all, I am Lida's father. . . .

Anna: Oh, as for your letters—at first I couldn't reply for the simple reason that I was in prison for six months. You know all about that. Then I was let out. Some people helped me find a job. My own earnings were enough for us. As you see, Lida's grown into quite a nice girl. Capable and clever. That's what she's like now. But believe me. . . .

Romodan: I understand.

Anna: Oh, it's simply not worth going back over it all. It would only upset me, and you as well. Now it's over and done with. Truth has conquered. . . . Even the man who threatened me with a concentration camp is now sitting in jail. The head of the Provincial MGB. They put him there when Beria was arrested. They took him the very next day—and, so they say, away by airplane to Moscow. Just like that.

Romodan: He was one of the same gang. I do understand. It's hard for you to talk about it, and not pleasant for me to listen. All the same, it's still harder not to talk. You'll have to tell me about it, Anna.

Anna: What can I tell? When you came back from the front and the head of the MGB showed you those anonymous letters about me, saying that I had been connected with the Germans during the occupation, did you try to defend me? No, you simply told them to check them thoroughly and then went straight off to Kiev. . . .

Romodan: I was ordered to report to the Central Committee.

Anna: I know. So they put me through it properly. . . . (*Pause. She reaches for the bottle*) Have a drink. . . . There, I've spilt it again. . . .

Romodan: Don't. (*He takes the bottle from her, and puts it down*)

Anna: It was lucky that some people refused to be frightened and gathered round to defend me. They dug out the people I saved from the Fascist slave camps. They knew me. Even people who knew very little about me believed me. . . . They could see it in my face. . . . That is what misfortune teaches. . . . They knew very well that the doctors did not go to the labour exchange of their own free will. . . . But you. . . . You knew me when I was a girl. We grew up together, and then we got married. . . . You knew everything about me; but all the same you had doubts. . . . But perhaps you didn't really believe. . . .

Romodan: It never crossed my mind that they would arrest you. When I heard about it I applied to the Central Committee at once. . . . I begged the secretary to do something. And he actually rang up that gangster while I was there. . . .

Anna: What did he reply?

Romodan: That it was a very complicated case and would need a lot of investigation. . . .

Anna: I did not know that you had tried to help me. Thank you for that. But all the same, Peter. . . . Here, give me a drink. . . . (*Romodan fills her glass*) And have one yourself. . . . Here's luck. I'm not going on being resentful. My heart just went dead at that time. And so it still is. . . .

Romodan: Anna, I came here to tell you. . . . I've suffered so much during these years. . . . The pain will be with me until I die! Oh, what you say is true enough. My belief in you *was* shaken. It was that sort of time. . . . But that doesn't excuse me. . . . I understood, understood very quickly, that a man who does not believe his dearest friend, whatever they may say about him, will never believe anybody. I understood that, but it was too late. . . . You sent back my letters unopened. . . . (*Pause*) Oh, what a terrible sum of evil and pain and tears has been spread about by that gang under the guise of vigilance! . . . . They threw dust in our eyes, but we believed them. How we believed them!

Anna (quietly): They hurt people. . . . They hurt people great and small. . . . (*Shining, simple words well up from the depths of her heart*) Our thanks, our deepest thanks, to the Central Committee! That horrible nightmare will never return again!

The Central Committee of the Communist Party of the Soviet Union: the giver of life . . .

Of course, there are plenty of people all over the Soviet Union who, while on the whole believing in the Communist ideal, do not see the Central Committee as a kind of composite St. George slaying a dragon who, only the day before, was himself St. George. But many see it very much like that, and they have to be reckoned with. The great majority of knowledgeable Party members, the eight million of the "vanguard," know very well that Beria was not alone to blame, that long before Beria appeared on the scene Stalin, through Beria's own predecessors, had committed more terrible acts than ever Beria was to aspire to. They know that General Ivan Serov, who has succeeded Beria on the Security side, although the office has been downgraded, was Beria's right hand when it came to dealing with any kind of political opposition, real or imagined, and earned for himself a reputation outstanding even in the Soviet Union for cold brutality. They know that Serov has lately been promoted in the Party. They know that it will take more than the word of a character in a play by Korneichuk, even if that word is inspired by the Central Committee, to abolish oppression and injustice and arbitrary police methods throughout the Soviet Union. But even these, men and women who have lived through hard and complicated times and have had their share of disillusionment, are not by any means as cynical as an outsider might expect. They will agree that in the thirties there was terrorism in the Soviet Union, but they will argue that this was a special action, demanded by the times, and that it was better that many who were innocent should suffer rather than that the system should be overturned. They will agree that in the early months of the war there was much defeatism and going over to the enemy; but they will argue that this always happened in the national republics, first in the Ukraine, then in the Crimea and Caucasia, and reflected nothing at all but an overflow of national-istic, anti-Russian feeling, the lingering product of bourgeois ideas, made possible by the course of events in lands not wholly assimilated to the Soviet system.

In a word, the thoughtful Soviet Communist will talk a great deal more sensibly about his own country, and the errors of the system, than any foreign Communist, or, if it comes to that, any foreign fellow traveller. I have heard deep, considered, and deeply troubled criticism of the regime from loyal Party members on matters which the Dean of Canterbury can find not the slightest fault with. It is possible also to read such criticism in the Soviet press.

In our very understandable preoccupation with the conspiratorial aspects of Communism we have fallen into serious error. In our concentration on the means we have forgotten the content of the idea. It is a very big idea, though somewhat changed since Lenin had anything to do with it. The contrast between the Communist idea and the blacker realities of life in the Soviet Union is so striking that it seems impossible to Englishmen or Americans that Russians who live with this reality and have suffered under it should still believe in the idea. In fact it is not impossible at all. And I think it is probably true to say that the tremendous majority of Russians, as distinct from members of the national minorities, believe implicitly in the general idea behind the Soviet system and, when they criticize it at all, criticize only its particular applications or perversions.

There is no hope for capitalism in the Soviet Union. There is no hope for anything but socialism of some kind. In the West, in Britain and America particularly, in France, Italy, and Germany as well, there are many people with what we can call only an instinctive and unreasoned horror of Communism and everything that it stands for. These are not the most gifted critics of Leninism; indeed, they do not know what Leninism is. But they exist. And they may be surprised to know that their opposite numbers exist in the Soviet Union, but in far greater numbers: men and women with an instinctive and unreasoned horror of what they call capitalism. They do not know very much about capitalism, or the bourgeois way of life—no more, indeed, than most anti-Communists know about Communism.

But they think it is an evil thing, a *basically* evil thing, beside which the inequities of life in the Soviet Union are trivial and superficial. Their revulsion from capitalism occurs on two distinct levels, and it is as well that we understand this. On the easy level, far too many Russians believe the lies of their own propagandists about the West. They believe, for example, that the England of Charles Dickens is the England of today: the England of the sweat-shop, the workhouse, of Gradgrind and Oliver Twist. They believe that the workers are directly exploited by the landlords and the factory owners as they were half a century ago. They believe that England is swarming with unemployed, as it was twenty years ago. They believe that Her Majesty's Government is a league of financiers, business tycoons, and landowners, united for the oppression of the masses, and backed by the Church. They believe that unemployment, poverty, and oppression are growing all the time. All this is hammered into their heads by propagandists, who can still find enough shameful fact to support the fabric of a major lie. And all this, I believe, is relatively unimportant: it makes many Soviet citizens feel sorry for the poor British and American workers, and perhaps it helps them to minimize their own immediate misfortunes. But it is only a matter of time, they are sure, before the workers revolt and the financiers are thrown down, and they are quite pleased to feel that their own country is acting as a guide and an example.

This, as I have said, is capitalism as seen on the elementary level. For the most part the ordinary Russian makes no distinction between, say, Conservative and Labour: Britain's Labour Party is simply an instrument of the big business interest, its historical role being to sell the pass to the bankers. On this elementary level the ordinary Russian is not unlike the ordinary American, who makes no distinction between Communist and Socialist, though for a different reason. It does not seem to me to matter very much either way.

What does matter, because it is not based on a lie and because it springs from a deep, perhaps fundamental difference of attitudes and outlook, is the revulsion from capitalism on the higher level. And this, I am convinced, would have developed in Russia had there been no Lenin, no Karl Marx: at the same time it is the mainstay of the present regime. It is far more than a revulsion from capitalism: it is a revulsion, instinctive in the mass of Russians, against a considerable part of what the West today understands by freedom. To the great mass of Russians, capitalism, or the bourgeois society of the West, is the caricature of the propagandists. To the intelligent Russian, Western democracy is a hollow sham which positively sickens the temperamentally antipathetic by its apparent hypocrisy, and is often incomprehensible even to the sympathetic. Just as we in the West can see nothing but hypocrisy in the system which magnifies the rights of the common man in its constitution and puts him in practice at the mercy of a tyrant, so they in the East can see nothing but hypocrisy in the system which magnifies the freedom of the individual and in practice puts him at the mercy of economic circumstances, which means big business. Just as we in the West can see nothing but a hideous lie in the regime which calls itself democratic and yet admits only one party, and that the instrument of a small group of rulers, if not of an absolute dictator, so they in the East can see nothing but a lie in the system which, under the guise of democracy, offers the people the chance to vote into power alternative groups of politicians who take turns in doing the same thing, if with a slightly different emphasis, to enjoy the fruits of office, and who appear to have far more in common with each other than with the people they are supposed to represent.

I have tried to explain this difference and examined its applications elsewhere. For the purposes of this book, which offers a picture, not an argument, there is no need to go into the historical causes of the Russian conception of freedom. It is enough to say that it is different from ours—how different anyone may see who cares to read the Russian thinkers of the nineteenth century and then, to bring himself up to date, the proceedings of the last Congress of Soviet Writers, held in December 1954. And the point I am trying to make is simply this: If the ordinary ignorant Russian finds his faith in the regime bolstered by lies about the regimes of the West, the educated Russian, who has perhaps travelled in the West and seen it for himself, shrinks no less from a system based, as he sees it, on usury, on the law of the jungle, on buying cheap and selling dear, and on the pretence that a man is free because he can say what he likes against the government and help to vote a political party out of office—even though the fear of unemployment may make him submit to all kinds of evils and indignities. And to the educated Russian these attributes of Western society seem no less intolerable than the more atrocious aspects of the authoritarian regime of the Soviet Union appear to us.

In other words, telling the Russians what we like to think of as the truth about Western society will not take us very far— not, at least, with educated Russians, who know something about it already. "Very well," they will reply to the Voice of America. "You can vote Eisenhower out and someone else in. So what? You have more Cadillacs, admittedly, and far more Chevvies. Your plumbing and your gadgets are the seventh wonder of the world. Hollywood is the eighth. But what are you doing with all these things which come to you so easily? And though you can stand up and say what you like about the President, what happens to a man who stands up and says 'Long live Communism'? You pretend you have freedom—and let it rot at the feet of the Statue of Liberty. We make no pretence of having what you call freedom; but we are working, slowly and laboriously—perhaps, indeed, not so slowly—toward a freedom that will be real, and not a sham."

Who is right?

Each man can answer for himself, and the answers will show a national line-up.

Perhaps the chief obstacle to credulity when it comes to believing that the Russians, ardent and idealistic Russians, really believe in the essential goodness of their system, and put down those aspects of it which arouse dismay in the West as aberrations rather than inevitable products of the system, is the fact that East and West have very different ideas of the real meaning of Communism. Communism, in so far as it stands for anything in the West, stands above all for egalitarianism and the withering away of the state. To Lenin it also stood for that: the early Communists permitted themselves maximum salaries which were very low, and forswore all luxurious living; Lenin, in his arrogant

innocence, for a time believed that all the administrative offices
could be filled by butchers and bakers and candlestick makers.
The retreat from this position, the exaltation of the apparatus
of state and the development of a stratified society with very
great, and planned, income differentials, has been such that the
foreign observer too easily concludes that the Soviet Communist
is now a total cynic, that the whole noble, if far-fetched, ideal
that inspired the early Bolsheviks has been thrown overboard. I
have no means of knowing what the higher leadership believes,
but I do know from conversations with many rank-and-file Party
members that they are far from being total cynics. Inside the
Soviet Union the Communist ideal has not been abandoned; it
has simply, over the years, shifted its emphasis—adapting itself,
if you like, to the living reality. Egalitarianism and the withering
away of the state are still seen as distant goals—but so distant
that for the time being there is no point on dwelling on them.
But their postponement has not left a vacuum. In order one day
to achieve this consummation it is necessary enormously to raise
the level of society, to turn the Soviet people into the sort of
people to whom egalitarianism and the withering away of the
state may one day naturally come. It was Stalin, as far back as
1931, who roughly attacked the egalitarian idea, calling it a petty-
bourgeois notion. He was concerned then with establishing a
steeply graded system of incentives to raise production under the
Five-Year Plan. But whatever may have been his real thoughts
about the matter, the egalitarian idea has not been lost, and
countless Soviet citizens look with regret, and sometimes dismay,
on the class differences that are growing up under the elaborate
system of differential rewards. If that were the whole of the story
there would be nothing more to be said, and Western critics who
say that Communism inside the Soviet Union is now an empty
husk would be right. In fact they are wrong; for although the
pure doctrine has been betrayed, and although very many governmental actions offend against the spirit of Lenin's revolution, that
spirit is very much alive. This is the precise opposite of what is
generally understood in the West: namely that the doctrine survives while the spirit is dead.

The spirit, which still dominates the minds of countless Soviet citizens, including the most active, says that by taking thought and projecting thought into action mankind can so improve his own material condition as to produce a new world, richer and more solidly based than anything dreamed up by the Utopians, because rooted in the historic truths proclaimed by Karl Marx. And what is happening in the Soviet Union today is the struggle of a minority to do good to a majority, often in the majority's own despite. It is the greatest "do-good" movement in history, and it has a wholly secular inspiration. It relies for its shock troops on the starry eyes, stout muscles, and mental drive of each new generation as it comes of age—which, as it tires and loses its impetus in disillusionment, is replaced always with another. And the disillusionment is rarely total. There, after all, the very real achievements in the chosen direction quite visibly are. The Soviet Union is more literate, more healthy, more developed in every way than the old Tsarist Empire. Its industrial achievements are stupendous, its cultural achievements, in spite of the regimentation of the mind, very much to be admired. And all this, no less than the labour camps, has happened under Leninism: the question whether all this could have happened, and without the labour camps, under any other system is neither here nor there; it did not. It was the Soviet system, and no other, that released the immense potential, frozen for so long, of the Russian people. And with their great and natural pride in the positive achievements of the past three decades the Soviet people, including many who have no use for the enthusiasts, the crusaders, the busy-bodies and the bureaucrats of the Communist Party, are not unnaturally inclined to identify the regime with the country, the object of their patriotism. When all is said, a regime round which a whole national way of life has grown is not to be shrugged off lightly. Too many people in the West talk of the Soviet regime as though it were simply a party programme. But in fact it is now in its best aspects taken almost wholly for granted, like Parliamentarianism in Britain, or the Constitution in the United States. Both these last are constantly modified in practice by changing emphases and values. So it is with the Soviet regime. And thus it is that even men who have suffered deeply under the regime, and men who are bitterly critical of some of its works, now equate it with their whole existence, believe in its fundamental superiority to other systems, and, in the last resort, would die for it—as many in fact did die.

None of this spirit is very manifest in the public places of the Soviet Union. Moscow in its bewildering complexity is to all appearances like any other capital city, with a strong Russian accent. The same is true of all the other great cities I have seen: Leningrad, Stalingrad, Kiev. The small provincial towns are like nothing more than the small provincial towns of the nineteenth-century novelists. The manufacturing towns are classic products of the industrial revolution. The peasants are peasants—with tractors added to them. To find the crusading spirit one has to go deep below the surface, past the stereotyped jargon of the propagandists, past the smug catchwords of intolerant, uncomprehending youth, deep down below the constant grumbling of the middle-aged—until one fetches up against the rock bottom of the system. I remember one evening in Moscow, after one of those interminable discussions about life and politics and attitudes, about the success and failures of Britain, about the potentialities of the United States, about the realities of life in the Soviet Union, a Russian friend—a very distinguished figure indeed, not a politician—finished an argument as follows, not dogmatically, but hesitantly and gropingly: "What it seems to boil down to is this: We believe that by taking decisive action we can improve the human condition; and we have the courage of our convictions; we are not afraid to make mistakes. You would like to see the human condition improved, but you have no convictions and are afraid to act in case you make mistakes." One comes across this attitude time and time again. It is a genuine attitude. The way Lenin put it was that you cannot make an omelet without breaking eggs.

And once one has touched this rock bottom, which really is the foundation of the Soviet Union, one discovers that the hectoring Party jargon and the smug catchwords are a great deal more real to most citizens of the Soviet Union than at first sight seems probable. We, when all is said, have our catchwords too, used by politicians every day scarcely less repetitively than the catchwords of the Kremlin. When businessmen or politicians extol in every speech the virtues of free enterprise, rugged individualism, liberty of the subject, Western democracy, Western values, the Christian attitude, we simply do not notice, taking such expressions for granted, in our stride; that does not mean that we do not believe in them, or some of them. And so it is with the Russians. Talk about free enterprise and Western democracy makes nonsense to them and must, they feel, be deliberate nonsense—as we feel, incorrectly, that the Soviet politicians are talking deliberate nonsense when they talk about war-mongers, People's Democracies, the peace-loving government of the Soviet Union, the wicked reactionaries of the British Labour Party, and the glory of Socialist Competition.

Not all Russians are ardent and idealistic. The vast majority, as in any land, live for the day and have to be managed. The only difference—and it is a vital difference—is that in the Soviet Union the ardent and idealistic, as a rule, are the supporters of Authority: in other lands they are usually the rebels.

Among the things that have lately been striking more intelligent and open-minded visitors to the Soviet Union are the unexpected—unexpected to them—reminiscences of Victorianism which are such a dominant feature of Soviet life. There is nothing new in this. Florence Nightingale and Queen Victoria have for long been the unknown spiritual heroines of the Soviet Union. Disciplined endeavour, self-denial, moral rectitude, have for long been the desired qualities of the new Soviet man. This was what I had in mind when I spoke, earlier, of moral rearmament without God. Or, imagine a YMCA without Christianity, but with all the power of the state behind it, and you have an image of the Komsomol as its organizers like to think of it. In fact the Komsomol today has nearly twenty million members: it is no longer the élite corps of self-denying youth that it was even before the war. It is now an immense and unwieldy cross-section of the Soviet young, reflecting much of the good and a great deal of the bad in the new society, and the Party is by no means sure of what to do with it.

5. *BLAT*

AS LIFE unfolds itself during a prolonged stay one becomes slowly conscious of aspects of life in the Soviet Union which have nothing to do with the aspirations of Lenin, which indeed contradict them. I am not thinking now of the more notorious manifestations of the police state: arbitrary arrest and no less arbitrary imprisonment, forced labour in unspeakable conditions. I am thinking of all sorts of things which, the Communists ask us to believe, are found only in the decadent bourgeois countries of the West: the ubiquity of "fiddling," or minor corruption; the frequent incidence of major corruption of a very high-spirited kind; the supreme importance of a phenomenon called *blat,* a significant monosyllable which stands for something rather stronger than "pull" and rather less than "graft"; the development of a class of irresponsible youth, called *gooligani,* or hooligans, when they are poor, and *stilyagi,* or playboys, when they are well off. With all this goes the stratification of Soviet society into clearly recognizable classes. And within this *ambiance* two new professions have established themselves and flourish exceedingly: on a sophisticated and wholesale level the *tolkach,* or "fixer"; on a cruder level, the *spekulant,* or "spiv." There is also the problem of drunkenness.

In face of all these, the ordinary police, or Militia, seem powerless, or unwilling to take action, although they are clearly no less "counter-revolutionary" than the most stubborn political offenders. And, for the time being, the fight against corruption of every kind is being carried on mainly by the propagandists, in an effort to mobilize public opinion on the side of puritanism against the forces of hedonism. It is now an open struggle. While Stalin was still alive one could read through a year's output of the Soviet press without being aware that drunkenness was a problem or that such a thing as a playboy or a spiv existed in the Soviet Union. Today it is very different. The papers are full of disgraceful and anti-social happenings, and the cartoonists of *Krokodil* and other satirical publications are finding in these a rich field for exploitation. Only the fellow travellers in the West, to say nothing of the Western Communist Parties, do not seem to have caught up with the times.

This is one of the reasons for my own personal gratitude to the new government. When Stalin was still alive, discussion of whole areas of Soviet life was virtually impossible, because nobody believed the returned traveller who had kept his eyes open and penetrated a little beneath the surface. Nobody would believe, for example, that the whole of the Soviet Union was one vast black market. There were occasional official reports of provincial Party and government functionaries' being arrested and heavily sentenced for embezzlement or the conversion of state property to their own uses. But those were always treated as exceptional. What was never understood was that during the hard times, when millions were starving, anybody, apart from privileged shock workers, who tried high-mindedly to exist on his legal ration and to obey the law in every particular quite simply died. And when the whole population of a great country is forced for survival on to the black market, the habit of mind induced is going to take a great deal of getting rid of.

The state itself, of course, had no choice but to legalize the black market in food. The government knew very well that there was not enough food in the country to keep everyone alive, and all kinds of devices were tried to ensure the survival of the most needed. These ranged from the simple failure to deliver any food at all to provincial towns which could contribute little or nothing to the winning of the war, through the establishment of special shops and canteens where adequate food could be had at low prices by those who were needed for the war effort, to the encouragement of the traditional kolkhoz markets in the towns where neighbouring peasants (they would come from as far as a hundred miles away) could sell their surplus products from their own plots for what they would fetch: this meant not only that the more able and better paid could supplement their rations, but also that, for the sake of heavy profits, the peasants would work harder and produce more food than they would otherwise have done. But even this was not enough. Factories would send out squads of workers on foraging expeditions into the countryside; and any individual who could by any conceivable means conjure up a truck, a car, and a few gallons of gasoline could keep himself alive and make a fortune into the bargain by driving out to a remote kolkhoz and returning in triumph with a couple of sacks of potatoes. The profits made by the *kolkhozniks* were all to be wiped out soon after the war by the great devaluation; but the black-market habit remained. It had, of course, been in operation since the revolution itself, all through the years of scarcity; but the desperate shortages of the war gave it a new life, so that it invaded every aspect of existence. And it continues to this day.

One of the biggest black markets deals with living accommodations. I found it impossible to discover the current illegal premium for a room in Moscow; but it was six thousand roubles in 1947, when wages were about half what they are today. The housing shortage is still acute, and, although official rents remain very low, there is another side to this picture: it is impossible to find a room in Moscow without an official permit which declares that your residence there is necessary. There are only two ways of getting one of these permits; the first is by being an indispensable worker or official; the second is through *blat*. At the same time, once you have a room there is little hope of ever changing it, unless you are specially privileged, by legal means. Hence the black market in rooms. And it is the same, to a lesser degree, in every city. Only a short time ago *Pravda* gave chapter and verse about the housing black market in Rostov, where, one would have thought, accommodations should be fairly easy to find.

Blat in its classic form stands for an extremely elaborate and all-pervading "old-boy" network: the granting of favours in the hope, the expectation, of favours to come. Everyone, including the most ardent Party members, deals in it—everyone, that is to say, who has anything to offer. If you have a friend who is a trade-union official he will probably have blocks of tickets to dispose of to his flock for everything under the sun, from theatres

to football games. He will let you have a couple of tickets to see
Ulanova in *Giselle* if he thinks you can put him in touch with a
man who can get him a new tire at list price, and without waiting, for his baby car. And so it goes on, through the whole of daily
life. With *blat,* enough of it, you can get anything: a ticket for a
sanitorium at Yalta; a seat on the Trans-Siberian; a length of first-
quality cloth to have a suit made to measure; spares for your
television set; a new electric stove; exemption from compulsory
political lectures; a man to mend the plumbing of your flat; caviar
when there is no caviar in the shops; nylons; a new edition of
Dostoevski; a rose-bush for your garden—everything you can
conceivably want, and pay for, in a land where scarcities in all
but the absolute necessities of life are general. *Blat* will get you all
these things, and access to any of these things will itself endow you
with *blat.* And the people with most *blat* of all are, as would be
expected, those who need it least: Party and government officials,
to say nothing of the political police, who are all well provided
for anyway, but who can add to their possessions by dispensing
patronage and favours of every imaginable kind. To him who
hath shall be given.

It should not be thought that *blat* has anything in common
with simple bribery. It is essentially the product of an under-the-
counter mentality which causes friends and acquaintances to
combine together to defeat the shortages, and the unlimited,
obstructive, entangling red tape of the bureaucratic machine.
The motive is self-defence; and the most incorruptible individuals deal in it freely. There is no other way to come through in a
land where there is still far from sufficient to satisfy all needs, even
at a price, and where the only legal channels are controlled by the
state—which means the bureaucratic machine. The English in
wartime were well acquainted with this atmosphere, which in the
Soviet Union is far more overpowering and all-pervasive, and
which will persist so long as there are shortages of anything, and
so long as every aspect of buying and selling is officially controlled
by the central government.

Bribery, I should say, is comparatively infrequent. *Blat* stands
for the exchange of personal favours and is human and warm.
Bribery stands for impersonal corruption. Obviously there are

innumerable cases every day where *blat* approaches bribery; but even then, more often than not, it is redeemed by the element of fair exchange, of barter. Straight bribery is frowned on: the new puritanism of the Soviet state has done its work there. But there is a point where the exercise of *blat* becomes almost professional; and when a man spends too much time exchanging favours, and develops a regular network of contacts with himself acting as a kind of middleman, he is regarded, sometimes tolerantly, sometimes with indignation, as sailing rather close to the wind. "He's a wonderful chap for making a *kombinatsia,*" his acquaintances will say, and shrug their shoulders, as one might say, "He's too clever by half!"

If *blat* is a country-wide movement of self-defence, speculation is something other. *Blat* is never mentioned in the newspapers; it is so widespread and universally necessary a phenomenon that it is quite taken for granted. Speculation is cold-eyed and selfish; and the government is active in trying to stamp it out. But that, too, will survive, so long as shortages exist, which means for a very long time to come. There are part-time speculators everywhere, but there are also full-time professionals, and these are regarded with distaste by upstanding citizens. They deal in everything from stolen goods to cheap money; from manufactures "diverted" between the factory and the state shops, to objects obtained by queuing longer than anybody else can afford to queue. And what they deal in at a given time gives a very fair indication of the social preoccupations of the moment. Last year the best speculators were dealing above all in spare parts for motor cars and motorcycles, spare tubes for television sets, illicit recordings of American jazz—and editions of the Russian classics. The generally accepted profit was one hundred fifty per cent.

Suppose you have been exploring one of the state gramophone-record shops in Moscow. There are not many of them—only two or three—that carry a large selection of records of the better sort. The shop is jammed with people, and because there are no printed catalogues the titles of the records are duplicated on foolscap sheets and displayed on revolving frames, rather like the revolving frames that display picture post cards in the West.

Soon you find that the densest crowds are trying to get at the
frames displaying dance music and popular songs—as they would
be in the West. They are fiercely pushing, sweating, rather short-
tempered crowds, possessed by an undoubted enthusiasm and full
of excited comments. They sway so much, and the frames revolve
so fast as people from every side catch at them to turn the lists
their way, that it is virtually impossible to write down the required numbers in the middle of the crush. Either you have to
learn them by heart and then butt backward through the people
breathing down your neck, or else you have to call out the numbers to a friend on the outskirts of the crowd. The fact that a
record is listed does not indicate necessarily by any means that it
is in stock, and the little girls behind the counter have a busy
time running to and fro, returning from the racks as often as
not empty-handed, and explaining to would-be customers that
they don't know anything about anything: they have only been
working in the shop three days (it is a remarkable thing that in
Moscow the more menial jobs, from taxi-driving to serving in a
gramophone shop, seem never to be held for longer than a week,
or at most ten days; the turn-over is astonishing, with the result
that nobody knows anything anywhere, and nobody can reason-
ably be blamed for it). The demand, in a word, is tremendous.
The whole city, it seems, must be possessed by a craze for gramophone records—dance records above all—until it is recalled that
Moscow has eight million people, and there are not more than
seven or eight gramophone-record shops all told, plus a few record
departments in one or two big stores. The comparative calm
round the frames showing classical music then seems all the more
surprising. For some of these records, especially the new long-
playing ones, are very good indeed. It is the hardest thing in the
world for an ordinary citizen of Moscow to get a ticket for *Boris
Godunov* at the Bolshoi Theatre; but with a little persistence
anybody can buy for a very moderate sum the same performance
on a long-playing record. Yet very few do so. The tremendous
and the fashionable attraction is jazz; and the sort of jazz until
recently permitted by the authorities is lugubrious in the extreme. So that for a young Muscovite to boast a couple of genuine

American records puts him in much the same position *vis-à-vis* the local young women as the possession of a Bentley in England or a Cadillac in the United States.

And it is here that the speculator comes in. He is lurking in the unpainted doorway of the shop. He has been keeping an eye on you among a hundred others; and when you come out he is there at your shoulder with the confidential insolence of a man selling dirty post cards. But he is not selling dirty post cards. What he has under his jacket, what he will show you if you give him the least encouragement, is the latest American hit—the latest, that is, to reach Moscow and be processed illicitly: perhaps only two years old. He produces a disk about the size of a saucer and remarkably heavy. It has a strange and cloudy appearance. It looks like glass. And indeed it is glass. It is nothing less than an old X-ray plate "won" from a Moscow hospital or clinic—by what tortuous process is anybody's guess—and serving as the base for a re-recording of the genuine American article. So that what you get is a revolving photograph of an unknown citizen's appendix, emitting the glad strains of Louis Armstrong's trumpet. Thus does a government policy discouraging hot jazz play into the hands of the manufacturers of collectors' pieces.

The speculators are not all as esoteric as this. A very thriving trade is done in spare parts of every kind. One of the failings of Soviet planning is that the provision of spare parts is almost always overlooked. This is a natural tendency in all industrial enterprises that can sell all they can produce and concentrate on quantity production with inadequate means. It happens in Britain with some of the more arrogantly successful organizations. And so the speculator steps in again; and here he serves staid citizens, who would not be seen dead conversing with a spiv on a street corner, through intermediaries. It is possible, as the cartoon from *Krokodil* shows, to see shady individuals outside motorcycle show-rooms, their pockets bursting with the valves and plugs and belts that cannot be obtained inside. But as a rule on this level speculation is organized through a middleman who comes between the client and the man who actually has the goods. It is in effect an illicit form of retail trade in a land where there is officially no private retail trade, and it is treated as such, with regular tariffs allowing for regular margins of profit. And it is true to say that it is impossible to run a private car or a motor-cycle in Russia today without employing, directly or indirectly, one of these speculating middlemen; to obtain the simplest spare part through the official channels in less than a year is an impossibility. So this sort of high-class speculator flourishes: he is a shopkeeper without a shop—without overhead. And speculation, with its connotations of risk, is hardly the word to describe his activities. He knows he can unload immediately as much as he can lay hands on at a very handsome profit indeed. And the only risk he takes is the risk of police prosecution, which, to judge by the newspapers, is not very great. There are speculators dealing in every conceivable article except the basic foodstuffs, some part-time, as I have said, some very much full-time. But for every transaction, such is the organization of Soviet society, there has to be an inside man; and the distribution and employment of these inside men, if they could ever be discovered, would make a fascinating sociological study. Some goods are stolen, of course; some are "cornered" by the manipulation of queues. But when it comes to spare parts and other desirable incidentals there is clearly a chain between the factory and the man who delivers the goods to the customer.

A little story illustrating the sort of thing that goes on all the time and everywhere was lately told in Moscow. One day when the workers at a certain factory were knocking off work an old packer with a beard and a sly, mujik look about him emerged from the yard pushing a push-cart piled high with straw and shavings. The guard at the gate stopped him and asked him what he had in his push-cart. "Shavings and straw," the old man replied, "just as you see." But the guard was not satisfied; he prodded the straw with his stick. The stick hit nothing hard, and so he made the old man take out the straw and spread it on the ground. There was nothing in the straw, and there was nothing in the push-cart, and so he had to let the old man through. The same thing happened night after night for a week. Increasingly baffled, the guard went through the ritual of searching the straw before he let the old man through. After that the guard gave up, and he and his colleagues made a joke of the old man—except that they were still convinced he was up to something, and every few months hauled him up for a quick check. It went on for three years. Every night for three years the old man came out with his push-cart piled high with shavings and straw—until the time came for him to be pensioned off. On his last night at the factory he came out as usual, but for once without his push-cart. He went up to the guard to say farewell, and the guard—the original guard, who liked the old man—having wished him well, said, "Now Uncle, come clean! We can't do anything to you now. You've got your pension and nobody can touch you. But just as a matter of professional interest—it won't go any farther—what have you been smuggling out of the factory every night all these years?" The old man smiled beatifically, and winked. "Push-carts," he said.

There is a lot of the Soviet Union in that story—from the factory guard who had no idea what the factory he was supposed to guard was making, to the fellow-workmen who knew very well and never tried to queer the old man's pitch.

It might be thought from all this—from the "spivvery" in jazz records and push-carts and motor-car spares—that Soviet society is wholly material and Philistine. But that is not so. England and other Western countries in wartime had black markets in almost everything. But no other country but the Soviet Union has a black market in books—not banned books, not what are called "curious" books, but the recommended Russian classics. These are printed in huge quantities, but the quantities are never enough. The works of Lenin and Stalin, and scientific text-books of every kind, are printed in millions; of these there are always enough. The works of the best contemporary novelists are printed in hundreds of thousands and given what one would think the widest circulation; but there are never quite enough of these. The pre-revolutionary classics are reprinted in editions ranging from fifteen thousand to one hundred thousand; and of these there are never anything like enough. The bookshops are besieged day after day when the word goes round that a new edition of *War and Peace* or *Fathers and Sons,* or Chekhov's plays is due to appear; but all but a handful of the hungry multitude are disappointed. Books, though cheap, are as good as any other merchandise; the speculators are at work. They keep their eyes and ears open; they have contacts in the publishing houses who tell them what is going on; and before the bona-fide customer arrives each shop's allocation is quite simply cornered—either "by arrangement" with the woman behind the counter, or by the simple expedient of paying people to queue. And so you have the remarkable sight of sober Soviet citizens bargaining on the pavement outside a state book-shop with disreputable-looking tricksters for a brand new copy of *Anna Karenina* or *First Love*—and paying cheerfully three times the price on the cover.

The spiv in times of scarcity administers to the appetites of the time, and there is no appetite in the Soviet Union more insatiable than the appetite for reading. The Russians read everything and everywhere. It seems that all Russians read: in the trams, in the underground, on seats in the parks, waiting in queues, at restaurant tables. Wherever you go, to whatever office, the girl or the man on duty will have an open book within reach. The floor girls and the elevator operators at hotels read day and night. The young people read, sitting on steps outside the theatres as they wait for their friends. The waitress will put down a book as you enter a café; and there will be an open book on the seat beside your taxi-driver. When they are not reading books the Russians are reading newspapers, which they devour, for all their deadly dullness. But books are what they like. And there are never enough to go round. The comparative newcomers to reading in this land where literacy has spread like a forest fire in the past thirty years are satisfied with almost anything. The more discriminating will read with pleasure only the more human contemporary Soviet writers, the Russian classics, and translations from abroad. The high intelligentsia and the truly exacting will read nothing but the classics and French and English originals. The more discriminating are growing every day, and the publishers lag behind in response to their demands. Hence the speculators. And it is amusing to see this junction of the most exciting and the most depressing aspects of Soviet life.

There is one kind of thing the speculators never touch; that is a book by Lenin or Stalin or any permitted revolutionary theorist. The bookshops are choked with these works. And I can say solemnly that in all the time I have been in Russia I have never once seen a Russian reading any book by Lenin or Stalin, or even the *Short History of the Communist Party*. I don't know who buys these vast editions. Some are compulsory for Party members, of course, which must account for several million copies. Perhaps the rest are distributed as prizes.

The attitude of the authorities toward the speculators has for a long time been curiously equivocal. There has been a powerful press campaign against these "anti-social parasites." The disease has been diagnosed and acknowledged. "The appearance of speculators and speculation in our time," said *Trud,* the trade-union daily newspaper (February 14, 1954), "is caused by the shortage of certain goods. Exploiting this temporary difficulty [*Trud* found it unnecessary to mention that the temporary difficulty has lasted for thirty-seven years] every kind of parasite and lover of easy gain buys up those goods which are in short supply in order to resell them, thus disorganizing our Soviet trade and causing the people great inconvenience. Like leeches they cling to the body of our society, in order to live at its expense. Thus do the repulsive survivals of capitalism manifest themselves—survivals which it is our duty daily and ruthlessly to root out." This sort of thing is going on all the time: a great deal of denunciation but very little action. The police are frequently attacked, sometimes by name, for their inactivity. *Evening Moscow,* for example (October 18, 1954), once went after a whole precinct, Section 108 of the Moscow Militia, whose officers were permitting the most elaborate illegalities to go on under their own noses. Section 108 includes the smartest shopping district in Moscow, including Pushkin Street.

Every morning . . . a senior sergeant of the Militia strolls unhurriedly along Pushkin Street. He is on his beat. The new, taut shoulder-straps and the glistening, polished numerals on his shoulder-pieces, show that their owner is a smart man and serves in the 108th section of the Moscow Militia. He walks on and does not see that near the entrance to a furniture shop there is being committed what on the Militia charge-sheet would be called a gross violation of public order —and, in ordinary speech, simply a disgrace. A handful of shop assistants are unsuccessfully trying to push a group of individuals in threadbare *tulups* away from the shop entrance. Ejecting streams of filthy language and breathing out alcoholic fumes, the owners of the tulups move aside reluctantly and then once more swoop back to their old positions. Here they brazenly importune would-be customers of the furniture store with one and the same phrase:

"You want a sideboard? What about a nice wardrobe? We'll fix it!"

And fix it they do. For an appropriate remuneration, of course—and not a small one. The statutory price for the services of such "supernumerary middlemen" is fixed at several hundred roubles. But the militiaman on duty in Pushkin Street does not see anything of this and passes by indifferently.

The press is full of such stories. There are speculators everywhere. "They work in an organized, coordinated way," *Izvestia* complains (March 20, 1955). "They know what goods will be arriving in the shops before the managers do. They have their representatives on watch at the depots. The extraordinary extent of the speculators' information inevitably raises doubts about some of the workers in these depots."

Sometimes the police take action, but only when things have gone so far that speculation merges into embezzlement—as in the case of Madame Profokevya, a storekeeper at the great Moscow shop for members of the armed forces. "How is it possible," *Trud* wistfully demanded (February 23, 1954), "that this unmarried storekeeper, with an aged mother to support, could appear one day at her work in a sealskin coat, the next day in a beaver coat, and the next in a Persian lamb coat without her colleagues' noticing something odd?" In fact the lady in question was not found out; she had bought herself a suburban villa for several tens of thousands of roubles—having the transaction ingeniously drawn up in the name of her brother-in-law, a university official. Miss Profokevya was not only a speculator; she had *blat*.

"In the great mirrored windows of the Tashkent fashion houses," wrote *Pravda* (February 11, 1954), "are displayed suits for both men and women, suits fashionable in style and elegantly cut." These are the windows shown proudly to foreign tourists, and duly admired by them on their conducted tours of Soviet Central Asia. But the foreign tourists are left to believe that anybody with the money may buy. *Pravda* went on to reveal what any Soviet citizen could tell the foreign tourists, if any Soviet citizen cared to stick his neck out. "Unfortunately at the moment the suits are worn only by dummies in the shop windows. Imagine that you have been bold enough to decide on one of these magnificent creations for yourself. You enter the shop. You are told, 'Alas, we have no suitable material.' If the material should by chance be available you will then be told that they have no lining material, no trimmings. If you overcome this difficulty, you will be asked to bring your own buttons. Along with the buttons it would be as well to bring a tailor. Otherwise you will have to wait a very long time for your order"—unless you have a great deal of *blat,* or unless you deal with a "supernumerary middleman," a speculator, as did Vladimir Vladimirevich Malyarov, occupier of a Chair at the Odessa Polytechnic, who was reproached by the Militia for buying from speculators. By employing rogues, the police maintained, he was in fact supporting them. " 'In what way was I supporting them?' he retorted with indignation. 'All that happened was that I found a man who could fix up a fur coat for my wife. It cost 2753 roubles, and I paid him 6500. . . .' " (*Literary Gazette,* April 24, 1954).

The publishing of the names of respectable citizens has so far been one of the main weapons of the Party against the wave of speculation. For example, *Leningrad Pravda* (May 23, 1954) blew the top off a remarkable black market in motor cars which involved some of the most respected luminaries of Leningrad. The black market was highly organized and had a name, "The Committee for the Observance of the Queue to Buy Motor Cars" and a headquarters, given by *Leningrad Pravda* as "Apraksin Yard, Cul-de-sac No. 2, Space between Dustbin and Old Barrel." "The plenary meetings of the Committee are held in odd gateways. . . . Scientists, artists, engineers, come to it to worship. It deals on the spot with hundreds of applications by letter and telegram, and organizes the sale and resale of motor cars with its own statutes and decrees." Among the members of this committee were a highly prominent engineer, the pianist Sverichevsky, and four members of the Leningrad Philharmonic Orchestra, all, among others, listed by name.

For a long time it was hard to see why the Militia were so powerless to put down a form of activity which stands for the negation of the whole idea behind the Soviet state. Good Communists in the Soviet Union were as puzzled as any outsider. It is true that the Militia, as distinct from the Political Police, do not enjoy a very high reputation for efficiency. They are amiable fellows, for the most part, who, in spite of their loaded revolvers, are happiest when looking the other way. They ignore drunks when they can, and are kind to them when they can no longer be overlooked. They turn a blind eye to the most remarkable goings-on, and seem to confine their constructive activities to blowing their whistles very hard when errant pedestrians cross the vast spaces of the main streets at the wrong places. Their easy-going and somewhat timorous ways are the precise opposite in every particular of the bland ruthlessness of their much more highly paid brothers of the political arm. And this is in the Russian tradition; under the Tsars, as under Stalin, the common criminal was always regarded as a venial offender, and the heavy punishments were reserved for the political.

And yet . . . there are crimes and crimes. And this offence of speculation attacks so directly the very roots of the system that it was hard to see why more was not done about it. The answer came last year in an elaborate study published in the legal journal *Soviet State and Law*: "Criminal Responsibility for Speculation under Soviet Criminal Law" (November 5, 1955), from which it emerged that speculation as normally practised was not in fact a crime, and the Militia failed to prosecute because they had no grounds for prosecution. The only kind of speculation recognized by the Soviet Criminal Law (Article 107 of the Criminal Codex of the RSFSR) was designed to combat "counter-revolutionary" trading in the early days of the regime. It defines speculation as the buying up and reselling, by private persons for the purposes of gain, of agricultural produce and mass-consumer goods. It was designed for a particular phase of the struggle to Sovietize the country, and it is full of loopholes as applied to present-day conditions. For example, as *Soviet State and Law* admits, "Jewelry, television sets, valuable furs, and motor cars may also be objects of speculation. These articles cannot be described as mass consumer goods in the strict sense, but there can be no doubt that their resale, like the resale of other similar articles at increased prices, does harm both to Soviet trade and to the interests of the consumer." The article goes on to demand a reformulation of the law to cover present-day contingencies, a reformulation based on the premise that "speculation is a crime of greed, in which the parasitic inclinations of certain backward citizens find their expression. Therefore the establishment of the intention to make a profit is of decisive importance in the substance of speculation." It further suggests that the punishments provided for under the 1932 statute —deprivation of freedom for a period of from five to ten years— are too severe. Thus the writer recomemnds at the same time a broadening of the law and a moderation of the penalties to fit comparatively small offences. "It seems to us that it would be possible at the present time to apply less severe measures of punishment to the less pernicious speculators. It must be kept in mind that the successful fight against any particular form of crime depends not only on the application of severe measures of punishment, but far more on the inevitability of punishment of some kind. It is therefore essential to create a situation in which not a single case of speculation in any shape or form shall remain unpunished."

This article has a very profound significance. I have written at length about the activities of the speculators because they form a great part of life just below the surface in the Soviet Union. They are a part of life as lived—the life that is not observed by the casual visitor. It is this sort of thing, not the state of the Communist Parties of Western Europe, that interests and preoccupies the ordinary Russian. And it is with this sort of thing that the energies of the Soviet leadership are increasingly occupied. Soviet speculation is amusing enough in itself; but I have not cited these examples out of malice. One of the most important requirements just now is that the West have some sort of idea of what it is to live in the Soviet Union, and what it is to share in the management of the Soviet Union. The forces eating away at the foundations of the Communist state are widely diffused, but they add up to something very strong. The deep need for consumer goods of all kinds in a country too long starved of them combines with the deep instinct for profitable trade—buying cheap and selling dear—to create what can be called only an illicit shadow retail network which spreads over the whole Union, makes many people rich, and corrupts many more.

For some time past a special government commission has been engaged behind the scenes in considering possible reforms in the Soviet penal code. Their findings are still unpublished; but it is clear that the *Soviet State and Law* article on the penal law as applied to speculators is a by-product of the deliberations of this committee. And a number of things emerge. In the first place the idea of crime as a product of environment—to die out automatically under a just social system—has been tacitly abandoned. In the second place there is a movement to change the law to fit this fact. In the days when speculation in "mass consumer goods" was regarded as deliberate counter-revolutionary sabotage by the relics of a discredited class, the massive punishment of five to ten years' penal servitude was logical; the whole effort was directed at stamping out the remnants and making the country safe for the faithful. The new suggestion that these punishments should be reduced and that various degrees of iniquity should be recognized by the law is nothing less than an acknowledgment that the Soviet state is a state like any other, inhabited by countless weak vessels, like any other, who must be kept on the narrow path of rectitude by the constant threat of minor penalties.

6. COMMISSARS AND RACKETEERS

SPECULATION is a crime, although the law at present is not fully equipped to cope with it. Embezzlement is a crime and, when discovered, is treated as such and heavily punished. The difficulty and tardiness with which major swindles are uncovered is an indication of demoralization in the Soviet trading and official world; cases in the last two years have ranged from the conversion of official motor cars to private use, with the connivance of the whole neighbourhood, to the simple embezzlement of hundreds of thousands of roubles by the managers of trusts and co-operatives and by high officials in provincial ministries. There is often a great deal of light relief in these cases; and one of the more remarkable things about life in the Soviet Union is the number of cases of swindling and impersonation that might have been taken straight from the pages of Gogol. The speculator in dead souls is still very much alive, though today he deals no longer in non-existent serfs but in equally non-existent boots or shoes or tractor spares. And time and again the Inspector General pops up out of the shadows and disappears again—a small official, or an individual trader living by his wits, impersonating a ministerial chief from Moscow and living like a prince for a few days at the expense of the local authorities of a small provincial town—staying at the best hotel, wined and dined by the town soviet, entertained by the local Party committee—until the fraud is discovered.

I referred earlier to another characteristic type, the tolkach. The term comes from the verb meaning to push, or thrust; but it is better translated as "fixer." Just as the speculator is a product of chronic shortages of consumer goods, coupled with faulty distribution, so the fixer is a product of shortages and bad distribution on a wholesale level, coupled with the endless muddles and bottle-necks produced by too rigid central planning. It is hardly too much to say that this cheerful and enterprising character in some shape or form is indispensable to the smooth working of the economy. And perhaps that is why he is not much attacked in the press, though lately he has been used more than once as a figure for satire.

He is much more than a speculator. On the face of it he is more often than not a solid citizen in the employ of a highly respectable trust or combine. But when one looks a little deeper one finds that he is employed not by one combine but by several. He is the contact man *in excelsis;* and although the life he leads has its risks and may very easily run into criminal ways, he can pride himself on his indispensability. His job is to make it possible for trusts and combines and factories to fulfil their plans without breaking down. He is the ingenious cutter of red tape, and he knows all the short-cuts which will secure access to goods and raw materials and spares which otherwise get lost in the official channels. One day he will be negotiating a barter deal between the manager of a bicycle factory and the inhabitants of the nearest collective farm: in exchange for a direct supply of fresh eggs, vegetables, and meat for the factory canteen, the factory will undertake to divert to the village as many bicycles as it requires. Or again, when *Pravda* complains that the manager of such-and-such a shoe factory has managed to obtain an illegal supply of leather straight from the tanneries, and not through the proper centralized channels, we know that the fixer has been at work, taking a rake-off from both sides. It may have been a straightforward deal: so much leather in exchange for so many pairs of finished shoes; but it is equally possible that it was something far more elaborate, for the fixer works on a broad front, and any of his deals may involve half a dozen principals; thus the shoe-manufacturer gets his leather from the tannery and is able to fulfil his plan with a bit of excess. The tannery may not want shoes; it may want a small power-plant unobtainable through the usual channels. The fixer is in touch with a manufacturer of power-plants who needs a new truck; but the manager of trucks is in despair because there are no shoes in his town and his workers are staying at home on rainy days. So the leather goes to the shoe factory; the shoes go to the truck factory;

the truck goes to the power-plant factory; the small power-plant goes to the tannery. Everyone is happy. Everyone fulfils his plan.

And the fixer has plenty to be pleased about. It is an interesting life. His activities take him all over the country; and he is equally at home in Odessa, Sverdlovsk, and Kharkov. Sometimes he works on commission, as a free-lance. Sometimes he leads a more sedate existence, acting as a permanent liaison man between three or four enterprises which stand in constant need of one another's services; then, as likely as not, he will be formally inscribed on the pay-roll of each. In Odessa he will be known as "our personal representative" by the button factory in Kharkov and the textile mill in Sverdlovsk; in Kharkov he will represent the Odessa ready-made clothing factory, as well as the Sverdlovsk textile mill; and so on. Also, as often as not, he is more than a mere go-between. He knows, none better, how the whole colossal, top-heavy system works. He has contacts not only among manufacturers but also in the ministries. In addition to obtaining desperately needed goods and materials in the shortest possible time he knows all the tricks of Soviet bookkeeping. He can conceal illegal reserves and arrange things so that the planned production of a given factory is fixed at a lower level than that factory's real capacity—to give the management a margin to play with. In the last resort he knows how to falsify the books, so that an enterprise may appear to have fulfilled its plan when in fact it has done nothing of the kind. In a word, the fixer is the very essence of the centrally planned society in its present stage of development. He will disappear when, and only when, there is more than enough of everything, and when the normal channels of distribution—including not only the overcrowded railways and the inadequate main-road traffic, but also the bureaucratic machine itself—are functioning smoothly and efficiently.

I have said enough, I hope, to indicate that Soviet society is not only a mass of extremely human irregularities, but, further, that these irregularities are multiplied by the nature of that society in its present form—particularly by the chronic shortages of consumer goods caused by the government's fanatical concentration on heavy industry, and by the extreme and sometimes fantastic rigidities caused by the centralized planning which alone makes concentration on heavy industry possible. Most foreigners see nothing of these irregularities, which, taken together, stop the machine from breaking down entirely. Most foreigners, however, see little or nothing of the real facts of life as lived and the true nature of the society in which these things occur.

The Soviet Union is more than Moscow. It is more than the other half-dozen cities so proudly shown to visiting delegations: Leningrad, Kiev, Minsk, Kharkov, Tiflis, Odessa, Gorki, and Tashkent. We have glimpsed the shop windows of Tashkent through the eyes of a candid *Pravda* correspondent. But it is the same everywhere. In Moscow on Gorki Street, on Petrovka, in the big department stores, there is a brave show of goods, and some of them may be bought by those who can afford them. But even if they could all be bought, the gay shop windows of the centre of Moscow can supply only a tiny fraction of that immense city's need, and what goes on in the inner suburbs is a very different affair indeed. We have already seen how even in Moscow and Leningrad the speculator thrives, because, in spite of the shop windows, there is not enough for everyone. Food is now fairly plentiful, though meat and butter—and, outside Moscow, sugar, too— are apt to disappear seasonally except at prohibitive prices on the free market. But nobody is hungry any more.

In the small provincial towns, however, it is a very different story. I could tell tales of drabness and near destitution over huge areas of the Soviet Union that simply would not be believed. So I shall content myself with one little story taken from a Moscow newspaper (*Trud*, September 19, 1954). It is not a very good little story, and it is written with that stilted coyness which has lately become the occupational manner of Moscow columnists in the new fight against corruption and inefficiency. But it gives a startlingly vivid idea of the manner of life in remote provincial towns, and also, thrown in for good measure, of the stubborn survival of the Russian habit of putting on a special act for distinguished visitors —including foreigners. The story is set in the town of Pavlodar, which lies on the River Irtysh in Western Siberia, halfway between Semipalatinsk and Omsk—where a new television station is now going up. It is called "Miracle in Pavlodar."

There was a day in Pavlodar which was a day of astonishment for everyone. From the smallest to the biggest, they simply threw up their hands. They threw up their hands and exclaimed:

"A miracle!"

This is what happened. The first thing was when people came out of their houses in the morning and thought that the old, familiar streets were looking different. Not exactly decorated for a holiday, but certainly not as they looked on an ordinary day. It was as though in a single night somebody had changed the shops and the kiosks, the canteens and the buffets. Shop windows which only yesterday had been thick with cobwebs gleamed in the sun. Walls, normally dirty, with the paint peeling off, had been newly whitewashed. The tins of crabmeat which had long occupied the shop windows had disappeared, and their place was taken by every kind of food. And the doors flung wide open seemed to invite:

"Come in, dear customers! Welcome!"

And the customers went in. What they saw inside astonished them even more. Incredible as it may seem, everything was where it should have been, and there was plenty for all. And the very first thing the people of Pavlodar demanded was matches:

"Have you any matches?"

"As many as you like," the salesman replied obligingly.

"And salt?"

"Yes, we have salt as well."

"You wouldn't have paraffin too?"

But indeed there was paraffin too, and one and all could have as much as they wanted.

In a word, on this great trading day, the townsfolk of Pavlodar were able to lay in stores of goods that for long had been "in short supply" in their town.

And so it went on. When lunch-time came things were even more surprising. In the canteens and the cafés,

instead of the customary menu of "fried egg and tea," or "fried egg and beer," trim waitresses offered tasty goulash, fresh Irtysh fish, vegetable salad, milk, and sour cream. Such was the state of affairs in the town for this one day and the next day too. But there are no miracles on this earth. The people of Pavlodar were convinced of this when the third day came round. On that day nobody any longer offered goods "in short supply," and the customers in the canteens and the cafés reverted to the familiar menu—"fried egg and tea," or "fried egg and beer."

What was it all about? The explanation was quite simple. "Pavlodar had been visited by an important official. The local traders had been exerting themselves not for the townsfolk but for him—and not so much for him as for themselves, such was the fear of these people in face of their superiors, so unclean their consciences toward their fellow townsmen." But by the local traders the newspaper did not mean the poor, wretched shopkeepers; it meant the officials of the provincial trading organization. *Trud* mentioned them by name. In one night these dignitaries had filled the shops with such an abundance of goods as had never been seen in Pavlodar before. And after two nights what was left of them was taken away. The visiting official, no less than the minister of trade of the Kazakh Union Republic, had gone away.

Even so, it was not really the fault of the provincial trading officials. These make useful scapegoats. But the reason why Pavlodar, and a thousand other towns, go chronically short of the necessities of life, down to matches and paraffin and salt, is that there are not enough of these things to go round. The local trading authorities cannot be blamed for keeping a supply of goods in store for emergencies. What they can be blamed for—though *Trud* does not do this—is throwing dust in the eyes of the minister. The reason why these small provincial towns have nothing, and also why there are constant shortages behind the gay shop windows of the Moscow stores—is that the government and the Party continue to starve consumer goods in favour of heavy industry. It is more than likely that the high officials and the Party chieftains sitting snugly in the Moscow offices and occasionally making well-publicized tours of inspection have no clear idea of the destitution of the Soviet Union as a whole. The reports they receive are glowing; when they travel, every place they visit is transformed, magically and instantaneously, for their special benefit. If the trading officials of Pavlodar had shown their minister the state of things as it really was they would probably have lost their jobs; but if every provincial official everywhere took his courage in both hands and spoke and showed the truth, then, I believe, very soon things would change. So that *Trud* was right in blaming Comrade Dvoretsky of the Provincial Trading Department for permitting the eyewash at Pavlodar, and Comrades Klimov and Tabuldinov of the Provincial Consumers' Cooperative for staging the performance. But it blamed them for quite the wrong reasons.

It is this sort of thing, too, that makes it so difficult for the foreigner to judge what is really going on. One has to be a Russian, or to have lived in Russia for some time, to have any idea of the extreme and elaborate lengths the authorities will go to to impress anyone they may think worth impressing. This is not by any means due to calculated deceit alone: deceit is there, but it is hopelessly mixed up with high and mighty standards of politeness, as well as what seems to me a splendid conception of hospitality. Thus, during the worst days of the war, the Soviet leaders would stage a Gargantuan banquet for distinguished visitors in the heart of a starving city, a proceeding which would strike guests used to the levelling austerity of England as callous in the extreme. What these people did not understand was that any individual Russian, struggling to keep body and soul together on black bread and watery soup, would scrape and hoard for weeks on end to provide a pathetic feast for his own private guests. He would not dream of portioning out a bottle of vodka, a pat of butter, a sliver of cheese, a handful of potatoes, a miraculous chunk of sausage— treasures which, used carefully, might stand between him and literal starvation; the whole lot would be shared with friends and blown in a single memorable feast.

Foreign visitors to collective farms—chosen collective farms, not too far from a great city—are more often than not sturdily convinced that the banquet put on for their benefit is an entirely spontaneous occasion. They are prepared to believe that the farm may be a show farm, as indeed it always is; they are prepared to believe that officialdom might go to some lengths to lay on an elaborate meal to impress them specially. What they cannot believe is that the kolkhozniks themselves would ever enter into the spirit of the performance. This is where they are wrong, because these occasions are not simply occasions of calculated deception; they are also red-letter days in the lives of all who participate. The Russian peasant is the most natural, as well as the politest, liar in the world. When, on orders from on high, he is bidden to give a party for some foreign visitors, with all food, linen, help, and cutlery, to say nothing of drink, to be provided, he does not repine or sulk. What is good enough for the foreigner is good enough for him. And when the foreigner, either very obtuse, or very cunning, or just plain silly, asks him solemnly over the suckling pig whether he eats and drinks like that every day, what is he to say but "Yes"?

One of my lasting memories of the Soviet Union is of a night stop in war time. It was early in 1941, in January, I think. The Germans had been held on the outskirts of Moscow, and certain foreign missions and Soviet officials were being transferred back to Moscow from Kuibyshev. There was no food on the train, and all day and what seemed all night the official in charge had been promising a hot meal at a wayside station "very soon." By midnight most of us had given up and gone to sleep. But I was awake when the train stopped just outside the station at Penza in the heart of the black-earth steppe. There seemed to be a lot of light and a great deal of bustle on the station and, to fill in time, I slipped down on to the track, deep in frozen snow, and plodded along the train and into the station. There was indeed a great deal of bustle. Officials in fur caps, NKVD guards in full uniform, porters with white smocks, were milling about.

"What's going on here?" I asked one of the guards, whom I had already met on the train.

He grinned. "Food," he said. "They're not ready yet. Go back to the train and you'll all be called in half an hour."

He turned away and started helping a colleague heave a heavy crate that was lying in the snow. I did not go back, and, in that confusion, nobody seemed to mind. Instead I wandered up the platform and arrived outside the station building just in time to watch one of the most extraordinary sights I have ever seen.

As is usual in large provincial stations in Russia, there was an immense waiting room of pitch-pine with a buffet at one end. The buffet was covered with huddled figures. The whole floor was covered with huddled figures—a horde of peasants and soldiers on leave, all in their tattered grey quilted jackets and their shapeless felt boots. Some had children; some were so old that they could barely hobble; many looked yellow with hunger. There was not an inch of space free on that floor. The doors had just been opened by two NKVD privates, and the smell and the stuffiness were overpowering. When I arrived a faint ripple of movement was passing through that solid mass. Those who were squatting looked up, some of them; some who were lying raised themselves on their elbows, cursing the strangers who had opened the doors and let in the cold. Then the doors leading into the station yard were suddenly flung open, and there, in the doorway, were two more NKVD men with fixed bayonets, muffled up against the killing frost. Now there was a stirring and a heaving in the huddled mass, and at that moment two more NKVD men, officers, with drawn revolvers, stepped up to the platform doorway and gave a sharp order:

"All out!"

Nothing happened, except that now everyone was awake and staring with fear or hatred or dumb bewilderment.

"All out, and quickly!"

A few weak spirits scrambled to their feet, tripping over their fellows, clutching their great bundles, dazed by the light. More curses; a whole dull wave of cursing. The mass stayed where it was.

Two more NKVD officers appeared, and now the four stood shoulder to shoulder in the doorway, their revolvers levelled at the living carpet on the floor. Together they took one step forward. The whole mass heaved and flinched away, not cursing now, but moaning. Those behind did not move, but slowly, and at the point of their guns, the police officers pushed back the ones in front, and their colleagues in the station yard started yanking at the stubborn spirits at the back. For about three minutes it was a grey inferno painted by Doré. Children screamed; men cursed; women moaned. The whole mass stumbled to its feet, trampling, snatching, lurching. And then everything was clear. Hardly a word had been spoken.

The NKVD men at the back shut and bolted and barred the doors to the station yard and came to join their colleagues. Through the steamed and frosted windows dumb faces could be seen pressed against the glass, where the poor wretches, so lately sleeping, found themselves herded, for what reason nobody knew, in the snow and the terrible cold of that deadly winter night.

They were soon to know the reason. Into the empty waiting room rushed a small army of cleaners and waitresses and porters. In ten minutes the great hall was swept. Long tables were set up, chairs brought in in towering piles. In another ten minutes the tables were laid with spotless linen. Crockery and cutlery were unloaded out of crates. Ranks of bottles appeared on the buffet, and fresh fruit in dishes, and plates loaded with fancy sweets. Then there were flowers. Heaven knows where these things came from: presumably most of them had been on the train all the time. And then, immaculately turned out in black frocks and starched aprons and caps, a dozen waitresses, young and twittering, buxom and slender, all with neat stockings and shoes, appeared from nowhere. And, at that moment, called by the official in charge of the train, the passengers came trooping up the platform, emitting cries of wonder and delight at the startling brilliance of the scene, chuckling at the astonishing way the Russians always managed things, sitting down at the long tables with their shining glasses for vodka and beer, and rubbing their hands as the little waitressess, having disappeared, returned, in procession, bearing tureens of steaming soup. I don't know how many of these distinguished guests could make out through the steamy windows those pale and yellow faces pressed against the glass and watching them as they ate. But certainly not many.

That is one way in which the spirit of Potemkin survives—Potemkin who caused to be built the bogus model villages to impress Catherine the Great on her great journey south through Russia to meet the Emperor of Austria. And the point is that there is a great deal more behind this remarkable behaviour than the desire to mislead and impress with false pretensions. There is also a deep feeling of the fitness of things. Nevertheless, it makes it very difficult for a foreigner on a short visit to know what to believe.

We begin to make out the image of a society which is not only human to a fault, but in which, also, people are widely separated in their conditions of life and great privileges rub shoulders with squalor and near destitution. And, indeed, the Soviet Union today offers contrasts of luxurious living and privation as great as anywhere in the world, and very much greater than in England. Paradoxically, the very fact that Soviet society is not yet a class society (and may, indeed, never become one) underlines these contrasts and makes them stand out more sharply than in other countries. The contrast between a French millionaire with his chateaux, his yacht, his race-horses, and a poor peasant in the Massif Central, or an unskilled worker in Lille, is absolute. So is the contrast between a British ship owner, motor manufacturer, or high-class financial operator, or spiv, and a plate-layer on British railways. Nothing could be more total than the difference between the Ritz and a Glasgow flop-house, or whatever the Scottish name for a flop-house may be. There is still a handful of hereditary peers whose way of life differs as fully as it is possible to differ from the way of life led by the old-age pensioners on their estates. The great foundations notwithstanding, the United States has numbers of the very, very rich, and still greater numbers of the very, very poor. It would be hard to imagine greater extremes than Hollywood in its more exotic manifestations and the poor whites of the deep South.

I mention all this because Western views about Soviet society cluster round one or the other of two poles. At the one pole is the firmly held conviction that the Soviet Union is, by profession and achievement, the land of egalitarianism; at the other the equally silly conviction, sustained by a great deal of nonsense written by ex-Communists, that it is the most unequal country in the world. Those who hold to the first view are either beatifically ignorant or knavish; those who hold the second view seem conveniently to forget the sort of examples I have just given. We all have our extremes. In the West they are sharper than in Russia, but on the whole they are growing less. In Russia they are still increasing. Also they hit the eye. And the reason they hit the eye is, above all, because the classes are not segregated. One sees the rich man's limousine pushing its way imperiously through shabby hordes. In the West it is only in Italy that one gets the constant impression of luxury living side by side with squalor. In other lands, because the very poor keep to themselves, it is possible to move in polite society without being much reminded of the very poor. And that brings us to the other difference. In the Soviet Union the poor are poorer, and there are more of them, so that a comparatively prosperous individual shows up vividly indeed.

When ex-Communists, and perhaps others, set out to prove that the income differences in the Soviet Union are greater than anywhere else in the world they invariably start talking about generals and private soldiers. They show that a Soviet general receives ten, or a hundred, or a thousand—I forget what the current figure is—times more money than the privates under his command. So we think of generals. We think of our own generals with their very modest pay and allowances; we think of their pensions and their often sad efforts to make ends meet in retirement, and come easily to the conclusion that income differences in the Soviet Union are indeed greater than in Britain and Western Europe and the United States. But in so doing we overlook an important fact—one which alters the whole complexion of the affair. In the Soviet Union the Army general belongs to one of the highest-paid groups in the land. In Western Europe he does not. Senior officers of the armed services; favoured writers; actors and ballet dancers; first-class scientists; aircraft designers and engineers of various kinds; Party chieftains—these form the most highly privileged groups in the Soviet Union. In the West, apart from rare exceptions, their opposite numbers come quite low down on the scale of income. In the West the most highly privileged groups are the financiers, the tycoons, the film stars of Hollywood, the successful lawyers. And the contrast between the incomes of a general and a private in the Soviet Army is a good deal less than the contrast between the incomes of a Western company promoter of the first rank and of the people who clean his office.

The general level of existence in the Soviet Union is pretty low. We have seen what it means to be a citizen of Pavlodar. In the great cities, as well as on the most prosperous collective farms, life is a great deal better than it is in Pavlodar. But for the masses it is still hard enough. Since 1947, wages have risen and prices have gone down, and this process continues. For an increasing number of Soviet citizens the problem today, as the flourishing of the speculator shows, is availability; they have money, but there is too little for money to buy. Nevertheless, for still greater numbers the dominant preoccupation is not availability, but cost. It is hard to convey an idea of prices. The exchange rate is bogus; officially about four roubles to the dollar, the real rate should be about sixteen to the dollar. Thus, in estimating comparative incomes and prices one has either to accept the official rate as a basis —the official rate multiplies incomes and prices four times—or else divide the official prices and incomes by four. Thus the average wage at the time of writing is about 200 roubles a week, which is $50 a week or $12.50 a week, according to which way you look at it. Similarly a ready-made men's suit of respectable appearance costs 1300 roubles, which is about $325—or about $81.25, according to your view.

Let us look at it this way: the lower grades of unskilled workers make 350 to 500 roubles a month; the lower grades of clerical workers 700 to 800 a month; the great mass of skilled workers, minor officials, and technicians, something in the neighbourhood of 1200 to 1500 a month; highly skilled workers and responsible officials, 2000 to 2500 a month; well-placed scientists, university professors, factory directors, 3000 to 5000 per month. As for prices: women's shoes cost from 240 to 600 roubles a pair; an aluminum teapot costs 50 roubles; a single metal teaspoon 12 roubles (36 roubles for a silver-plated one); a cheap razor 15 roubles; a bottle of beer 8 roubles; a poor-quality man's shirt 60 roubles, and a rather better one 100 roubles; kapron stockings (equivalent to inferior nylon) 30 roubles.

It is plain that people with an income of less than 600 roubles a month are engaged in a desperate struggle for survival. There are plenty of these. It is clear that people with less than 1200 roubles a month will have difficulty in making ends meet (and these are the great majority). It is equally clear that people with 1500 roubles a month and more are no longer chiefly preoccupied with keeping alive at all and are prepared to spend proportionately very large sums on small luxuries. With 3000 roubles a month and more, the problem is to know how to spend your money. With 5000 roubles a month, and windfalls in the way of special royalties, bonuses, and Stalin prizes, the very height of Soviet luxury is reached.

The summit of Soviet luxury means something like this: a four-room flat in Moscow in one of the most modern blocks; a villa in the countryside not far from the city; a motor car of your own, usually a small Pobeda or Moskvich, and the use of an imposing limousine that goes with your job; everything in the world to eat and drink; good furniture and probably a collection of pictures, or Meissen china; clothes from abroad; money in the State Bank. All these things, except the Moscow flat, are your own absolutely and may be left, together with royalties posthumously accruing from your work, to your widow or your children. To earn this much you must be an important person and of value to the state. The state, as a final gesture, will endow your widow with a solid pension; and if you are extremely distinguished your children will have pensions as well.

All this, compared with the possessions of Western bankers, is not very imposing: the equivalent of $7500 (or $30,000) a year (according to the valuation of the rouble) in a land where the average wage is $625 (or $2500) a year; plus, of course, the chance of a big money prize, which is often 100,000 roubles at one blow; plus the fact that income tax is low, and grows proportionately lower as one's income increases.

There are no statistics about the distribution of income in the Soviet Union. Indeed, there are no statistics about anything that might conceivably interest the interested foreigner, as distinct from the specialist in Soviet affairs. But the number of individuals in Russia with an income of between 60,000 and 120,000 roubles a year is proportionately very much less than the number of individuals earning between $3750 and $7500 a year in England. They stand out from the mass, just as the owners of motor cars stand out from the mass. It has been calculated that there are at present some 300,000 passenger cars in the whole of the Soviet Union, only a tiny fraction of which are privately owned; this means a car for every sixty people, as against a car for every three people in the United States. And this reflects fairly well the proportion of people earning comfortable incomes to those on or a little above subsistence level. The only individuals who live as the very rich live in the West are the handful of top Party leaders, who have every luxury and live in palaces in the grand manner. Then come the highly privileged groups, a very long way behind; then the greater numbers who think themselves well placed but would not dream of aspiring to a car or a villa or a flat with more than two rooms; then the immense majority whose preoccupation is the cost of living, who live in one room, or a part of a room, and share a communal kitchen—often in buildings which are literally falling down. These are the Soviet people, as one sees them in the streets. They have enough to eat now, but still not enough butter or meat or fresh vegetables; they can afford to buy waterproof shoes, which is a great advance on 1947, and to dress themselves adequately against both heat and cold. Since they have only one room to furnish, furniture is not a great problem. Curtains are unknown, and among the most fascinating sights in the world are the great new apartment houses at night time, with every room occupied by a separate household, and no curtains, so that each window is lit. After food and clothing and the barest essentials in the way of crockery, cutlery, and kitchen utensils—all of which are proportionately fabulously expensive— people have little money over for anything at all. But they will save until they have a television set, which the government has made available for 1300 roubles—the price of a decent suit of clothes or four decent pairs of shoes.

It should be remembered in this connection that until the very high income brackets are reached, married women almost invariably go to work, and often earn as much as their husbands. It is this that makes possible the television set for the home and the cherished "best clothes" for both husband and wife. But for the very poor there are no best clothes. And the gulf between the masses and the few with motor cars and villas, though smaller than the gulf between the masses and the very rich in Britain or America, *seems* greater than it is because the general level of living conditions is so low. A Rolls-Royce in the mean streets of a Western city looks no more out of place than well-cut clothes of good quality material in the streets of Moscow or Leningrad or Kiev. The masses have inherited these cities, and dominate them. But riches keep breaking in.

7. THE YOUNG IDEA

"HE WHO does not work shall not eat": thus the quasi-Biblical language of the Stalin Constitution. It was more or less true in 1936, when the Constitution was laid down. Today, twenty years later, it is anything but true. It is too early yet to speak of a leisured class in Russia, but there are a great many leisured individuals; and in another generation their children will harden into a class, unless the government takes action of a kind it shows no signs of taking—and a remarkably irresponsible leisured class at that. I have tried to show that income differences in the Soviet Union, although great and occasionally spectacular, are still not as great as in the West; but this is not at all to say that these differences in practice are not producing a form of society entirely alien to anything dreamed of by the early Bolsheviks.

The division of the Soviet Union into two nations was for a long time obstructed by the hazards and uncertainties of life under Stalin. There were plenty of individuals earning handsome incomes; but they made their careers by sheer hard work of a sustained intensity unknown in the West save to the exceptionally determined and ambitious. At the same time they lived in a period of chronic instability, in which a man on top on Monday would find himself in a labour camp or condemned to be shot by the end of the week; it was a period of rapid, slogging success and lightning disaster. Their families profited by their rise but shared their disgrace. There could be no question at all of a new upper class, still less a new leisured class, crystallizing in this atmosphere of "here today and gone tomorrow."

For the survivors of this period—and every man in a distinguished position who is over fifty today is, precisely, a survivor, with something of the survivor's mentality—the story is very different. In spite of recent upheavals in the higher reaches of the Communist Party and in the Security Police, the atmosphere is comparatively relaxed and stable. The survivors have now reached safe harbour and brought their families with them. They still form an élite of individuals, and not a class; but their children are intermarrying; and there we have the makings of a perfectly distinguishable class. *Their* children, now in the nursery, will, if life goes on as it promises, know nothing at all of life as it is lived in Soviet Russia by the masses, will start with immense advantages and comparative luxury behind them, assuming high positions or a leisured existence as their right. I am speaking now of the uppermost drawer. For example, the two daughters of Marshal Zhukov have married the sons of Marshal Voroshilov and Marshal Vassilievsky. I could name plenty of other examples. The result is the birth of a new Soviet aristocracy.

These creatures are still rare. They have all the money they can want and all the opportunities the Soviet Union offers for spending it. That is to say, they spend most of their lives in one another's villas in the Moscow countryside or on the Black Sea, according to season. They wear Western clothes, and they get their entertainment from private cinemas and imported gramaphone records. Their life is a round of parties—and they are bored! There is only one thing they want to do, and that is to travel abroad. They are seen rarely if at all in public. They regard the government, even when their husbands belong to it, as a sort of joke in rather poor taste. They regard the masses, not unkindly, as cattle. They will attend gala performances at the Bolshoi Theatre (closed performances, that is), and an occasional Kremlin reception. Their shopping is done for them by servants. Most of them in youth have taken a university degree of sorts, but there their interest in work has stopped. Their estrangement from the country as a whole and the masses in particular is more absolute than anything known in the West since 1914.

These, in the nature of things, still form a very small group. They form a problem chiefly because of the well-known fact that the children of great men are apt to be third-rate, which means that a class is growing up, endowed with every worldly privilege, which, unlike its begetters, will be in no position to make an adequate return to the state. They are protected for the time

being by the simple fact that they are all dependents of the most
distinguished figures in the land, who can be relied on to look
after their own.

But there is a far bigger problem than this. It is set by the wives
and children of the able administrators and technicians and the
new intelligentsia, who, without being great men, in effect among
them run the machinery of state. These are numbered in hundreds of thousands, and their distaste for the masses and their
sense of superiority is even more self-conscious and acute than
that of the children of the really great, because they are closer to
the masses. Their parents are determined that, come what may,
the advantages they have won shall be handed on to their children. These youngsters sooner or later have to work. Their parents
have not accumulated fortunes. But they can afford to choose
their work. And their parents can afford to keep them in idleness
until they choose—until, that is, a suitable opportunity arises.
What seems to them a suitable opportunity is an easy job in one
of the few great cities, preferably in Moscow. These youngsters
are for the most part intelligent. They are all well educated.
Their parents can afford to keep them at the universities, even
if they are incapable of winning scholarships. Indeed, they are
taking up more and more places in the universities, particularly
in Moscow. And more and more the graduates are ·refusing to
leave the cities and go where they are required. Newly qualified
doctors refuse to go to the country; newly qualified agronomists
refuse to take jobs on farms; newly qualified scientists refuse to
leave Moscow, or Leningrad, or Kiev, to work in the new towns
beyond the Urals. And their parents can afford to support them
until, through nepotism or influence of one kind or another under
the general head of *blat,* they find some job of the kind they want
where they really want it.

I am talking now not of ne'er-do-wells, but of the decent children of decent parents. It is not a new problem. The Russian has
always been notorious for his reluctance to get mud on his boots.
It is not only the young who scheme for attractive jobs in the few
attractive places in the Union. In the nineteenth century Chekhov's "To Moscow!" was the standing *cri de coeur* in the provinces; and ever since the revolution the authorities have had the

greatest difficulty in getting the gifted out of the great cities and spread through the country. Only members of the Communist Party had to go where they were told—at one extreme; and, at the other extreme, deportees of the Security Police, whose numbers at one time ran into millions, and without whom the more insalubrious areas of the Union would never have been opened up. Nevertheless, until lately, economic pressure told. And to the devoted Party members and adventurous youth were added many pioneers who went East for the sake of better pay.

Large numbers of the new generations do not need better pay. It is not simply a lack of adventurousness which makes them think twice about leaving Moscow for Omsk—or Pavlodar, that salt-less, match-less, paraffin-less paradise on the Irtysh River. *Izvestia* was wrong when it attributed the reluctance of so many graduates of Moscow University to sacrifice themselves for the cause of Socialist Construction to idleness and lack of adventurousness. An agitator had been addressing a body of these students and asked for volunteers for necessary jobs on remote "collectives." He got none. Instead he was jeered. "You might just as well ask us to go and be cobblers and have done with it," one of the students retorted. *Izvestia* was shocked. "Why indeed not?" it demanded. "What nobler calling could there be than that of a cobbler?" And it went on to read a lecture extolling the virtues of Soviet labour, in the best spirit of George Herbert, but without the charm:

> A servant with this clause
> Makes drudgery divine:
> Who sweeps a room, as for Thy laws,
> Makes that and th' action fine.

Unfortunately the laws recognized by *Izvestia* are the laws not of God but of Lenin, and they lack the requisite authority.

Also, the students know very well that the production of cobblers was not what the fabulous sky-scraper on the Sparrow Hills was built for, and they know that *Izvestia* knows it. It is not a lack of adventurousness. It is more a clinging of the offspring of the new "gentle" class to the few points in the Soviet Union where "gentility" has established itself and where they can live among their own friends. Instead of going out as solitary pioneers to spread civilization in the wilderness, they prefer, not unnaturally, to cluster round the small points of civilization that already exist. They have to be stubborn to defy the pressure of the government. Their parents have to be adroit in exploiting contacts. And the harder the struggle, the more stubborn they become and the more they exaggerate the difference between themselves and their kind, on the one hand, and, on the other, the brute masses from whom they have so recently risen. That is why, in casual conversation with members of the new Soviet intelligentsia, one hears charming, highly educated youngsters speaking of the masses, of the proletariat to whom the country is supposed to belong, with a callousness and a brutality which has not been met with in the countries of Western Europe for many decades. It is the new respectability.

In its more extreme forms this revulsion from everything the Soviet Union is supposed to stand for takes on very curious shapes, and what they all boil down to is a tacit rejection of the regime. It is not easy to sort out and label these manifestations, and the attitude of the authorities, who are deeply worried by them, does not help. Authority, if it had its way, would call the whole lot "hooligans," write them off as juvenile delinquents produced by unfortunate survivals of capitalism, and leave it at that. But there are too many of them, though still only a small minority of Soviet youth, for this to be feasible. They include large numbers of Komsomols. Furthermore, in the higher income brackets many of the offenders are the children of distinguished pillars of Soviet society and, in the lower income brackets, of highly respected working families—children at both extremes, in a word, who have been brought up in the very bosom of the Soviet state and given every opportunity to become good Stalin-fearing citizens —given, indeed, no opportunity to become anything else.

Yet large numbers of them have become something else. Every Soviet citizen today under the age of forty was born into Bolshevism. The majority of today's university students are the children of parents who know nothing of pre-revolutionary Russia. We are told—how often are we not told?—that years of conditioning from the cradle onward will turn any individual into an obedient instrument, unspeculating and unresisting, of the master's will. It is clear that Stalin himself believed this and expected the Soviet educational system reinforced by Party training in the Pioneers and the Komsomol to eliminate all undesirable characteristics and to mould the masses to the pattern preordained by him. Nothing was overlooked. Children at a tender age were taken out of the hands of their parents, who were regarded simply as providers of house-room and food and clothing. From the infant school onward they were taught to be on guard against their parents. Propaganda for the regime and hatred for all other regimes was drummed into them in school and out of school. Writers and painters were forcibly enrolled into the honourable corps of engineers of human souls and compelled, by every sort of pressure, to subordinate their talents to the propaganda of the moment. In public places the radio blared all day, and what it blared was propaganda for the regime. Every conceivable pressure was put on every individual to conform and obey; every conceivable inducement was offered to make him enjoy obeying. Never before in the history of Europe had a whole nation been so completely at the mercy of a single tyrant; never before in the history of the world had a tyrant disposed of so elaborate and all-embracing an apparatus of mass persuasion. In 1934 all the preconditions existed for 1984. And what is the result?

A great many Russians, the majority, believe that "capitalists" are bad men, given to making war on peace-loving nations. A great many Russians, the majority, believe that the Moscow subway is unique, which it is. There is no knowing what can be done with propaganda—from making people conscious of "B.O." by reiterated advertising to making people believe in Britain's mass unemployment by reiterated lying. But my years in Russia have proved one thing finally and beyond all doubt; and that is that although a dictator disposing of all the apparatus of propaganda can make people sacrifice themselves, he cannot for long kill the speculative element in the human mind. Two young Russian friends of mine, girls, can serve as an example. They were brought up in the faith. They lived for the day when, at sixteen, they would be eligible for the Komsomol (this was in the days when the Komsomol meant something other than an approved club for all Soviet youth with a political bias, which is what it has degenerated into today). But when the day came, they refused that fence, first one, then the other. Solemnly, priggishly if you like, they confessed to me, a known heretic beyond the pale, assuring me that as a capitalist I would not understand the delicacy of their feelings or the matter of a deeply troubled conscience ("In Russia," the younger of them, sixteen, expounded, "we have a sense of what we call the individual conscience, which you, as an Englishman, would never understand; but since we like you, we shall try to explain")—they confessed that having arrived at the moment of initiation they were unable to reconcile the teachings of the Party with many of its actions and so thought it proper to remain outside, in all humility, and subject to subsequent correction. Both are now in their middle twenties; neither has yet joined the Komsomol or the Party. They were clever girls and got good degrees at the university. The Komsomol would have helped them with their careers.

That is one example of unsuccessful conditioning. Here is one on a more every-day level.

It will be remembered that, after the eleventh-hour salvation of Moscow, the war continued badly for the Russians and they had to wait a long time for a major victory—until Stalingrad, in fact. I was in the Soviet Union at the time; practically every Russian believed, as I myself believed, that Stalingrad would fall. It was a gloomy prospect. But, as we all know, Stalingrad did not fall. Instead, the city held, while Marshal Rokossovsky, then a national hero, now the effective governor of Poland, carried out his fabulous encircling action. While the Western world hung on his movements, the Russians listened to the daily communiqués with sullen, inattentive scepticism. And when the news finally came through, bellowed out by the loud-speakers all over Russia and received, I was told, with delirium by the Western allies, most educated Russians simply did not believe it. It was nearly three weeks before I could convince a certain friend of mine that a victory really had been won, a victory of supreme importance. "I can't understand you," he would say. "I can't understand how anyone of your intelligence can believe what he reads in the papers." (He himself, so unpredictable is the influence of propaganda, believed, without realizing it, quite a number of things that he read in the papers.) "But it's not just your papers," I would reply rather helplessly. "It's in the London papers too." And he would look at me pityingly. "What conceivable difference does that make? Why should you think your newspapers are any more truthful than ours?"

I could go on like this, illustrating the strange, the uncanny mixture of unconscious conditioning and conscious rejection of conditioning. But it seems to me that a great deal of what I have already written in earlier chapters has gone to show just how far the Soviet Union is in spirit from 1984. It is not a thing that surprises me in the least, any more than it surprises me that Stalin and his colleagues should have made the gross error of assuming that, given time and power over a human being from the cradle onward, they could in fact be able to do what they liked with his mind. What does surprise me, though I suppose it shouldn't, is the eagerness with which Christians and humanists outside the Soviet Union have rushed to endorse this vulgar error, loudly proclaiming their dismay at the absolute destructibility of the human mind, and thus, without apparently realizing what they are doing, betraying the fundamental principle that underlies all they are supposed to stand for.

Perhaps they would be surprised by the stilyagi. I was not—though I myself would not have expected young Russians in leaderless revolt against Stalin's conditioning to duplicate in every particular the "Teddy Boys" of London. I say duplicate, not imitate, because I have been quite unable to learn how these youngsters could have discovered so quickly for themselves the costume and manners favoured by their Western counterparts. There has been no delegation of Teddy Boys invited to Russia by the Woman's Anti-Fascist League, to my knowledge. And although occasional copies of women's fashion magazines brought home by diplomats, soldiers, returning delegations, are treasured in Moscow and passed half-furtively from hand to hand, it is hard to imagine Teddy Boy fashion-plates penetrating in sufficient numbers to start a new fashion in no time at all.

The stilyagi form only a part of disoriented youth, but it is the most spectacular part, and so far authority has been able to do nothing about them, although they parade themselves publicly with all their flaunting eccentricities: the long draped jackets in loud checks of yellow or green, the painted "American" tie, patch pockets, padded shoulders, turned-back cuffs, peg-top trousers, and—pride of the whole outfit—yellow or light tan shoes, with thick crepe soles, worn a size too big so that they turn up at the toe. Their haircuts are works of art, and they favour side-whiskers. They are not attractive, and they spend their evenings in bars and billiard saloons, or dancing where dancing may be had. You can see them any night in any Soviet hotel that has a dance band; but they prefer dancing to hoarded records of American jazz. And with them are the girl stilyagi, "whose dresses are stretched over their figures to the point of indecency. They wear slit skirts. Their lips are painted with bright colours. In the summer they wear 'Roman' sandals. They do their hair in the style of 'fashionable' foreign cinema actresses" (*Soviet Culture*, January 18, 1955).

In the words of *Komsomolskaya Pravda*, which has always a great deal to say about the stilyagi, many of whom, astonishingly, are members of the Komsomol:

Our readers write that by no means infrequently they still encounter those young people whom our youth scornfully call "stilyagi." They dress in loud clothes, take pride in their ignorance of classical music, but play vulgar ditties with enthusiasm. Such individuals have their own pretentious language, their own way of expressing themselves, which seems incomprehensible to others. Try to tell them that this is not good, not beautiful, and they repeat to you the words of Viktor K., "That is our taste; and about taste, as they say, there's no arguing."

The Viktor K. referred to above was cited by *Komsomolskaya Pravda* as an example of the better-educated kind of stilyag: "A student in one of the higher educational establishments of Odessa, he usually turns up at lectures in tight green trousers and a bright yellow jacket. The pride of Viktor's wardrobe is a foreign tie with a parrot painted on it."

The incomprehensible language they talk among themselves is a sort of stilyagi slang, interspersed with English or French. Above all they favour English. *Krokodil* (December 20, 1953) satirized one young stilyag who formally changed his name from Grisha to Harry. Their dogs (they are strong on keeping dogs, otherwise rare in Soviet cities) have English names: Bobby, Tommy, Joan. I have heard youngsters in a bar talking about the Militiamen and calling them Bobbies. They like calling towns and streets by their pre-revolutionary names: Petrograd for Leningrad, Tsaritsyn for Stalingrad, neither of which are at all well thought of. They call Gorki Street in Moscow "Broadway." "Good evening, ladies and gentlemen!" they call out on meeting their friends, even if there is only one lady and gentleman present. There is no nonsense about "Comrade"; "Hello, Mister!" is preferred. Kopeks are cents; roubles are dollars. They may be watched and observed in summer on the bathing beaches by the Muska River, and in certain unofficial night haunts; they do not much patronize the official "dancings" in the big Moscow hotels. Their language is full of be-bop and boogie-woogie. They drink far too much, dance a great deal, and offend deeply against Soviet puritanism with their philandering. "It is impossible," exclaimed *Komsomolkaya Pravda* (January 18, 1955), "to acquaint oneself with this side of the stilyagi's life without feelings of disgust and disdain."

In spite of the constant flow of censure poured out by the Party press, exhortations to parents, to school teachers, to Komsomol leaders to stand up against the stilyagi, nothing much can be done about the cult. It goes too deep and is too widespread—and the youngsters too often have parents in high positions. They flaunt their foreign neckties and shoes, brought in from East Germany and the satellites, or even farther afield, by diplomats, returned delegates, members of trade missions, soldiers in the occupation forces home on leave. They find hair dressers to satisfy their peculiar and exacting needs, and tailors to make up bizarre materials into their remarkable outfits. The barbers and the tailors are not proceeded against. Sometimes indirect action is taken; for example, after a series of newspaper attacks on the young patrons of Moscow's notorious cocktail bar, the Cocktail Hall on Gorki Street (where, in the difficult days of the war, I myself suffered a mild but disconcerting attack of wood-alcohol poisoning), this outstanding pleasure haunt was closed and re-opened shortly afterwards as an ice-cream parlour. Sometimes individual offenders are pilloried by name. But nothing happens to them. Thus *Literary Gazette* (June 11, 1955) carried a direct attack on a not so young man, the son of the Soviet Union's most celebrated surgeon, who became a national hero during the war because of his sacrificial services to the Red Army, all but working himself to death in the process. Afterward he fell into disfavour with Stalin, but was able to make some sort of comeback before he died a few years ago. And he left a good deal of money. He also left behind him a number of standard textbooks, which continue to bring in royalties. *Literary Gazette*'s tirade was based on the manner in which his son Yuri managed to get through the twelve thousand roubles which formed one instalment on the royalties for one of his father's books, called *Restorative Surgery of the Alimentary Canal*. The article was a vivid piece, describing a drunken orgy in the classical nineteenth-century Russian manner on the eve of young Yudin's departure for a holiday at a Crimean *plage*. It expressed the deepest sympathy for Madame Yudin, the great surgeon's widow, but concluded that since she was herself evidently quite unable to discipline her son, she would no doubt be grateful for the public intervention of the Party press.

This kind of thing is not new. Children in the Soviet Union have been running through their inheritances for some years past; but it is only lately, with the opening up of life after the privations of the immediate postwar period, that they have been able to do it with a flourish. Now it has become something very much to be reckoned with, and the new idle rich are making themselves felt and becoming increasingly arrogant and flamboyant. Who can blame them? *Literary Gazette* offered fulsome sympathy to the surgeon's widow for being afflicted with an irresponsible and ne'er-do-well son. It did not, however, apologize for the disgraceful treatment of the old doctor in his closing years—treatment calculated to turn any children of his into cynics and rebels against the regime.

The second edition of the *Large Soviet Encyclopædia* (Volume 5, 1952) has this to say about juvenile delinquency in "bourgeois countries": "It arises on the one hand as a consequence of economic crises, unemployment, and the extreme poverty of the working masses, and, on the other, of the moral corruption of the children of the propertied classes."

That seems, also, quite a good definition of juvenile delinquency in the Soviet Union. But there is something to add, with particular reference to Soviet society: in addition to the "extreme poverty of the masses" and the "moral corruption of the propertied classes" a very strong motive behind the really terrifying wave of juvenile delinquency in Soviet Russia is an inarticulate revolt against the tedium and emptiness of the Soviet way of life.

It is to emphasize this point that I have come to this subject by way of the stilyagi and the idle rich. The stilyagi, as a whole, are not delinquents; they are youngsters bored to distraction by their grey surroundings and the interminable preaching and nagging of the authorities. Spiritedly, but a little pathetically, they try to make a more colourful world for themselves.

The authorities have something else to say. Thus *Soviet Culture* (January 18, 1955): "Faulty upbringing in the family, the inculcation of an irresponsible attitude and contempt for honest work, kow-towing to everything 'foreign' (which means to the taste and manners of the 'gilded' youth of bourgeois societies)— it is all this that has given birth to 'style' and the stilyag." *Soviet Culture* does not go on to say who made the Soviet family what it is, who did their level best to destroy all family feeling, who for decades strove systematically, and with all the apparatus of state-controlled education, to alienate the children from their parents, who physically destroyed innumerable families by sending fathers away to Siberia and teaching children to act as informers and wives and mothers to ostracize husbands and fathers arrested on trumped-up charges.

The wonder is that it is possible to find any family life at all. And for every case of a woman deserting her husband or her lover when he found himself in trouble, there are many more in which the woman carried on, worked for two to bring up her family, and refused to let go. Some wives have begged, pleaded, and demanded to go to Siberia with their husbands, touching heights of nobility; but in most cases such gestures could serve no purpose:

a home of sorts had to be kept together and the children educated. And while the mother went out to work, the household chores, the shopping, the queuing, the care of the smallest children, devolved on the grandmother, the babushka, without whom (crèches notwithstanding) the whole system based on woman's equal right to work (which means in practice, for ninety-nine out of a hundred Soviet women, woman's need to work) would have long ago broken down.

On the other hand, and particularly during the hard years of the great purges, many wives of the suddenly disgraced rushed to *Zags*, the office for marriage and divorce, with indecent haste and disowned their husbands then and there, throwing off their whole past life in a matter of minutes. But even in the worst times this was not taken for granted, and public feeling against it ran very high. I remember one very well-known, and popular, ballerina, well married with two children, who, being tipped off about her husband's impending arrest, instead of warning him ran home, packed up her belongings, and rushed off to her mother's apartment with the two children, leaving her husband to the NKVD—or so it was said. The important thing is that the Leningrad public believed it; and the next time she appeared at the Kirov Theatre (the old Mariinsky) she was hissed off the stage. Many months passed before she dared appear again.

It is not only among the children of the well-to-do that the revolt against the regime and everything it stands for is manifesting itself in anti-social conduct. A far bigger problem is the swelling wave of what is called "hooliganism." The campaign against hooliganism has been under way for three years. It was sharply intensified during my last visit in the autumn of 1954— and it was high time. Now it is moving to a climax. Even as I write this chapter the authorities seem to be working up to a really violent effort to stamp it out of existence. In *feuilleton* after *feuilleton* the Militia is nagged and bullied not merely for failing to cope with hooliganism, but actually for siding with the hooligans against respectable citizens; and what looks like a new move in the campaign was the recent dismissal from the head of the MVD, which controls the Militia, of General Kruglov, Beria's one-time lieutenant, and the only MVD officer to have received a

high order (the GCB) from a British sovereign: he got it for looking after the security arrangements at the Yalta conference. As
I shall suggest later on, Kruglov's fall was certainly an incident
in the power struggle that continues; his replacement by a career
Party official, Comrade Dudorov, was part of Khrushchev's quiet
activity directed at getting his own nominees into key positions.
But there is very little doubt that the failure of the Militia to
deal with hooliganism provided a handy pretext for the operation; only a few weeks before his dismissal Kruglov presided at
a remarkable meeting in Moscow, which was in effect a prize-
giving ceremony and a recruiting campaign in connection with
an auxiliary force of Komsomols, raised to help the police tackle
the hooligans.

Who are these hooligans? Even the Soviet propagandists have
at last given up the pretence that they are isolated misfits, survivals of the past, relics of capitalism (how can a seventeen-year-
old son of good Soviet citizens be thought of as a relic of anything?). Even the party press is recognizing that they form an
acute problem, which is getting out of hand. The government
does not make the solution of the problem any easier by lumping
together all delinquents under the general label of hooligans. On
the other hand, once it recognizes the existence of a variety of
quite different types of offender, produced by a variety of quite
different causes; once it tries to analyse the problem objectively
to find out what is really going on in the land where crime should
long ago have withered away; once it abandons the crass formula
about relics of the past—once all this is done, then how will it
any longer be able to pretend that Soviet society is superior to
every other society? As I shall show in the next chapter, the government has tied its own hands. It admits the existence of crime
and delinquency, but the moment anybody suggests that these
are inherent in the system it utters cries of outraged indignation.

There are all sorts of hooligans. Stilyagi may be hooligans,
even when they are well enough off to own motor cars of their
own; and there have been a number of cases lately reported in
which stilyagi have broken out into senseless acts of violence, or
have unaccountably taken to stealing and embezzlement, though
they do not need the money (unaccountably only in a land which

refuses to admit the findings of the psychoanalysts). War orphans, deserters, children from shattered homes, children from the countryside conscripted into the training schools of the Ministry of Labour Reserves (up to half a million of the least bright children from the collectives are taken each year in this way to feed the insatiable demands of the "industrial base"), natural degenerates —all these are liable to band themselves together in an anti-social sense and form gangs to terrorize the streets.

This is no new problem for the government. All the world knows about the *bezprisorni*, the hordes of fatherless, motherless children who roamed the countryside like animals after the Revolution, the civil war, the famine. A decade later, after the liquidation of the kulaks during the collectivization, the same thing happened again on a lesser scale; but by that time the country and the forces of order were better organized. At the end of the last war there was a new outbreak of gang terrorism. In Moscow in 1947 decent citizens refused to go out at night except in sizable groups anywhere off the main thoroughfares; they feared, justifiably, that they would be set on and robbed, and perhaps injured or killed in the process. The government was aware of all this, and although it took time to clean things up, it no doubt believed that it had the measure of the problem, and it saw fit in 1953 to amnesty all common-law prisoners serving up to five years and to halve the sentences of the rest—with what looks like dire results: although times are very much easier the released hooligans have not shown any propensity to settle down and mend their ways, and the Soviet courts are discovering the problem of recidivism; corrective labour has not done its vaunted job of re-education.

These are the real hooligans. It is not my word. Hooliganism is a peculiarly Russian concept. It is one of those elastic terms that may cover any offence, from swearing in public, "committing a nuisance," or being drunk and disorderly to brawling lethally with broken bottles. In any open society it would be perfectly easy to sort out the various types of offender and treat them appropriately—to sort out, that is to say, the hardened thug from the swashbuckling juvenile; the natural degenerate from the stilyagi's working-class (the word is not mine; it is an official Soviet term) equivalent. But the Soviet Union is not an open society; and the authorities are making a bogy for themselves by lumping all these categories together—and, at the same time, making it all too easy for the uncouth but innocuous to assume the attributes of the real criminal.

What seems to have happened is simply that some years after the war, when supplies—above all, vodka—became more plentiful, and people had a little more money in their pockets, all the suppressed impatience of working-class youth began to manifest itself and find expression in drunkenness and general loutishness. Everything that has ever been said in the West about broken homes' and sordid environments' producing juvenile delinquency applies in the Soviet Union, but on a nation-wide scale. The youngsters are crammed together in tenements, two or more families to a room, or segregated in barracks-like hostels close to the factory sites. They are bored. They are desperate. Cinemas are inadequate, to say the least. In all but model establishments club facilities are virtually non-existent. There are not even comics. Their working lives are hard, and when it comes to social and cultural facilities, their existence compares unfavourably with the existence of prisoners in the labour camps since the postwar reforms. I am speaking of life in the factory districts of the great cities, in the wholly industrial cities, in the dreary provincial small towns. So they drink and band together and roam the streets. They must either do that or sit listening to interminable and meaningless political lectures, delivered by barely literate "agitators" who have not the least understanding of what they are trying to say and reduce the theory of Leninism and the problems of Communist Construction to a hodge-podge of slogans and clichés from the columns of *Pravda* or the *Agitator's Notebook*.

And so the young louts go out into the streets. Often they are no more than a nuisance, calling out at the girls and yelling rude remarks at harmless citizens. Even when they have money and get drunk, the Militia ignore them. But more and more of them, as though driven to defiance by this lack of reaction on the part of authority, are taking to violence; and recently the press has reported at length some very strange cases in which it is the harmless citizen who has been punished for having the temerity to defend himself, while the hooligans have got off scot-free. It has begun to look as though the Militia are not only timid, but positively corrupt; and it may well be that the feverish attempt to whip up enthusiasm among the tougher young Komsomols, who are now brigaded as auxiliary Militia volunteers expressly to help put down hooliganism, springs not only from the need for physical help but also from the need to spy on the Militia's activities.

Certainly the government is worried. The evil is not confined to Moscow, Leningrad, Kiev, Odessa—the show cities. These, because the richest cities, have the most stilyagi; but hooliganism is everywhere. The extraordinarily savage sentences passed on a group of toughs who disputed a referee's decision at a football game in Erevan, and started a fight, indicate a measure of panic. The top sentence for this kind of thing, under the relevant article of the Criminal Code (Article 74) is five years, but at the Erevan trial in November 1955 the ringleaders were charged under another article of the Code. One was sentenced to twenty years in prison, two were sentenced to fifteen years, and two to ten years' deprivation of freedom—all these with confiscation of their personal property and deprivation of electoral rights for five years. Others received lesser sentences. This trial was very widely publicized, evidently as a warning. Since then a number of Soviet organs have been demanding the amendment of Article 74, to allow for heavier sentences.

This kind of thing, however, obscures the real problem. Thugs and gangsters can be dealt with, but disoriented youth, whether expressing itself politely in a passion for jive or impolitely in general loutishness, is a product of the system; and until this fact is recognized it will remain as an increasing problem. The government has moved further in recent months toward recognizing the reality and the complexity of the problem, but it still denies the root causes. These are two, each breeding lesser causes: first, the continued priority for heavy industrial development at the expense of civilized living conditions; second, the deliberate killing of mental and spiritual life by the forced imposition of total orthodoxy. To the first is due the housing shortage with resultant overcrowding, the breaking up of family life by the segregation of youth in industrial hostels (and now in agricultural hostels in the virgin lands), the squalid shortage of amenities of any kind outside half a dozen show cities, from cinemas to sports equipment—leaving only vodka. To the second is due the substitution of inane political lectures for honest and speculative discussion, leading to excruciating boredom; the production of huge quantities of books, made to order, which nobody wants to read; and the hideous and dreary uniformity of the Soviet press.

All these sub-causes are now recognized by the government. During the past two years there has been a ceaseless outcry against local authorities for falling down on the housing programme; against the management of trusts and combines for allowing shocking living conditions in the new industrial areas; against various ministries for leaving the settlers in the virgin lands stranded on the Central Asian steppes without the first aids to civilized living; against the writers for producing unreadable books and plays; against the film industry for producing intolerable films; against the musicians for producing nothing to compete with American jazz; against municipalities for tolerating a too free sale of vodka (state-produced) in cafés and liquor shops that offer nothing else at all; against parents for neglecting their children's upbringing, or spoiling them; against local Party and Komsomol organizations for their total failure to provide proper recreational facilities. The evils are admitted. Only the first cause is never mentioned: the considered policy of the Communist Party and the government of the Soviet Union to sacrifice everything to a heavy industry that battens on the living people, and the dissemination of an ideology which, year by year, is left farther behind by the realities of life.

To give the impression that corruption and racketeering, idleness and snobbery, drunkenness and hooliganism, dominate the Soviet scene is the last thing I want to do. *Blat* and speculation are another matter, these forming the necessary and all-pervading lubricants of the whole monstrous, ramshackle, and ludicrously over-centralized machine that is the Soviet state. It is because the evils just mentioned are not yet dominant (though there are many decent Soviet citizens who would disagree with this) that I have stressed them. They exist, they are rife, but the casual visitor to Moscow, to Leningrad, to Tiflis, to Kiev is scarcely more conscious of them than he is of the hidden labour camps. There is next to no drunkenness in the Intourist hotels, and the stilyagi are also kept out. And even if an enterprising visitor with roubles to spare manages to break away from the National, the Metropol, or the Savoy in Moscow (these are the Intourist centres, shrouded in Edwardian splendour: museum pieces, like the treasured, varnished, dusted, pre-Revolutionary *wagons-lits* of the Soviet state railways)—even if he breaks away and gets as far as the terrace restaurant of the Moskva Hotel, overlooking the Kremlin, and finds every other table occupied by parties in a state of high intoxication, the impression will only be one of a rather startling and inexplicable departure from the established norm. The ordinary tourist, or delegate, will not be offered American jazz on X-ray plates when he makes his obligatory round of the GUM department store; will not, in a backyard off Gorki Street, be offered a place in the queue for a Pobeda motor car for a matter of two thousand roubles down; will not be invited to a wild party by stilyagi students in the country cottage, or *dacha,* of the father of one of them, who turns out to be a deputy minister for this or that. He will not even be offered, at a price, spectacular and shiny post cards depicting Miss Betty Grable in the full panoply of fish-net tights against a dubbed-in background of palm trees enclosed in a cut-out heart. He will simply see the workaday face of a workaday city with the interminable crowds for ever drifting, window shopping, or engaged in the two main spare-time occupations of the privileged city dwellers: visiting friends, or making excursions to far-away shops which are rumoured to have a stock of darning needles or electric-light bulbs or even oranges.

He will see the great Metro, which, as Richard Chancellor, the first English visitor to Russia, would have said, is "a wonder to behold." He will see the new sky-scrapers, looming against the heavenly blue of the Moscow sky, lately the pride of Muscovite officialdom, now condemned for extravagance by Khrushchev. He will, if he is wise, spend every moment of his evenings at one of the great theatres, above all the Bolshoi for its ballet, rapt in enchantment at the full flowering of the Russian spirit—but possibly not fully realizing that here and here alone, in that vast

land with its multifarious activity, is the Russian spirit ever permitted to flower. He will meet, if he is sufficiently important, a
chosen VIP of the regime, a departmental minister concerned
with his particular specialty, and he will be spellbound by the
exhibition of ability, charm, and high idealism to which he will
be treated. The effect will be all the stronger because he probably
has not reflected that a minister of state in a country of the size and
power of the Soviet Union, who is also in effect the supreme head
of a whole sector of industry, must of necessity be a man of outstanding ability. As for the charm and the high idealism, he may
not know that, when it comes to blarney, the Russians are second
only to the Irish, and they are the more formidable in that they
bring to their blarney a cool and massive dignity of manner.

One morning, in Kiev, I was hospitably received by a very
smooth and powerful figure, the deputy minister of agriculture for
the Ukraine. There were no flies on him. We were talking of Mr.
Khrushchev's campaign to grow vast quantities of corn for cattle
fodder, often in places where corn had never been grown before,
and should not in fact be grown by anyone with any respect for
economics. In the deputy minister's office there were no doubts.
"You would like to see what we are doing? Ivan Sergeyevich, be
good enough to bring in the latest sample!" An assistant slipped
away. "Now you will see and will never doubt again!" And sure
enough, a minute later, two little men staggered in bearing between them a great sheaf of corn-stalks fully twelve feet high, each
with a number of fat ears eighteen inches long! Who wouldn't
have gasped? Certainly I did. It was a stupendous product. "There,
what did I tell you? Now you can go away and tell the world just
how we grow corn!"

The day before, I had passed through fields of corn, stretching
for mile after mile, some of it passable, most of it weedy, imma-
ture, and burned up. My host knew all about those fields. But
when I gently suggested that this sample of his was exceptional,
he good-humouredly demurred: "Very good—yes. Excellent—yes.
But exceptional—not at all. Not at all!" And, bursting out laughing, he clapped me on the back.

I don't know what I was supposed to believe. I don't know
what I was supposed to believe when, later in the conversation,

this same host blandly denied the existence of any troubles on the collectives, assured me that all was well with cattle breeding, that there was no shortage of meat, or butter, or anything at all—anywhere in the Ukraine. It was not as though he thought me a total greenhorn. He knew from my questions that I had some knowledge of agriculture. He knew I spoke Russian. He knew I had read Mr. Khrushchev's speeches in which he detailed the troubles on the collectives, and complained among other things of the failure of the cattle-breeding programme and of the shortages of butter, meat, and vegetables. He knew that I knew that over vast areas the corn planting had been a folly in conception and a fiasco in execution. And yet, plump, polite, well-shaven, beaming, he cheerfully denied that there was any difficulty about anything anywhere, and slapped me on the back. So we both had a good laugh together. Whether we were laughing about the same thing it was impossible to tell; but I am inclined to think we were.

So much for the tourist's Russia.

That, then, is why I have laid a good deal of stress on the things that go on just beneath the surface—or, rather, except for omnipresent *blat,* just round the corner. It is necessary to know something about them before trying to understand the domestic policies of the Soviet leadership. Until lately it was hardly possible to speak of such things. Their very existence was ignored in the Soviet press. Apart from released prisoners, only a handful of foreigners who had lived in the country long enough to penetrate below the surface were aware of them. It was not easy, it was almost useless, for these to write about them because their stories, affronting the preconceptions not only of Communists and fellow-travellers, but also of anti-Communists, could never be substantiated. There was no documentation whatsoever. If I had reported the case of two young Russians, sons of eminent fathers, who ran an amateur brothel in the heart of one of the most select villa suburbs of Moscow, who would have believed me? But when the case is reported circumstantially in a Moscow paper (*Soviet Culture,* January 10, 1955) not as a unique and unheard-of outrage but as symptomatic of a new and distressing development in Soviet life, then it can be talked about. That is why I have confined myself to examples cited in the Soviet press. Since I first wrote about the X-ray-plate jazz records I have even discovered official references to these (*Pravda,* October 31, 1955), which surprises me, as I had imagined this particular fantasy was not known to the authorities. And I have described it as observed, not in a spirit of censoriousness. I myself am old enough to remember ragged bare-foot gangs of children in the East End streets of London, and the roar and turmoil of fighting drunks outside the pubs on Saturday nights. These, like the hooligans of the Soviet Union, were the products of extreme poverty and a blank environment. Now we have the "cosh-boys," young gangsters, who no longer dress in rags, and the self-conscious, silly, and innocuous Teddy Boys. These, like their opposite numbers in the Soviet Union, are the products of broken homes and a general sense of futility. We also have slums, the welfare state notwithstanding. And, during the war, when everything under the sun was hard to get, we had our fill of spivs and speculators.

When I was in Moscow before, in 1947, all the practices I have touched on were in full swing; but it was hard to decide what they amounted to because the subsistence margin was so low that decent citizens of the highest integrity were being forced, as they had been in the war, to degrade themselves every day in order to survive at all. The change between then and now seems to be due, above all, to two things: the abundance and cheapness of vodka and the inarticulate, only half realized, entirely un-political revolt of the young, in very large numbers, against the system—not against its political foundations, but against the way it works.

Not, as I have said, all the young; far from it. The great majority still take life as it comes, and a sizable sector—how sizable is anybody's guess—finds fulfilment in the better aspirations of the Komsomol. These are filled with burning indignation against all the baser manifestations of life in the Soviet Union. They seek to purge it of everything ignoble and unworthy. And the irony in the situation of these young idealists is that what they are attacking in the name of the Party are evils created by the Party, and sustained by it.

Most, of course, are neither crusaders nor stilyagi nor hooligans. They are the ones who take life as it comes, and somehow, clinging tenaciously to every tiny gain, carve out for themselves a

niche in that swarming and still unstable society and in it mature
and bring up their families and pursue their own private interests. They achieve what in any society would be called normality,
and so far in the teeth of fearful difficulties. They combine in
their attitude to the world that mixture of credulity and scepticism toward official propaganda upon which I have already remarked. One can never be sure what they will believe and what
they will reject. They maintain an unsleeping and uninstructed
curiosity about the outside world. They lead their own private
lives with immense zest, but always with a wary eye in the direction of the authorities.

How they get themselves educated I have never been able
to fathom. I was asking one young girl, charming and upstanding,
occupying a well-paid and responsible position, about her childhood. Her father, an engineer, had been killed in the war. Her
mother had taken work in a factory, and in the evenings did
sewing to make extra money. There were two younger sisters.
The widow and the three girls had a single small room, but they
were forced to take in a lodger, who snored and talked in her
sleep (this was at the time when in order to keep alive at all
Muscovites had to expend immense sums on tiny scraps of sup-
plementary nourishment in the kolkhoz markets). During the
worst winters there was no heat, next to no gas for cooking, and
only intermittent light. Yet during all this time this young woman
worked through school, bringing her homework back every night
to puzzle over in pandemonium, and on an empty stomach. She
worked so well that she got a good scholarship to the university,
taking history and modern languages. She devoured every English and French book she could lay hands on. Things were better
during her student days, but there were still the lodger and the
single room, and the two sisters now needed help at school. But
she took an excellent degree, working for money in vacation
time. Soon she was paying for the higher education of her sisters.
Now the lodger has gone, the mother no longer works, the sisters
are at the university, and the heroine of this tale is earning two
thousand roubles a month and supporting the whole household.
She still reads furiously and voraciously. At the same time she
has accumulated a really well-thought-out wardrobe, so that for

evenings out she can appear by any standards adequately dressed, by Soviet standards smart and elegant and colourful in the extreme. Her latest acquisition, cherished in tissue paper like a rare jewel, is one of those feather hats that were smart in London three or four years ago, and in Moscow today it looks like something from another world. The clothes all live, carefully wrapped, under the bed, where her university books once had to go. Home is still the single room in a tumble-down nineteenth-century backyard house. I asked her how on earth she had been able to concentrate on homework in the noisy chaos of that tiny room. She had no desk to write at, and her study was the window sill. She laughed and shrugged. "What else was there to do?" Then she checked herself, as though struck by a new idea. "Do you know," she said, "I never thought of it. Until this very moment I never thought anything of it. If I had thought of it I don't think I could have done it. So it's a good thing that I didn't. Goodness me! Now that you've asked, now that I look back, I don't know how it was done."

I don't know either. But it was, and in innumerable cases. This particular young woman is not typical in that she is good-looking by any standards, more than usually intelligent, and has a taste for elegant clothes and the figure to carry them off. But in other ways she is entirely typical. She is not a Communist, or anything like it; but, although she wishes the regime were less stiff and harsh and stupid, she thinks the leadership means well—while doubting the capacity of Messrs. Khrushchev and Bulganin to stand up to "the bureaucracy"—of which she, charming and inconsequent creature, is herself a part! She does not believe at all in the picture of the West offered by the official propagandists—though she has some queer ideas about it; she is aware of the very dark sides of Soviet life; but she is pleased and proud to be a Russian and sees the pattern of the future in the best achievements of the present. In the cities there are millions like her. Like the English middle classes of fifty years ago, they are the backbone of the system. One of the big questions is whether the Party will drive on, breeding corruption and spivvery until decency is swamped, or whether it will adapt itself to decency.

8. THE THAW

THERE are signs that it will adapt itself to decency. All the virtues now being officially extolled are the classical middle-class virtues: sobriety, chastity, industry, solvency—in a word, respectability. The Komsomol, the Young Communist League, has been imperceptibly transformed. Instead of being a limited society of starry-eyed youth dedicated to the task of carrying out the commandments of the Party, ideological stalwarts, it is now a vast organization with a membership of nearly twenty million which catches in its net pretty much the whole of presentable Soviet youth. The idealists are still very much there, and they form a hard core, but for the rest, for the majority, the Komsomol has degenerated into a more or less compulsory club, or fraternity. And the main object of the movement is no longer to catch the cream of the younger generation and turn them into good Communists, but to raise the moral tone of youth as a whole so that they may become good and sober citizens. Ideological training of all kinds still forms a large part of its activities; but this, to judge from my own observation of the Komsomols and Komsomolkas of today, is increasingly perfunctory. The difference in atmosphere between the Komsomol of ten years ago and the Komsomol of today can perhaps be summed up like this: then, in order to be a Komsomol and serve the Party well, the individual had to be a model citizen; now it is the task of the Komsomol leaders to turn their members into model citizens.

This change of emphasis, it seems to me, is one of the most vitally important developments in the history of the Soviet Union. Once upon a time the prime task of the Party was to instil the Leninist ideology into the best and most receptive elements in the Soviet Union. Today it is the prime task of the Party to set an example of blameless conduct to the country as a whole. Their own model performance is based on the precepts and practice of Leninism—which the decadent bourgeois societies do not have. Thus Leninism has been transformed from an ideological dynamic into the source of the new respectability.

I think I have said enough in earlier chapters to show that this is so, and how it works. Any reader who is in doubt about the matter is invited to peruse the samples of Party pep-talks printed in the Appendix. These, which offer a minute fraction of the immense mass of such writings current during the past few years, provide a more revealing commentary on the true nature of Soviet society today than anything a single observer can hope to provide. It will be seen that the true nature of Soviet society today is about as far removed from the preconceptions of the West—of Western Communists and fellow-travellers as well as Western anti-Communists—as it is possible to be.

The next question, then, is whether our ideas of the Soviet leadership are equally out of line.

Writing in 1950, three years before Stalin died, I committed myself to the view that the fearful strains and rigours imposed on the Soviet people by Stalin's cold-war policy were too heavy to be endured for much longer, even by the Russians, who can endure almost anything. It seemed to me impossible that this policy could lead to anything but disaster. On the other hand, it seemed unlikely that Stalin, in his old age, was capable of changing his ways.

At the end of 1952 the proceedings at the Nineteenth Party Congress indicated that in fact Stalin was preparing to ease his pressure at home and abroad. At any rate his celebrated thesis on the economics of Socialism offered an ideological basis for easing the cold war and beginning to raise the standard of living at home. Whether he was prepared to take the requisite measures to work seriously toward these goals will never be known. For shortly after the Nineteenth Party Congress, which met in October 1952, Stalin either went off his head or fell mortally ill.

There is no other possible explanation than one or the other of these for the terrifying "vigilance campaign," with its rank flavour of anti-Semitism, which culminated in the arrest of the

Kremlin doctors and was about to plunge the Soviet Union into a new terror such as it had not known for over a decade and a half. Either the sick and aging tyrant was visited in the last months of his life with visions of treachery and conspiracy against him which brought out the dreadful, paranoid rages of his final victory in the middle thirties—visions and suspicions no doubt deliberately strengthened, if not actually instigated, by some of those closest to him seeking to use the old man's fury to crush their own rivals —either that, or else Stalin lay stricken and impotent while his would-be successors unleashed the new terror as a by-product of the struggle for power among themselves.

I prefer the first explanation. It is in character—not only with Stalin the Georgian eagle, but also with the tradition of the Tsars. I have frequently been reproached for invoking this tradition, which ran through two dynasties, of paranoiac violence. One would not, people say, dream of associating the House of Windsor with the murder of the princes in the Tower. Indeed one would not. But Richard's coronation took place in 1483. Ivan the terrible with his own hands murdered his son and heir in 1580. The deposition and murder of Peter II at the hands of Catherine took place in 1762. The deposition and murder of Paul, the mad Tsar, took place in 1801. In 1917 Nicholas II, his Empress, and his children were murdered by Bolsheviks in a cellar at Ekaterinburg (now Sverdlovsk). In 1937 Stalin ordered the shooting of Bukharin, Zinoviev, Rykov, and practically all the survivors of the original revolutionary party. And in case these selected fatalities still seem to have no bearing on the matter in hand, it was in 1953 that the Communist Party of the Soviet Union uncovered a conspiracy which was said to have been responsible for the death of Shcherbakov and Zhdanov, two of the highest leaders in the land, and to be actively engaged in plotting the death by poisoning, at the hands of the Kremlin doctors, of the greater part of the Soviet military higher command. After Stalin's death this charge was denounced as a fabrication. As recently as 1954, Lavrenti Beria, one of the first three men in the Soviet Union, was arrested by his own comrades and shot for treason; and it was stated in the indictment that this man, one of Stalin's most trusted lieutenants for decades, chief of the Security Police since

1938, and a senior member of the Politburo, had been a British agent since 1922.

It seems to me that a government which asks us to believe (a) that some of its highest luminaries were poisoned, at the instigation of unseen plotters in the highest places, by Stalin's own doctors; (b) that after all they were not, and that the whole story was a fabrication of the highest officers in the Security services, including an individual of ministerial rank; and (c) that one of the senior and most trusted members of the inner circle had been a British agent since 1922—it seems to me that a government which asks the world to believe this, and a great deal more besides, cannot have it both ways. Not all of these things can be true; (a) and (b) directly contradict each other. None of them need be true. But if none of them is true, then the Soviet government and the Communist Party of the Soviet Union convicts itself of lying pushed to the level of high fantasy. And if any of them is true, then, on its own admission, the Kremlin is a place where very remarkable things take place—the sort of things that have not happened in England since the time of the late Tudors (with the exception, as some hold, of Charles I). In a word, in the light of their own announcements about the manner of life of the highest Soviet leaders, those who remain can hardly be choosy about what the outer world believes. The outer world, indeed, is not only justified in believing the worst if it feels so inclined, but is positively obliged, in its own interests, to believe something pretty bad. We have never given as much power to the British home secretary (or anybody else), as the Soviet Communists gave Beria: but supposing Mr. Chuter Ede, or Mr. Maxwell Fyfe, or Major Gwilym Lloyd George had been arrested, and hung, for being a Bolshevik agent since 1922—I feel the outside world would be justified in leaping to the conclusion that there was something rotten in the state of Britain. And supposing Lord Horder, Lord Dawson of Penn, Sir Farquhar Buzzard, Sir Stewart Duke-Elder, and a number of others, had been arrested on the information of a house surgeon at Middlesex Hospital and charged with having murdered the late Sir Stafford Cripps and the late Lord Halifax and of plotting to murder Lord Alexander of Tunis, Field Marshal Montgomery, Air Marshal Tedder, Admiral Sir Dudley

Pound, and Lord Louis Mountbatten—I feel that at the very least there would be some critical comment on the British way of life in *Time* and *Paris-Soir*. And to anyone who says such suppositions are nonsense, the answer is that indeed they are nonsense; but in the Soviet Union, the most progressive country in the world, they came true. And the charming, inconsequent Russians seem to expect to get away with it. And quite often they do.

I have no intention here of trying to sort out just what happened in and around the Politburo between the Nineteenth Party Congress, five months before the death of Stalin, and the arrest of Beria three months after that climacteric. Nobody knows. It is possible to construct a variety of engaging and plausible theories, circumstantial to a degree, any one of which may be true, each one of which is likely to be wrong. It seems to me, moreover, that this kind of deductive theorizing, or instructed speculation, or guesswork, or whatever it is called, is (though I myself have indulged in a fair share of it) open to sharp criticism. It serves no useful purpose, unless to familiarize the reader with the names of the Soviet leaders. It can lead to no firm conclusions. On the other hand it very certainly distracts the eye from the fundamental issues. The interpreter of Soviet affairs is apt to fall in love with the creations of his own imagination. It becomes a matter of the most earnest importance to demonstrate, by reasoning that is often brilliant, based on facts which only a handful of fellow specialists can appreciate, or even remember, that Comrade X is more liberal that Comrade Y, and that Comrade Y is assisted in his dedicated task of scuppering Comrade X by the ineptitudes of the British Foreign Office which, by turning a deaf ear to the peaceful pleadings of Comrade X has lost him credit in the eyes of Comrades A, B, and C. In a word, until we know a great deal more than we do, or are ever likely to know, speculations about the internal groupings are irrelevant and misleading. What matters is that every individual in the government of the Soviet Union and the highest organs of the Communist Party of the Soviet Union was a creature of Stalin's, and helped Stalin to carry out those policies at home and abroad with which we are all familiar. On this count, until there is conclusive proof to the contrary, there is nothing to choose among the lot of them. They were all the satraps of the most terrible tyrant in modern history; they were all murderers on his behalf.

Having said that, we are in a position to see them in perspective —I mean, above all, Messrs. Khrushchev, Bulganin, Molotov, Kaganovich, Mikoyan, Malenkov, and the rest of their closest colleagues. The fact that Ivan IV established a reign of terror in sixteenth-century Russia, strangled his son, and died of remorse, did not mean that he was not a ruler of genius; nor did it exclude sixteenth-century Russia from useful relations with Elizabethan England. The fact that the present rulers of the Soviet Union can look back on a past packed with treachery and violence does not mean that they are incapable of anything but treachery and violence or that they cannot change their ways to meet changing times. Quite clearly they are capable of all sorts of other things. And equally clearly they changed their ways very quickly when their lord and master died—so quickly, indeed, that they gave every appearance, with the exception of Mr. Molotov (who was clearly grieved and at sea), of deep relief at the departure of their master, who was a tyrant to them also, and of disapproval of many of his policies.

The change was much greater than most of us in the West were allowed, or allowed ourselves, to suppose. It was epoch-making, in the literal sense of the term. Throughout the whole of 1953, after Stalin's death in March, and well into 1954, taking the arrest and execution of Beria in its stride, the new leadership, with Malenkov as prime minister, presided over a process of general liberalization inside the Soviet Union, so strong that, although the process has since been checked (but not reversed) its effect has come to be regarded as permanent and enduring. The check to the process began in the spring of 1954, and in some sense appeared to be confirmed and strengthened by the fall of Malenkov early in 1955 and the end of the dream of a steep rise in the standard of living and a swift abundance of consumer goods. But there is a good deal of confusion here—not inside the Soviet Union, where people understand what is going on, but in the outside world. And I shall try to show that in fact the substitution of Bulganin for Malenkov and the dizzy rise of Khrushchev is not seen by Russians as a reversion to Stalinism; further, that the

abandonment of immediate solicitude for the consumer in favour
of renewed priority for heavy industry was due to causes far more
complicated than the outcome of a straight argument about guns
before butter. The vision of the West was distorted because most
observers were barely conscious of the reality of the great thaw
before the check was put on in 1954—just as the real meaning
of Geneva was obscured by certain developments on both sides,
which we shall consider later.

The post-Stalin thaw can be studied usefully only in its effects
inside Russia. In the international field there have been so many
complicating, local, and changing factors outside the control of
the Kremlin that it is very difficult (though not quite impossible,
I think), to establish a coherent line. And probably the best mirror
of developments at home in the past three years is offered by the
proceedings of the Writers' Union, since writers are by nature
articulate and express trends in their work more clearly than
scientists or soldiers.

The first open sign of the change did not, of course, come from
the writers; it came from the new government. It was the broadening of the base of the government; the inclusion of the popular
hero, Marshal Zhukov, who had for long been relegated to obscurity; the immediate demolition of the cult of Stalin as the all-
wise, all-seeing, infallible leader and teacher—and the substitution
for this cult of the conception of collective rule. The idea of collective rule was carried so far and so demonstratively that in
months to come the new leaders frequently put themselves to
extreme inconvenience to appear all together in the same place
on every possible occasion—to the extent, sometimes, of sharing
the same motor car, even though it meant sitting almost in one
another's laps, to solve the question of precedence. The dropping
of all but the most perfunctory references to Stalin was so swift,
so sudden, as to be uncanny: it was as though a whole continent
had vanished from the surface of the globe. It was meant as a sign,
and it was taken as a sign by the Soviet people. So, a few months
later, was the arrest of Beria and the vigorous down-grading of
the Security Police: Beria was to be the scapegoat for all the
evils of Stalinism, and the MGB were no longer to enjoy almost
absolute power over everyone in the land. The third major sign

was Malenkov's speech to the Supreme Soviet in August, when he assured the country that the industrial base was secure, that there was bread for all in plenty, that Soviet industry could thus afford to pay a great deal more attention to the manufacture of consumer goods. A fourth sign was the throwing open of the Kremlin, or parts of it, to the general public, after it had been so long a closed fortress, both the seat and the symbol of the mystery in which Stalin enveloped himself and the whole vast land.

All these, and other things besides, happened in the first year of the new government. They were landmarks, signs from on high. And the Soviet people, for whom they were primarily intended, have not forgotten them. In spite of subsequent waverings of the Party line they are still full of meaning.

The case of the writers should be viewed against this background.

Already at the Nineteenth Party Congress, while Stalin was still alive, several of the speakers showed extreme dissatisfaction with the state of Soviet literature, as well they might. Malenkov, in particular, went out of his way to protest against the stereotyping of permissible situations, unreal "type" characters, the absence of genuine conflict. He tried to explain the sort of conflicts that could be regarded as legitimate in a land where a steady upward progress on the broadest possible front is the order of the day; but although Malenkov is a highly gifted man, and a Latin scholar into the bargain, he did not succeed in making himself very clear, and Soviet writers went on playing for safety. They were still cowed by the Zhdanov edict of 1946 with its harsh and rigid prescription of the permissible in literature and the arts in general. It was all very well for Malenkov to talk about the creation of genuine characters and the presentation of real conflicts, but this simply could not be done under the Zhdanov formula, which required nothing but the presentation of the new Soviet man, seen as an apanage of the expanding industrial economy, moving steadily onward and upward in a mood of manic optimism, without a doubt, without a question, without a backward look, and triumphing over all opposition with scarcely a visible check; the opposition, of course, came only from villains.

Nevertheless, there was, it later transpired, a movement behind the scenes. The first sign of the thaw, the faint gurgle of free-moving water somewhere underneath the solid mass of ice and snow, occurred in April 1953, barely a month after Stalin had died. The heroine, whose name will always be dear to me, was Olga Berggoltz (I do not know Miss Berggoltz), a poet from Leningrad, who has since shown herself to be an irrepressibly high-spirited critic, with a cheerful sense of humour. Miss Berggoltz started the ultimate avalanche with a resounding and circumstantial attack on the state of Soviet poetry—lyric poetry. It seems unlikely that the editor of *Literary Gazette* picked up his telephone and ordered this piece while Stalin's body was still lying in State. It is far more likely that it had been written while Stalin was still living, but after the Nineteenth Party Congress the previous October, in anticipation of an official change of policy toward the arts.

Be that as it may, it was a revolutionary document. Miss Berggoltz pleaded on behalf of the heart. She had lately performed, she said, at a Leningrad poetry reading, together with a number of her colleagues, and she had been deeply perplexed because, at the end, the audience had begged for "something lyrical" to finish up with. "Something lyrical" was precisely what she thought she had been giving them. But she thought again, and when she got home she conscientiously sat down and read through the year's output of verse in four separate literary magazines.

Perplexity then gave way to shock. In not one single poem was there any attempt at the lyrical treatment of the heart, of love. That started her thinking again, and this is what she thought: "In a great many of our lyrical works the most important thing of all is lacking: humanity, the human being. I don't mean there are no human beings in any of these poems. Indeed there are; there are operators of bull-dozers and steam-shovels; there are horticulturalists, all carefully described, sometimes well and even brilliantly described. But they are described from the outside, and the most important thing is lacking in all these poems—a lyric hero with his own individual relationship to events and to the landscape." This externalization, she went on to say, simply will not do; the poet himself must be involved and identified in the "the image of man" in his verse. For only by revealing himself openly, candidly, and without reserve will he win the reader to his side in a sort of "partnership."

Having diagnosed the evil, Miss Berggoltz boldly sought the cause. This she found in the influence of those critics who accuse poets of "pessimism and decadence" if they ever, even for a moment, allow themselves to express a shadow of doubt or irresolution, or even grief—even, "God forbid, sorrow at, let us say, parting from the beloved." Sorrow, she went on to say, has become a forbidden emotion in Soviet lyric poetry, or, if it ever finds expression, must be counteracted immediately in its pernicious effect by some constructive action—"by, for example, the jilted lover's buckling down to it and exceeding the hay-making plan."

This, of course, was a frontal attack on Zhdanov and the critics who took their cue from him.

The next major contribution to the rediscovery of the literary impulse came from the poet Alexander Tvardovsky, who, in the June issue of *New World,* which he himself then edited, published a narrative poem about a long railway journey, one of those fantastic and interminable Russian railway journeys, in which he, Tvardovsky, was grilled by his fellow-passengers for the shortcomings of his colleagues—and found himself forced into agreement with them. Then writer after writer came up with his own reflections on the same theme. And in the early autumn, at an All-Union Congress of Young Critics, the individual voices were joined into a chorus. The avalanche was under way. Vera Inber, another Leningrad poet, declared roundly that nobody was reading Soviet poetry because it was so bad and dull and imitative, always about "the same old dam, the same old steam-shovel, the same old road" (the steam-shovel, as well it might, seems to have become a symbol of everything the Soviet writer was secretly feeling about the æsthetic tastes of the late Colonel General Zhdanov). She attacked the critics, with their inflated claims for Soviet literature simply because it was Soviet. She sprang to the defence of Tvardovsky, who had been heavily attacked for his poem about the railway journey. In a simple anecdote she summed up the state of Soviet criticism. There was a well-known critic, she declared, who, solemnly analysing the construction of nursery songs and lullabies, had committed himself to the following: "In bour-geois societies lullabies put children to sleep; but in our country they must rouse them."

It was at the same meeting that the critic Tarasenkov made a spirited demand for more controversy: "We forget that the truth is born in controversy, in the clash of opinions." Another writer, Paukovsky, called for a universal heart-searching on the part of all Soviet writers and pleaded for a return to the conception of the writer's "high calling."

All this was less than six months after the death of Stalin.

The stage was now set for two events: the intervention of Ilya Ehrenburg and the Plenary Session of the Writers' Union to dis-cuss the state of Soviet drama. Both took place in October 1953.

Until now the voices had been unofficial. They were the voices of individuals, though speaking in concert, and clearly with the general approval of the Party. But Ehrenburg is more than an individual; he is a portent. He is the highly gifted spokesman of the government, who knows how to infuse with the passion of creation a statement of whatever Party line happens to be in fashion at any given moment. The meeting of the Writers' Union was presided over by Fadeyev, the novelist, a member of the Cen-tral Committee, who was then, in effect, the Party commissar for literature. It was also blessed in person by Comrade Ponomarenko, a member of the Party Presidium, and for a brief time minister of culture.

These two events more than confirmed the new idea that had gradually been finding expression. Writer after writer stood up at the Plenary Session and said things he had been wanting to say for a very long time; the picture they drew between them produced the final answer, crushing and inescapable, to the claims of fellow-travellers about the healthy state of Soviet literature. Nobody outside Russia need ever again bother to argue the case against the Zhdanov edict and its paralysing effect on the mind. All that is necessary is to quote the Russians themselves— as their speeches, one after another, were recorded in the proceed-ings of the Plenary Session. Nobody in the West could have at-tacked the Zhdanov line more bitterly or devastatingly. But it was attacked always by implication, never directly. Its absurdities were attributed not to Zhdanov and the Party, but to the people who had been wearily trying to follow the line. The Party itself was not much mentioned by speakers—not enough, as it later turned out. But Fadeyev and others made it quite clear that it stood above criticism. The sins of the Party were to be visited—but mildly—on its victims. The Party remained, as always, the wise counsellor and guide in all æsthetic matters. Those who took its advice to heart could never go wrong. All this was said by Fadeyev speaking as a member of the Central Committee, regardless of the fact that the advice the Party was now tendering was diametrically opposed in every particular to the advice it had offered— or, rather, enforced—only the day before.

(It is important to remember that at this dam-bursting session at the Writers' Union, in October 1953, no pretence was made that the Party was not omnipotent in æsthetic matters. Unless that is remembered—and it is too often forgotten by Western critics—it is impossible to see subsequent events in any sort of perspective at all.)

The first thing the Congress revealed was a new interest in people, a realization of the importance of the reader, the audience. "The dramatist must not forget that he has to earn the right to take up four hours of the time of one-and-a-half thousand Soviet people." This observation by A. Popov, chief producer of the great Theatre of the Soviet Army in Moscow, summarized that aspect of affairs. Then came the theme of backwardness, announced by the poet and dramatist Simonov, another member of the Central Committee, and the most reliable and sensitive (two qualities which do not always go together) weathercock, or turn-coat, in the Soviet Union—which is saying a good deal. It was an instructive episode.

Four years earlier the celebrated critic Stein had recklessly tried to start a little avalanche of his own. Sick to death of the endless succession of plays and novels about life on collective farms, which had no contact with reality at any point whatsoever, turned out by hacks according to the Zhdanov formula—but without the Zhdanov conviction (that insufferable man, whose timely death, from whatever cause, saved the Soviet people from calamity, was at least an impassioned Communist)—he lashed out at them, and got himself into fearful hot water in consequence. He gave his recipe for the writing of a successful play about a kolkhoz. He had read twenty of them, he said, and they all had the following points in common:

"First Act. A kolkhoz which has suffered under the Nazi occupation: (a) there are no seeds; (b) there is no fuel; (c) the tractor station has been destroyed; (d) the chairman of the kolkhoz is either away or on a drinking bout, or he has lost faith, or he is simply a dolt. . . . Curtain of the First Act: (a) the district party secretary arrives on the scene; (b) also the assistant chief of the Political Department; (c) a war veteran is made chairman of the kolkhoz. . . . Second Act. The new chairman tells all the kolkhoz members 'the earth is given us for our eternal use; we must gather in the harvest; comrades, let us work!' "

And so on.

That was one of the episodes that led to the venomous official attack on a whole group of Jewish critics. Then the weathercock Simonov stamped on poor Stein with both feet. There was nothing wrong with the Soviet drama, he fulminated. "We have had enough of these crocodile tears over the lack of talent in our Soviet drama! We have had enough of these Hottentot dances provoked by the first error which can be discovered in the work of a given dramatist."

Now, in October 1953, it was Simonov's turn to do a Hottentot dance. The Soviet drama, he declared, "had been in a state of backwardness for a number of years." He proceeded to explain why, beating the big drum for progress and liveliness, sneering at the dullness and rigidity of his colleagues. (Simonov himself, it should be said, is an engaging and talented playwright who has become a millionaire not only by virtue of his flair for knowing which way the cat is going to jump but also because he is rarely dull, knowing how to turn the Party line into drama.) He, too, demanded the presentation on the stage not of stereotypes (Malenkov's word) but of complicated characters.

The dramatist S. Mikhalkov went further. He launched into a downright attack on the utter falsity of contemporary Soviet plays. He said flatly that Soviet audiences had been "taught to see on the stage that which departs from the truth of life, from the real difficulties, misfortunes, joys, and sorrows of living Soviet people." Indeed, he continued, burning his boats, many people had come to feel "that the divergence of dramatic literature and reality is almost compulsory." He gave examples. He was not alone. The dramatist Lavrenev, who preserved a tone of slightly detached irony throughout the debate, as though he were not at all sure that he really believed in the new era but was determined to have fun while it lasted, if only for a day, came to Mikhalkov's support. He boldly attacked the preoccupation with regional novels and plays, with novels and plays about the building of dams and the irrigation of deserts. He reminded his listeners that the proper concern of men was "with the clash of passions and characters typical of the whole of Soviet society, not only of the builders of a specific dam, or the lemon growers of a specific district." He cited a well-known play which, he said, had characters speaking extracts taken straight from a text-book on the oil industry. He said there were others which could be understood only if the spectator had in his pocket a technical manual of the industry under discussion. Above all he attacked the totally frivolous attitude adopted toward the human emotions by many dramatists seeking to concoct the grounds for a "spurious conflict." Thus, "the agrotechnician Vanya, who is madly in love, has just married Tanya, the brigadier of the field station; and now he casts off his beloved wife as a backward element, because Tanya holds different views on the correct methods of clamping potatoes." Such contrivances, he concluded, "testify to the author's fundamental lack of respect for his heroes, Soviet people . . . for when bosom friends, lovers, fathers and children become mortal enemies, and with astonishing thoughtlessness part for ever because of a difference of opinion on a question of agronomics, this is nothing but a distortion of the image of Soviet man."

And so it went on. Other speakers elaborated the idea of reflecting the movements of human emotions as the supreme concern of the dramatist, and demanded the abandonment of flat, cut-out shadows masquerading as people. Others ranged beyond the problems of the contemporary dramatist. Simonov, remarkably, put in a plea for the rehabilitation of certain works belonging to the early years of the revolution which had for long been virtually banned because they were full of dangerous thoughts. He attacked "the timid, distrustful attitude to the majority of works . . . describing the epoch of the inception and early development of Soviet society, with all its complications and contradictions." Editors, he said, behaved as though in publishing or considering plays of the twenties and the thirties "they were dealing with something that might burn them." In particular he demanded the reissuing of a number of works, including a once well-known play by Afinogenov, which had been banned because their ideas, though apposite when they were written, were no longer applicable. Fadeyev himself, from on high, appealed to editors, publishers, and critics not to boycott an author because he had made individual mistakes in the past, but to rally round and lend a helping hand.

It was against this background that Ilya Ehrenburg, in the October number of *The Banner,* published his celebrated confession of faith. He had been asking himself, he said—and others had asked him too—whether all was well with the state of Soviet literature. And he had to confess that all was very far from well. He went on to discuss at length the reasons for the *malaise,* and in the end came to the *clou* of his argument, which was an author's plea against prescription from above;

An author is not a piece of machinery, mechanically registering events. An author writes a book, not because he knows how to write, not because he is a member of the Union of Soviet Writers and may be asked why he has published nothing for so long. An author does not write a book because he has to earn a living. An author writes a book because he finds it necessary to tell people something of himself, because he is pregnant with his book, because he has seen people, things, and emotions that he cannot help describing. . . .
——That is why I cannot understand some critics when they blame such-and-such a writer: he has not written a novel about the Volga-Don canal, about the textile industry, or about the struggle for peace. Would it not be better to reproach another author, who has written a book, although he felt no spiritual compulsion to do so and could have quietly left it unwritten? . . .

In pre-revolutionary times an author's life was not an easy one, and in Chekhov's letters there is mention of how the editors of a newspaper or magazine would order a story from him. But even the most

impudent of editors refrained from suggesting to Chekhov the subject of his story. Can one imagine Tolstoy being given an instruction
to write *Anna Karenina* or Gorki being ordered to write *Mother?*

Ehrenburg's colleagues, alas, could all too easily imagine precisely that.

All through the autumn and winter writers and critics revelled
in the new freedom. There were occasional harsh voices raised
in protest or warning. There were reminders that freedom of
expression does not mean freedom from responsibility. But the
general mood was one of hopefulness and high spirits—finding
expression in experimental practice first in criticism, magazine
articles, newspaper *feuilletons.* In addition, the Party organs increased their cry for more and better satire, first demanded by
Malenkov at the Nineteenth Party Congress. There were all
kinds of evils in the Soviet Union, it was agreed; and these had to
be attacked and lampooned and flayed. Everywhere there was
an atmosphere of emotional and intellectual stimulus and ex-
pansiveness.

The same sort of thing was going on in the other arts, most
notably in music, for painting, never strong in Russia, was still
dominated by the aged Gerasimov, one of the most deadly and
cantankerous old fudges in the history of academic painting—and
that includes the history of the Royal Academy in Britain. But
in music Khachaturian came out with a most moving defence of
his dead friend Prokofiev, and boldly denounced the men who
had made his closing years unhappy. In science the same current
was moving strongly. The doctrinal excesses of Stalin in his last
phase were recanted. The symbol of this was the unseating of
Lysenko from his arbitrary throne. The symbol of the new mild-
ness was the retention by Lysenko of a respectable position.

It seemed too good to last, and so it turned out. Already in the
new year there were dark mutterings. In the previous December,
New World, edited by Tvardovsky, had printed a long and impassioned article by V. Pomerantsev called "Sincerity in Literature." In it he took up Ehrenburg's point, under the slogan "A
bad book is worse than no book at all," and attacked the Writers'
Union, that holy of holies of the Soviet literary world ("I have

heard that Shakespeare was not a member of any union, yet he did not write badly!") and the doctrinaire critics. He exalted sincerity above all other qualities. He attacked playing for safety as the worst of all sins: "At the very least it is all of ten sins." It was, in effect, a perfectly reasonable appeal to the artist's self-respect; and only in a society of the kind we have just seen revealed out of the mouths of the Soviet writers themselves would it appear as anything but trite.

But it was too much for the Party, and it offered a useful pretext to the counter-attack that had been brewing. It was answered in *Literary Gazette,* a month later (January 20, 1954), by Vitaly Vasilievsky. Vasilievsky made some quite good points (Pomerantsev had laid himself open to all sorts of valid criticism), but there was only one point that mattered: "He [Pomerantsev] claims that 'the degree of sincerity—that is, the directness of things, must be the first test.' No, the first test for the Marxist has been and will continue to be evaluation of the ideological-artistic quality of the work. Thus, under close scrutiny, the basis of the article is seen to be false."

Within a few months Pomerantsev, together with other contributors to *New World,* was officially denounced, and Tvardovsky, the editor, dismissed from his post.

The new masters had seen the absurdities of Zhdanovism—and not only the absurdities, but the very sharp and real threat to all intellectual initiative. They showed themselves eager, some of them at least, to slip the strait-jacket from the arts of the Soviet Union; they massaged tenderly and solicitously the numbed and paralysed members. They were all for free expression and spontaneous creation; they saw that the arts, above all literature, could not flourish if every situation, every word, was prescribed from above; they urged with paternal benevolence that writers should be themselves, that they should not look over their shoulders to see what the next man was doing, play for safety, and for ever reinsure themselves, to use the current catchword. But when at last the writers began to stretch their limbs and give expression to their real thoughts the new masters were appalled at the depth of pent-up feeling they had unleashed—and convulsively clamped down again.

When they clamped down, many people (but not in the Soviet Union) concluded that this meant the end of a beautiful dream, that the ghost of Zhdanov was firmly back in control, that the new masters had either relaxed their pressures out of weakness, and once more began to feel strong, or regretted their experiment and would have no more of it. But this has not turned out to be true at all. The situation three years after Stalin is far more complicated and entirely fluid. Since the attitude of the new masters to the writers and artists of the Soviet Union offers a very close reflection of their attitude toward many other things it is worth seeing what happened next.

9. FREEDOM WITHIN BOUNDS

THE big row started not with Pomerantsev and Tvardovsky but with a number of playwrights. Plays take less time to write than novels, and four dramatists, encouraged and made a little light-headed by the unprecedented freedom of discussion at the October drama session of the Writers' Union, proceeded to profit by the new mood; they were I. Gorodetsky, A. Marienhov, N. Virta, and A. Zorin. All their plays were pilloried for basically the same reason: they exposed evils and bad characters, but presented these evils and these characters as endemic to the Soviet scene, if not actually products of the system, instead of as disgusting relics of the bourgeois past. Gorodetsky's play *A Man of Action* had for its main character a typical careerist who had become in all his corruption chairman of a city Soviet. Marienhov, in *The Crown Prince,* showed "a group of young idlers and good-for-nothings in the last stage of moral degeneration," to quote *Pravda.* "Instead of presenting the struggle against these negative phenomena, A. Marienhov's play offers cynical speculations about them . . . does everything in his power to lend these insignificant moral monsters, who kow-tow to the morals of American gangsters, the semblance of some kind of 'drama' and 'interest,' a nuance of cheap 'demonism.' . . ." In other words, Marienhov was interested and depressed by the phenomenon of the stilyagi, and in his play tries to find out what it is all about.

The chief sacrifice, however, was Zorin, who had written a play called *The Guests.* This play, when published in the monthly *Theatre* had been praised by none other than Simonov.

The Zorin case tells us almost everything there is to be told about the Party's attitude to the writer. I do not know how often he has been attacked, but I have six major broadsides: the initial attack by A. Surkov in *Pravda* on May 25, 1954 (Surkov has lately achieved an unpleasant prominence as secretary of the Writers' Union; he is either a rabid Zhdanovite or an unscrupulous yes-man); a leading article in *Literary Gazette* (May 27) entitled "A False Play"; an attack by Yrmilov in *Pravda* of June 3, called "For Socialist Realism"; a report of a meeting of the Moscow playwrights to discuss (i.e. condemn) *The Guests* (*Literary Gazette*, June 5); the report of a special meeting in the Collegium of the Ministry of Culture of the USSR, condemning *The Guests* as "ideologically defective, inartistic, and alien to the principles of Socialist Realism" (*Soviet Culture*, June 5); an attack on the magazine *Theatre*, for publishing *The Guests* and other plays (*Izvestia*, June 9). The loyal memory of Zhdanov was evoked both by Comrade Surkov and by the Ministry of Culture.

In a word, poor Zorin was given the full treatment. Why? What did he do wrong?

His unforgivable error was that he connected the shortcomings of his main character with certain shortcomings in the Soviet system. We have already in earlier chapters glanced at some of these shortcomings and seen them to be deep-rooted and extensive. Zorin had done the same.

The Guests presents a conflict between the old and the young generation of Bolsheviks. Peter Kirpichev is a Communist careerist in the Stalinist manner, a man of influence and privilege, with high official position, motor cars, and country villas. He goes on a visit to his old father in the country, and a very real conflict arises between the old man who fought for the Revolution and did not count the cost, who devoted his life to it, all for no reward, and the son who inherited the Revolution and cashed in on it. It is, as those who have read this book so far can easily imagine, a fascinating real-life problem—though, in fact, not many old Kirpichevs survived Stalin's purges. Some did, however, and Zorin has created a recognizable type. Furthermore, not content with the simple opposition of old and new, of father and son, with the new disreputable and the old full of honour, Zorin has complicated matters by making one of his younger characters, a girl of decent instincts and high aspirations, side against Peter Kirpichev with his father.

The attack on Zorin was carefully managed. It was nowhere

denied that Peter Kirpichevs exist in Russia. He is a recognized character. There are, it was admitted, soulless careerists inside the Communist Party, and they must be exposed. But they must be shown as anomalous survivals of the disreputable past. Zorin's sin is to show Kirpichev not as a survival but as a representative man thriving on the unhappier aspects of the Soviet system—as, indeed, an inevitable product of that system, though not the only kind of product. This is a deadly sin, because "it distorts the very nature of Soviet society and the state system, thereby undermining in its readers their faith in the insuperable power of our society to develop uninterruptedly forward along the path to Communism."

Interval for prayer.

The central idea of the play is summed up by old Kirpichev: "The country has become stronger and the people have become richer. But alongside the toilers and hard workers there have appeared, imperceptibly and abundantly, such people as you: white-collar aristocrats, greedy and conceited, far from the people."

Here, in a sentence, is the basic tragedy of the Soviet Union. No writer had ever dared state it. The vehemence of the reaction, the massive repetition of anathema on Zorin, indicates, more clearly than anything else could, not only that it goes too close to the knuckle, not only that the Soviet leadership is aware of its truth, but also that it knows that the people too are aware. And in this lies the basic dilemma of the Soviet leadership.

Even so, it is when Zorin elaborates his theme and seeks the reason that he offends most deeply. The mainspring, he finds, is love of power. "I simply worked side by side with the great toilers of our land," old Kirpichev exclaimed. "I worked. And I did not know the taste of power. But you have known its taste since childhood; and it has poisoned you." And the young girl echoes, "Yes, it all comes down to one small, simple word—power."

For some reason, which psychologists may fathom, the official rage is focussed on Varvara, the young girl, for that remark. Old Kirpichev they forgive, comparatively speaking; but that a young girl, nurtured in the bosom of the Soviet system, could speak those words is something unheard of, unnatural, positively wicked.

Her remark has become a sort of slogan running in a crescendo of horror through the criticisms. One feels almost sorry for the Soviet leadership because it is driven into incoherence by this —evil. It is incoherent because, being atheist by conviction, it cannot believe in the devil—and poor Varvara, to it, is the devil. It has no word for her. It has no ritual of exorcism. It is at a loss.

Soviet power is benevolence, is goodness. Zorin's conception of power, declares *Soviet Culture,* "is false and harmful from the very first word to the last. It carries a deep distortion of the very nature of the system and a deeply false idea of the nature of the public relations which have been instituted in our country during the years of the great victories of Socialism. Only a person totally ignorant of the facts of life and intentionally closing his eyes to what goes on every day in front of us all could talk such pernicious rubbish. Who is there who does not know that the aim and content of the whole activity of the Soviet organs—ministries, departments, and the rest—is daily concern for the vitally important interests of the working people, and that the very word 'power' has become here, because of this, something lustrous, gladdening, the embodiment of the finest hopes and aspirations of every Soviet man and woman, and that our people regard their popular power with unshakable trust and warm, filial love?"

Who indeed?

Simply reading these outraged criticisms of Zorin, with the invocation of the memory of Zhdanov, it was fairly natural for observers outside the Soviet Union, particularly those who, for one reason and another, know a great deal about Communism but not much about Russia, to believe that the expected reaction had set in. And this belief was immensely strengthened and apparently confirmed to the hilt by some (but not all) of the events of the subsequent two months. There are five considerable literary reviews in the Soviet Union (apart from the quasi-official *Literary Gazette*): *New World* (*Novy Mir*); *October* (*Oktyabr*); *The Banner* (*Zhamya*); *Theatre* (*Teatr*); and *The Star* (*Zvezda*), the celebrated Leningrad review, always, because it belongs to Leningrad, irrepressible and unquenchable, in the van of any trouble. In the midsummer of 1954 each one of these reviews was heavily censored, and the editors of three—*New World, October,* and *The Star*—were summarily dismissed.

At about the same time there flared up the great Ehrenburg controversy.

There is no need to go into this in great detail. When, in October of the year before, Ehrenburg published his revolutionary reflections on artistic integrity and spoke of an author's being pregnant with a book he was evidently thinking of himself. And six months later the book appeared; its symbolic title was *The Thaw.* It has since been translated into English, and is thus accessible to all. It is not very good. But it is a serious attempt, though stilted and barren, to picture certain aspects of Soviet society as they really are. There is the woman who falls out of love with her husband and into love with somebody else. There is the husband, on the face of it a fine figure of a factory director, who is shown up as an empty windbag and a decided crook, condemning his workers to live in hovels because he diverts money from the housing fund into the machine-shop—not because he is in love with production, but so that he can fulfil his plan and ingratiate himself with Moscow. (It was Pomerantsev in his ill-fated essay on sincerity who had said of another writer of an "industrial novel": "The author had nothing to say about the dormitories and dining-rooms of the factory he had in mind when writing his novel; and they were atrocious ones.") Above all, and close to Ehrenburg's heart, there is a prolonged debate, or conflict, between two young painters: one who paints according to the book, does very well, and despises himself and everybody else, and one who starves for the sake of his own vision, though a much better painter. There are frequent references, not always oblique, to the Terror and the spiritual and intellectual paralysis of the bad old days. The two most sympathetic characters are a woman doctor, profoundly devoted to her work, who finds herself in trouble at the time of the "doctor's plot," and an old revolutionary teacher, the real hero, who has sacrificed his health and everything he has to help the boys of his neighbourhood—but in vain: his gifted pupils either turn out to be too poor to continue their education or get into bad company and go to the dogs.

The Thaw, first serialized in *The Banner,* appeared in May 1954 and was avidly sought after; it was the first truly human novel to have appeared in the Soviet Union for many weary years. Then, in July, the attack began. It was launched by Ehrenburg's colleague, Simonov, in *Literary Gazette* (July 17). Simonov at this time, it will be remembered, was seeking to erase the impression produced by his earlier unfortunate praise of *The Guests.*

It was not, however, the Zorin story all over again. Zorin was a young playwright, and the authorities had decided to make an example of him. Ehrenburg was a veteran fox and an important figure into the bargain. On several previous occasions switches in the Party line had been marked by inspired attacks on Ehrenburg, who would submerge for a time, and then surface, paddling strongly in the new direction. It is hardly too much to say that his role as official whipping-boy (the public whipping has never in the least affected the comforts of his private life; he is a very rich man) is the price he has to pay for being received back to the Soviet fold after his years of exile in the West. At any rate, Ehrenburg was allowed to reply, and did so three weeks later —again in *Literary Gazette* (August 8). It was a strong and vigorous reply, but it avoided the main issue, which was, precisely, that he had created wretched characters and shown a rotten state of society and implied that these were characteristic. All through the summer the attack was pressed home, until finally, in October, on the eve of the All Union Congress of Soviet Writers, the editor of *Literary Gazette* summed up and gave a verdict against Ehrenburg. *The Thaw,* however, was not withdrawn. It was, indeed, reissued, but in a small edition of 45,000 (250,000 would have been the appropriate figure by Soviet standards). And that was that.

In the middle of this row the Party's theoretical journal, *Communist* (November 9, 1954), pronounced formal judgment on the state of Soviet literature, reaffirmed the hegemony of the Party and restated the principles of Socialist Realism. Simonov recanted his error about *The Guests* in *Pravda* on July 4. The stage was set for the Congress at the end of the year, at which all Soviet writers were expected to pledge their loyalty to the Party directives, and did so. On the face of it full circle had been turned, but in fact nothing of the kind had happened.

I am not telling the story of the Soviet writers during those two critical years, 1953–54, for its own sake, though it seems to me fascinating in itself. I am telling it because of the light it throws on the new Soviet leadership, on the activities and problems of Messrs. Khrushchev, Bulganin, Malenkov, and the rest. The "spirit of Geneva" and the *obiter dicta* of Mr. Khrushchev may seem very far removed from the backbiting of a bunch of Soviet intellectuals, or even from the abortive flirtation with freedom of expression; but they are not. And to understand why they are not it is of the first importance to distinguish between the effects of this story on the Western reader and on the Soviet reader. To the Western reader the whole situation must appear so alien, the limited victories for freedom so insignificant, the reassertion of authority by the Party so absolute and crushing, that he will be hard put to it to understand what all the fuss is about. To the Soviet reader it does not look at all like that.

The most interesting thing about the attacks on Ehrenburg's novel is that nowhere at any time was the general conception held in question—the general conception being that the Soviet people had been through a very terrible time, gruelling for the body and numbing for the spirit, from which they were now beginning to emerge. Nor was there any censure for his preoccupation with the human element, with the ordinary man as distinct from the Stakhanovite in stainless steel, with the problems of the heart and the individual conscience, as first projected by Miss Berggoltz of Leningrad a year before. All this was quite taken for granted. So that what in effect happened as a result of all the hullabaloo of those summer months was that Soviet authors were forbidden under pain of excommunication to ascribe existing and acknowledged evils to the workings of the system. Just that. Everything else they were allowed and encouraged to do, with one exception: they must not exhibit serious doubt, or pessimism, or speculate about the ultimate meaning of life.

The poet Boris Pasternak, for example, who had long been under a cloud, once again found a publisher (*New World* of Pomerantsev fame) in the first careless rapture of the new self-expression. *Pravda* picked up a stanza from one of these poems as an example of everything that was false and shameful. "The struggle for the truthful portrayal of actual reality," it declaimed (June 3, 1954), "in its revolutionary development is the main element of Socialist Realism. The art of decadence, on the other hand, which preaches pessimism and despair, calls for a retreat from objective reality and declares real life to be an illusion, a dream, and subjectivist dreams to be reality. These ideas are entirely hackneyed and have been in existence ever since subjective idealism has existed in the world."

The lines that gave offence were these:

> Life is also but a moment,
> A merging
> Of ourselves with all that is:
> A semblance of a gift.
> A marriage, a desire
> Striving upwards from below,
> A song, a dream,
> A grey dove.

"Life is only a moment, only a dream, only a grey dove in frantic pursuit of a dream," spluttered *Pravda*, "of an apparition which has appeared but momentarily and which merges into everything and everyone, into the clouds, into the air—such is the content of B. Pasternak's poem. Subjectivist art has always tried to prove that life is 'but a moment,' 'but a dream'; and that therefore it is senseless to strive to improve it, to waste energy on the struggle for a better future for one's homeland, for mankind."

In a word, evils must be acknowledged, denounced, satirized; but no attempt may be made to discover their real cause: above all, they must not be attributed to the regime. At the same time, there must be no pessimism or questioning of the meaning of life, as exhibited by Pasternak and the Leningrad poetess Anna Akhmatova; there must be nothing that might cast doubt on the ability of the Communist Party to remake the world. Within this framework there is a great deal more freedom than there was. There is very real scope for satirists and iconoclasts who are prepared to ignore the root cause of the evils they attack. Further than this, there is a quite new emphasis on individual human values, provided always that in the end it is always the "positive" values that triumph.

The result is confusion—not by any means a reversion to Stalinism, but simple confusion. The confusion of the outsider, watching developments, as in a serial story or a comic-strip, is as nothing to the confusion of the man on the job—the Soviet novelist, playwright, or critic, trying to keep his soul and live up to the demands of the Party. He is perhaps more uncertain of himself today than he has ever been before, even under the first impact of the Zhdanov edict. Zhdanov at least knew what he wanted, and said so. What he wanted made no sense, but it could be produced; and produced it was, in quantity: those who felt they could not produce it kept as quiet as they could and cultivated their gardens. The new masters have seen the absurdities and perils of Zhdanovism. But they want things both ways: free and spontaneous expression, yes, but it must, of course, fit into the permitted framework of ideas. They demand satire and the bold exposure of the evils of life in the Soviet Union. But only some evils. And when they are taken at their word they become uneasy. "I know nothing about literature, but I know what I don't like." That negative version of the ancient Philistine cliché sums up quite accurately the attitude of the Party pundits. So unhappy writers, urged to be original, have to guess what the Kremlin does not like. Gone are the happy, dreary, days when to write a play you used a simple formula. And as they proceed by trial and error new definitions are painfully hammered out.

Confusion . . . I have tried in these pages by illustrating many contradictory aspects of Soviet life to bring out the impression of confusion which must assail any foreigner who is able to dig a little below the surface in the Soviet Union. The case of the writers, which I have gone into at some length, expresses the whole basic confusion in one compact story. Among the writers are all sorts of men and women. I shall not mention names; but in the Writers' Union are to be found highly articulate and often cultured representatives of all the trends which go to make up present-day Soviet society. There are honest fools of fairly low intelligence who are parrot Marxists and think, if you can call it thinking, in terms of Party jargon. There are opportunists and careerists developed to a very marked level of efficiency, able to turn their coats in a night and turn their talents to anything. It is in these two categories that the Party finds its strength. There are also idealists of the purest kind, usually young, who believe with a burning faith in the sacred mission of the Party and the Soviet Union. Then there are the cynics, usually soured idealists, who lack the glibness of the careerists, and perhaps the skill, and are apt to end in trouble by taking to drink or peculation. There are the total sceptics, who are interested not at all in problems of man in society but only in problems of man in relation to the universe; these may no longer publish. Finally, in great strength, are the representatives of honest doubt who fight each day afresh the battle with their own consciences and in varying degrees of honesty strive to adapt themselves to a system which, in spite of clearly seen shortcomings, is the only one that seems to them to offer an ultimate solution to some of the major ills of humanity. This category, which is large and various, covering a broad range of scepticism, is the strongest of all and includes some of the finest and most impressive of the contemporary Soviet writers, as well as a mass of minor ones.

It could be said that this division, or something like it, could apply equally well to the writers of any country in Europe; and so it could be. But it is made uniquely significant because in the Soviet Union, as nowhere else in the world that counts for anything, all categories are subjected to an unremitting pressure from the arms bearers of a central orthodoxy; and it is complicated beyond words by the fact that all but the smallest handful of Soviet writers, artists, musicians, and the rest, are more or less deeply imbued with the traditional Russian attitude that the artist must be, above all, a servant of social progress. Even the cynics feel this. The leadership takes it for granted.

So that the next and most immediate question is what, in the context of the Soviet Union, is social progress?

10. THE MATERIAL BASE

SOCIAL progress in the Soviet Union is no longer simply a matter of electricity and steel. For twenty-five years it was almost entirely that. A whole people was sacrificed to the production of steel and electricity in order that steel and electricity should form the solid base of the new society in which each should receive according to his needs. Everything was subordinated to the stupendous industrial revolution, so that even education became a by-product for this. And during the process the means, as so often, loomed larger than the end, which many forget. The discipline necessary to make people work year in, year out, too hard for too little, became a terror; and the men, under Stalin, who organized the terror became the most powerful caste in the state, perpetuating for its own sake that system which had raised them up. In the end, in Stalin's last years (in a situation worsened catastrophically by the German invasion), steel became the synonym for social progress. Communism is electrification plus soviets, Lenin had once said, looking out into the far distance where he saw material progress marching hand in hand with his own peculiar brand of democracy to make the desert blossom like the rose. Thirty years later Communism had come to mean nothing at all but steel—plus Stalin. But the industrial revolution was achieved.

St. Petersburg was founded on the broken bodies of innumerable slaves. Peter the Great is remembered with a shudder for his fearful demon, but with mingled awe and pride for creating Russia as a European power. Ivan the Terrible strangled his son, the Tsarevitch, with his own hands, scourged his nobles with unspeakable cruelty, and, on his death-bed, tried to rape the young wife of his second son. But today in Russia his name is venerated for his unifying mission. Other Russian autocrats committed vile outrages and condemned their subjects to unmeasured suffering, not only in the Middle Ages, but also in the Age of Reason. When Nicholas I had the vast Winter Palace rebuilt within a year of the disastrous fire that destroyed it, thousands of artisans were condemned to work in rooms which were heated like ovens to dry them off while the work was going on. Many died each day. Victoria was on the throne in England.

Stalin will be remembered with a shudder for his atrocities. But all Russian autocrats commit atrocities. And he will also be remembered with Ivan and Peter and Catherine for his colossal achievement in a land where nothing material has ever been achieved unless it was colossal, nor without an infinity of human sacrifice.

Ardent mountaineers, we are told, regard with scorn and deep contempt all those who use funiculars to scale the snowy heights. Nothing, they assure us, least of all the vision of the sunrise on Mont Blanc, is worth achieving without sacrifice. By half-killing themselves they receive, it appears, an afflatus. The Russians carry this general idea some stages further; in one mood they seem to feel that nothing is worth achieving unless ten thousand souls have died for it.

Stalin achieved a great deal. His vision demanded ten million, not ten thousand, individual sacrifices.

Peter the Great picked Russia up by the scruff of her neck and thrust her bodily into the lap of an apprehensive Europe. Afterwards there were back-slidings; but the Russians were never the same again. Stalin made Russia into a power strong enough not only to dominate Europe but also to face the only power strong enough to dominate the world. That is not nothing. His methods were the methods of the Russian autocratic tradition carried to their atrocious conclusion with the help of twentieth-century science. Let the Russians judge them, those millions of Russians who, while broken by Stalin, still take a mystic pride in the magnitude of his despotism. Our judgment is irrelevant.

The Revolution was a negative, not a positive action. The revolutionaries hailed the break-down of the old society with the slogans of liberation. What was liberated showed its true metal by collapsing. The Russians shook off their rusted chains and promptly went to pieces. Men of good will, aristocrats and businessmen with modern ideas, then Socialists with ardent vision, exhorted them to pull themselves together. Lenin stepped in at the moment of total disintegration, first to promise peace and land, then to dragoon the country in the name of a scarcely existent proletariat. The tones of despotic authority sounded in his proclamations of universal brotherhood. And after an orgy of anarchy cut short by civil war, the Russians responded. But Lenin died before the dragooning could start.

Stalin, burning for power, had also quite clearly a vision of a better Russia. But it had first to be a strong Russia. Strength in this century is measured in steel and what it makes. Russia had to have steel, and the Five-Year Plan was conceived and launched to give her steel. New towns had to be constructed and the workers fed; but the peasants, with their primitive holdings, could not or would not feed them under any system which a Socialist regime could tolerate. They were coerced.

The dreadful epic of the collectivization, which Stalin confessed years later was for him a more perilous struggle than the worst days of the war, was designed and carried out to get control of the peasants, break their political independence, and make them feed the towns in return for practically nothing—because there would be nothing to give. The peasants struck back and destroyed their livestock and burned their crops, making a desert of productive land. In a bitter civil war, in which one side had all the guns, their resistance was broken—and then industry had to be furiously distorted to mechanize the ruined agriculture.

It was a scene of lunacy. But Stalin had to throw in his hand, commit suicide, leave Russia in chaos, or go on. He went on. And at the height of the lunacy he kept his vision, the vision for which he will be remembered: "No, comrades . . . the pace must not be slackened! On the contrary, we must speed up to the limit of our possibilities. This is dictated to us by our obligations to the workers and the peasants of the USSR. It is dictated to us by our obligations to the working-class of the whole world. To slacken the pace would be to lag behind; and those who lag behind are beaten. We do not want to be beaten. No, we do not!"

He went on to invoke the history of Tsarist Russia. He pre-

sented the history of Russia as the history of Russian defeats. And
these defeats, he said, had invariably been due to Russian backwardness: "She was ceaselessly beaten for her backwardness. She
was beaten by the Mongol khans. She was beaten by the Turkish
beys. She was beaten by the Swedish feudal lords. She was beaten by
the Polish-Lithuanian *pans*. She was beaten by the Anglo-French
capitalists. She was beaten by the Japanese barons. She was beaten
by all—for her backwardness. For military backwardness; for
cultural backwardness; for political backwardness; for industrial
backwardness; for agricultural backwardness. She was beaten because to beat her was profitable and could be done with impunity.
You remember the words of the pre-revolutionary poet: 'Thou
art poor and thou art abounding; thou art mighty, and thou art
helpless, Mother Russia.' "

And finally: "We are fifty or a hundred years behind the advanced countries. We must make good this lag in ten years. Either
we do, or they crush us."

That was the first trumpet-call of the revolutionary inter-
nationalist to that Great Russian nationalism which later became an obsession, using the revolutionary dynamic in different
lands to harass the outer world, and the power and prestige of
Russian arms to extend its effective sway far beyond its frontiers.

The cost was immense. The reforms of Peter were epoch-making;
but to carry them through he had to regiment the Russian nobility and give the bodies and souls of the common people absolutely into their hands. The rigidly graded hierarchy, in which
each man's position depended not on birth or wealth but on his
merits in the despot's eyes, left Russia suffocated. The ruthlessness required to carry out the revolution from above crushed the
spirit of the people. It was not until late in the nineteenth century
that it began to recover, soaring in the springtime of Russian
liberalism.

Stalin brought upon his people limitless physical suffering. He
calculated that if he could drive they could endure; and he was
right. But just as he ruined Russian agriculture in the process of
improving it, so he crushed the minds of his people in the process
of educating them. Again, he sought strength and security for
Russia and made her to all appearances stronger and more secure

than ever in her history—and in the process of so doing wakened
and quickened the sleeping might of a civilization greater than
his own. He killed by excess what he sought to build. This may
be the way of dictators everywhere. It is certainly the way of autocrats in Russia.

But no matter what convulsions may lie in store for that unhappy land, what has been done has been done. The great achievement to which most people would point has been the forced industrialization of a backward agrarian land. History, writing an
ironic footnote to the pretensions of the Bolsheviks, may well
say that Stalin's supreme gift to Russia was to provide her for the
first time with a strong middle class, called into being by the quest
for steel, without which, in the modern world, no civilization
can begin to ripen.

That tribute to Stalin is an interpolation in this book, but, it
seems to me, a relevant one. It was written in March 1953, the
day after the announcement of his death. It is ironic that throughout the length and breadth of the Soviet Union no tribute to the
great leader has yet appeared, or is likely to appear for decades,
remotely comparable with this in its recognition of Stalin's great-
ness. Russian historians will one day make amends, but for the
time being the great man's colleagues and successors are deny-
ing to the people he left behind a vision of his real achievement.

In the end, of course, Stalin outstayed his welcome. His successors inherited a system which had fulfilled its purpose and out-
lived it. In 1953 it was rotten and unviable. There had to be
change. But change at first meant nothing but confusion. Stalin
had gone, leaving behind him a small army of lieutenants who
were intelligent enough to see that Stalinism in its final phase
had all but killed the vital spark, but also shrewd enough to see
that without the use of certain Stalinist techniques they could
never maintain their own positions. It was a nice dilemma.

In a word, the new leadership first had to sort themselves out
and then subject the economy, the administration, and popular
morale to a thorough investigation, so that they might diagnose
the danger-spots of the system and then take measures for a com-

plete overhaul. The investigation and diagnosis were to take just about three years. It was still in progress when this book was started, and then it seemed likely that I should be compelled to argue fairly closely, to give elaborate and circumstantial reasons for my conviction, held ever since the day of Stalin's death, and strengthened greatly by what I saw and heard in Russia nearly three years after his death, that the new leaders, as a collective of sorts, had turned their backs on Stalinism. But now the necessity is passed. The new leadership has found its feet and made up its mind where to go. After a great deal of wavering, at the Twentieth Congress of the Communist Party of the Soviet Union which met in Moscow in February 1956, the men who helped Stalin to supremacy and were, in due course, enslaved by him, at last broke free. This Congress was more than the occasion for a formal statement of policy in the years to come; it was, above all, a ritual ceremony of exorcism. Stalin had been thrown over as soon as he was dead, and, in the very moment of liberation, his colleagues began to cast about in all directions, trying to pick up new bearings. But the world they inhabited, the apparatus of the Communist Party, was still dominated by Stalin, who had made it with his own hands. And to break the spell finally they had to call the Party together and go through the motions of remaking it. That was what the great Congress, "the most important Congress since the time of Lenin," as it was designated by Mikoyan, mainly signified. The spell was broken; and everyone who counted publicly danced on Stalin's grave in the presence of all the others.

Social progress is no longer simply steel, though this, goodness knows, is still supremely important. Social progress in the Soviet Union today means raising the standard of living fairly quickly and turning the Soviet people into a prosperous and contented society. The very lives of the new leaders depend on this, and the historical moment demands it. Steel has been put in the shade by the hydrogen bomb, which makes nonsense of a number of time-honoured Bolshevik assumptions—among them the article of faith which laid it down that so long as capitalism existed major wars were inevitable—or that the global revolution could be achieved only through war. Khrushchev's amendment to this

sacred tenet of Lenin's at the Twentieth Party Congress marked
an epoch in the history of the Soviet Union and of the world as
a whole. We shall consider its international implications in a
later chapter. For the moment we are still concerned with the
Soviet Union from the inside. And here Khrushchev's rejection
of the principle of the inevitability of war was the logical end of
a great deal that had been happening. While Stalin lived the
whole economy of the Soviet Union had been based on the assumption that war was indeed inevitable. The Second World
War was seen by Communists everywhere as the justification of
this thesis; and immediately after the Second World War Stalin
startled the world, still dazed by the shock of the first atomic
explosions over Hiroshima and Nagasaki, by solemnly declaring
that the epoch of wars was not over and that the Soviet people
must buckle to in order to be ready for the next. He was speaking
at the victory banquet given to his marshals and generals in the
gleaming white Hall of St. George in the Kremlin, and, at his
words, a great moan went up from every town and village in the
Soviet Union. It was too much. The people had suffered starvation, fire, massacre, and rapine to make their country safe—for
ever. And now they were told they must build up everything
again to see it destroyed once again. They had nothing. They
were hungry, they were unshod, they were dressed in rags, they
were exhausted. But they were not allowed to rest. They had to
make more steel, more steel than ever before.

"No comrades . . . the pace must not be slackened! On the
contrary, we must speed up to the limit of our possibilities. . . ."
The words came grimly echoing down the weary years.

"We must achieve a situation whereby our industry is able to
produce each year up to fifty million tons of pig iron, up to sixty
million tons of steel, up to five hundred million tons of coal,
and up to sixty million tons of oil. Only under such conditions
can we regard our country as guaranteed against all accidents.
This, I think, will require at least three new Five-Year Plans, if
not more."

That was in 1946. It did not mean that Stalin wanted another
war. He did not—not, at any rate, until he had his sixty million
tons of steel, in 1960. It did mean that he wanted to be ready if

war should come, and that he believed that sooner or later war
would come, because the bourgeois societies would never submit
to revolution, guided and dominated by the Soviet Union, without putting up a fight.

So steel had to be made. And because steel was essential to the
survival of the Soviet Union, steel was social progress.

It is no longer so. The new leaders have given up talking in
terms of primary products. Stalin either took little stock in the
atom bomb, or (and this seems more probable) he deliberately
played it down in order that its menace should not discourage
the Soviet people fatally. He also believed that long before 1960
there would be a disastrous slump in America, which would shake
to pieces the economy of the West as a whole. But the atom bomb
existed; and the hydrogen bomb has brought home to the new
rulers (as it has brought home, and with much the same time-lag,
to the governments of the West) that no country can ever be guaranteed any more against all accidents. Also, instead of slumping,
the American economy has continued to expand at a rate beyond
all possible foreseeing—and with it the economies of other Western countries. So that Stalin's figures for 1960 now seem pathetic
as an insurance against all possible contingencies. It is ironic
that Stalin's 1960 target is going to be reached well before the
earliest date he considered possible, and surpassed. But, at the
same time, it will not be enough. Steel is no longer the master,
though still a very necessary servant.

For very many years one of the showplaces of the Soviet Union
has been the huge automobile factory at Gorki, named after
Molotov: *Zavod Imena Molotova,* where the Zim cars are made.
It was a pride of Soviet industry, and a popular symbol of Soviet
power. Another is the Zis automobile factory in Moscow, named
after Stalin. In a long report to the Central Committee of the
Soviet Communist Party, published, rather belatedly in *Pravda,*
July 14, 1955, Marshal Bulganin rudely upset the complacency
of the managerial staff of Zim. He attacked particularly the wasteful dispersal of effort. "What we have here," he said, "is not an
automobile works but a universal production works." He said the
same applied to the Zis factory in Moscow, and to a great many
other factories of all kinds. He explained what he meant, and at

the same time inaugurated a revolution in Soviet industrial thinking and technique.

This was the fruit of the radical investigation into the state
of Soviet industry which started after Stalin's death. It cleared
the way for the new Five-Year Plan, the draft of which was approved by the Party Congress in February. The new men had
made up their minds about one aspect of the economy.

Bulganin was criticizing the Zim works because it had allowed
itself to be side-tracked from its proper business of producing
motor cars. Only sixty-seven per cent of its total production, he
said, came out in the form of motor cars: "In addition to motor
cars, this factory produces bicycles, machine tools, forging, stamping, smelting, and welding equipment, small electrical installa-
tions, electrically welded piping, and much else. Each month this
works produces for its own consumption tens of thousands of oil-
cans, which could be successfully made by any workshop employing craftsmen." And he continued: "A wide range of production impedes the organization of output, the use of flow methods
of production, complicates the technological equipment of production processes, and acts as a brake on the introduction of
highly productive automatic equipment. All this leads to increased production costs."

In other words, it is interesting to work in a great Soviet
factory—as interesting as working in a small-town garage; more
interesting, even, because there is more scope for messing about.
But it is not modern industry. The qualities required are the
qualifications of the super-handyman; the worker's horizon is
being constantly widened. But the result is not all that is needed.

At Bryansk, for example, there is a great locomotive works;
but according to Marshal Bulganin a great deal of the floor space
is occupied by anything but locomotives: "In addition to producing several types of wagons, it is manufacturing steam tur-
bines, trains for electric power stations, trolleys for conveying
molten pig-iron, small rolled metal items, cast iron and steel
for other works, tractor and locomotive spare parts, spare parts
for electric power stations, and various other items. In short, this
factory is working on the principle, as the popular saying goes,
of tinker, tailor, baker, and candlestick maker."

And not only that factory. Marshal Bulganin had other re-markable examples. He said they were typical. He revealed that it is the practice of most engineering works in the Soviet Union to manufacture their own nuts and bolts. The average cost of these, he said, is fourteen times greater than that of the same articles turned out by one of the few specialist factories, and almost twice as much metal is consumed. That is to say, "in order to produce one ton of bolts, a specialized works uses one thousand kilograms of metal, while a non-specialized works uses two thousand kilo-grams." The position, he said, was particularly bad when it came to metal castings and forgings: instead of taking their castings and forgings from specialized shops and foundries, individual enterprises of all kinds were producing their own—at treble the appropriate cost. The same, he said, applied to components and accessories of all kinds. More than this, each individual ministry (meaning a ministry responsible for a specific industry) goes in for making its own machines and tools, often unskilfully, always at the expense of far more money, material, and labour than would be necessary in a specialized works. Marshal Bulganin in-stanced a particular design of mechanical excavator, production of which had been "mastered" by the Ministry of Road-Making-Machine Building. Manufacture is not concentrated; instead, the same design is copied and turned out independently by factories under the control of the Ministry of Construction for the Coal Industry and the Ministry of Construction for Petroleum-Indus-try Enterprises—at a cost of between fifty to a hundred per cent more.

I have no intention of discussing the development of Soviet industry in detail and for its own sake; but since it is the base upon which the whole system stands, its nature and condition are important. Bulganin's report to the Central Committee was the first statement by any Soviet minister since 1931 that attempted to tell the truth about Soviet industry. It is a mine of information and enlightenment. It is also some thirty thousand words long, with very little padding. It acknowledges all those shortcomings of Soviet industrial organization which have been familiar to the student for decades—and which have been steadfastly and mo-notonously denied by the Russians themselves. It admits that much of the finest Soviet engineering is obsolete or obsolescent. It compares with extreme frankness Western performance with Soviet performance, and instructs Soviet engineers and designers to jump out of their complacency and look to the West for ideas —and not only to America: Britain, Italy, Belgium, Scandinavia, and Western Germany are all cited as producing some kinds of goods and machinery, from synthetic fibres to bull-dozers, superior to their Soviet counterparts. It was, indeed, the first call on the highest governmental level to Soviet industrialists to learn from the West.

After the sterile years when the Russians were told by Stalin that they had nothing to learn from the West, that any interest in Western achievement was indicative of "kow-towing" and sub-versive "cosmopolitanism," this call was dramatic indeed. For nearly a decade a whole corps of researchers had been kept busy working through the Imperial archives to discover "proofs" that Russia had been first in the field with every conceivable inven-tion. It was enough to turn up a memorandum from an ingenious subject of Nicholas, outlining a theoretical idea for any sort of machine under the sun, from a flying-machine to a submersible vessel (no blue-prints were required, no prototype, not even prac-tical specifications), for the Soviet Union to claim priority of invention over all comers—attributing the unimportant little detail that the machine, or apparatus, was never in fact con-structed in Russia until some foreigner, such as Marconi or Wil-bur Wright, had shown the way, to the obscurantism of the Im-perial government. Suddenly all that changed overnight, and the call to learn from the West, first clearly stated in Bulganin's re-port, has become an urgent and reiterated chorus.

Marshal Bulganin did not confine himself to brave generali-ties. He went into minute particulars. For example he made fas-cinating comparisons between Soviet, American, and British ma-chines of comparable design—mainly to show the waste of ma-terial in the Soviet products. He said that the Zis automobile chassis weighed three tons, compared with the two tons of its American counterpart (the Studebaker was the one he chose). He said that the British Fordson Major Diesel tractor weighed only two tons, compared with the three tons of the pride of the MTS, the Belarus tractor from the Minsk tractor works—simply because the designers lavished too much metal on them.

These are random examples offered not for their own sakes but to illustrate the difficulties facing the Kremlin as it enters the final phase of the Soviet industrial revolution—and to show why the elemental drive for steel is no longer enough, even without the H-bomb! Marshal Bulganin introduced a new slogan into Soviet industry: specialization. What he meant was rationalization. What he was saying in effect was that Soviet industry, notwithstanding its mighty achievements, had reached a crucial phase; if it was to move forward and become comparable with American industry it must take a deep breath and rationalize itself from top to bottom.

This is really what Marshal Bulganin's speech was about. And it is what the new Five-Year Plan is about. It is the first major change of direction since the inauguration of the Five-Year-Plan era in 1928. The change is from sprawling, wasteful *extensive* growth to the *intensive* development of industrial resources. For nearly three decades Soviet industry has proceeded on the general assumption that it had at its command unlimited man-power and natural resources. It did not matter at what cost the machines were produced—at what cost, that is to say, in terms of man-power, money, raw materials, and human suffering—provided they were produced.

In countries liable to flooding, the construction and maintenance of dams and dikes proceeds normally in a planned, orderly, and economical way; but when the floods rise beyond bounds and a dike bursts, everyone and everything is flung into the breach, regardless of cost, regardless of the dislocation of normal services, until the waters are held. Such a time is like a war. And this was the mood in which Stalin undertook the forced industrialization of the Soviet Union. Starting more or less from scratch, he gave himself ten years to make the Soviet Union strong enough to withstand invasion by mechanized forces from the industrialized West. Nothing else mattered. Thus the Soviet industrial revolution was started under what were, effectively, war conditions. Then came the real war, with the accelerated development of heavy industry east of Moscow and its more or less total destruction west of Moscow; then, in 1945, in the great reconstruction, a repetition of the early days—but on a more gigantic scale, and with the experience and techniques accumulated in twenty years, and with the hands and brains of new generations born to a mechanical age.

The expansion has been spectacular. Stalin's goal will be achieved long before 1960. Thanks to the swift development of rich new oil-fields the 1960 figure is already passed, and one hundred and forty million tons are promised by 1960. But elsewhere the rate of increase is already dwindling. The most easily worked coal and ore are being exhausted; the man-power problem is already acute and will grow still worse when the annual intake begins to fall in a year or two because of the decline in the birth-rate during the war years. The Russians find themselves in a spiral, familiar enough in the West, which works on the principle that the higher the national production the more men must be taken away from primary production and put into factories and public services to exploit the products. The Soviet transport system, for example, if it is to be made adequate to cope with the increased level of production, will make tremendous demands on man-power and material; under the new Plan no more steam locomotives are to be built, and the whole system is to be changed over to electric and Diesel haulage. Finally, the conditions under which Stalin carried out the exploitation of his country's wealth were inimical to the development of a balanced relationship between skilled and unskilled labour. The demand for unskilled labour in its crudest and cheapest form, as expressed most absolutely in the forced-labour system, which devoured millions of human brains, militated against the growth of that huge army of skilled artisans and technicians now required to make the best use of the industrial machine.

I do not want to give the impression that the whole of Soviet industry is in a muddle; on the contrary. There have always been priorities. I have never toured a naval shipyard in the Soviet Union, or a jet aircraft factory, but I have seen the most modern power-stations, remotely controlled down to the last detail, and I have talked to British and American steel-masters who have been impressed beyond all their expectations by the extremely high level of accomplishment in the Soviet steel industry. I have no doubt that that whole immense sector of Soviet industry which falls directly under the control of Mr. Ustinov, that unknown and almost anonymous figure, the minister of the defence industry, whose estimates never appear in the Five-Year Plan, who is never seen at public functions, is on the same high level. It has the first call. The rest is patchy in the extreme. It is patchy because it has grown up, in spite of the planning, in a higgledy-piggledy manner, because of over-centralized bureaucratic direction, because, to escape the bottle-necks of the Plan, every enterprising factory director has become something of a law unto himself, doing side-deals with other factories, either directly or through "fixers," turning out turbine parts in a motor-car factory to oblige a friend, and generally producing the sort of chaos outlined by Marshal Bulganin in the passages already quoted.

Recently Western statesmen have expressed acute alarm at the very high annual output of scientists and technicians in the Soviet Union. And, indeed, wonders have been done in this field; for decades an expanding higher educational system has been devoted almost exclusively to the incubation of scientific and engineering cadres for the service of an expanding industry. But Western statesmen forget, or perhaps have never understood, that the science graduate is one thing, the skilled and conscientious artisan with inborn mechanical sense, who thinks with his hands, quite another. Both are necessary in this age, and the Soviet Union is critically short of the latter—as the leadership will no doubt discover for itself in the course of the next few years—and is likely to remain so for some time to come.

It is clear that to continue its expansion the extremely patchy industrial economy cannot persist in its present haphazard manner. It is clear also that in its present form it is in no position to supply the Soviet people with the consumer goods they must have if they are to be turned into a modern and upstanding society. And here, I think, is the crux. Beyond reaffirming the Party line on continued priority for heavy industry, Marshal Bulganin had little to say about the consumer. But the consumer must have been very much in his mind. The draft of the Sixth Five-Year Plan proved that conclusively.

One of the first acts of the Malenkov government after Stalin's death was to declare that heavy industry was in such good shape that thenceforth the government proposed to devote a far higher proportion of the country's resources to the needs of the consumer and to work for a steep rise in the standard of living. New factories were to be built for light industry; existing factories were to divert a proportion of their floor space and man-power to turning out consumer goods on the side (it was this expedient that was partly responsible for the chaos in the Zim factory and others, condemned by Marshal Bulganin); the disproportion between the output of capital and consumer goods was to be corrected immediately. In 1940, Malenkov said, the ratio of heavy industry to light industry was 60:40; in 1953, in the year of Stalin's death, it was 70:30. This disproportion could be put in another, more dramatic way: at the end of the Fourth Five-Year Plan, in 1950, it was claimed that industrial output as a whole had increased over the 1940 output by 73 per cent, but the increase in light industry had been only 17 per cent. The disproportion was all the more striking because heavy industry had largely surpassed its target, while light industry had been allowed to fall behind; the Plan had been distorted in the process of execution to increase the burden on the unfortunate consumer.

In the Fifth Five-Year Plan, begun while Stalin was alive, the first serious attempt since 1938 was made to satisfy, or begin to satisfy, consumer needs. On paper the attempt looked more impressive than it really was. Heavy industry was scheduled for an 80-per-cent increase during the five-year period (1950–55), consumer goods for a 65-per-cent increase. But in contemplating these figures it is necessary to bear in mind that the 65-per-cent increase for consumer goods referred to an intolerably low figure, and that the consumer goods turned out in this period were virtually the first available to the Soviet public since 1941. Malenkov pledged himself to increase this figure; and in fact it was increased—from 65 per cent to 72 per cent. As I have already said, the rise in the standard of living in the great cities seems almost startling. But outside the great cities the story is very different, and chronic shortage of everything desirable is still the order of the day.

The new leadership knows very well that it is impossible to turn Soviet peasants and unskilled labourers into sober, alert, and responsible members of a modern society, fit to cope with the skills, the tempo, the obligations of that society, without raising their living standards very steeply. There is a stage in every industrial revolution in which production is best and most economically served (taking the short view) by housing the workers in hovels, compelling them to toil long hours, and treating them as mindless "hands." The English industrial North before the factory acts offered a perfect example, the first in history, of this state of affairs. It is not much more than a hundred years ago that Lord Shaftesbury, then Mr. Ashley, harrowed the consciences of the brash new middle class by describing the fiendish horrors of child and female labour in the coal-mines and the Lancashire textile mills. At that time Engels, also in Lancashire, was making the observations which were to convince him, and Karl Marx, that in the mad rush for profits, and uninhibited by any considerations of humanitarianism or long-term self-interest, the capitalists would inevitably drive their workers ever more furiously, until these, in desperation, would revolt. Marx and Engels were wrong. Expediency combining with an awakening social conscience reversed the process; the proletariat, instead of being ground underfoot, began to improve its position, until it, no less than the *bourgeoisie,* began to have a stake in the system—with what results we know.

The industrial revolution of the Soviet Union is now passing out of the era of slave labour and barracks factories. The days of a primitive society's wastefully and clumsily operating twentieth-century machinery are numbered. It is not that the new Soviet leadership has discovered that the machine is not enough; it has discovered that the machine cannot be worked efficiently by a depressed proletariat. After Stalin's death the new leaders started to take immediate action to raise the standard of living—only to discover that the industrial machine as it existed was incapable of swift adaptation to the production of consumer goods without total dislocation. They called a halt and thought again. While Khrushchev on the agricultural front launched his stupendous effort to increase food production to feed the towns more adequately without increasing the rural labour force, Bulganin (who, before he became a statesman, was one of the most able industrialists in the Soviet Union) was evidently sitting down with his advisers to diagnose the basic ills of Soviet industry. His report to the Central Committee was the fruit of this labour. He said, in effect, that unless the whole industrial machine was reorganized and stream-lined, unless more advanced technicians could be got into it and the most gifted organizers given their heads, unless the Soviet Union opened its mind to Western ideas, there could not be the over-all increase in production necessary to raise the standard of living of the Soviet Union. What he did not say was that until this standard is in fact radically raised the Soviet Union, for all its high peaks of material achievement, will remain a backward country. The Soviet industrial revolution has turned Russia into a first-class power. The question was whether it could be continued so as to transform her into the sort of prosperous modern society which alone can sustain great power.

As far as industrial development is concerned, I think the new Five-Year Plan provides the answer, a positive answer. I think that too many Western observers have here, as in other matters, confused practice with doctrine. This is not the place to argue the real meaning of the great blast which, early in 1955, appeared to blow the consumer-goods programme out of the water and reaffirm the old Stalinist line of heavy industrial expansion at all costs. For a time Soviet propaganda was full of the iniquities of those who, it was maintained, had allowed themselves to imagine that priorities had changed and that henceforth heavy industry could play second fiddle to light industry, capital goods to consumer goods. They were accused of total heresy, of "right-wing deviation," and were lumped with the ill-fated Bukharinites. Since all this was going on at the time of Malenkov's fall, and since Malenkov had publicly stated the case for more consumer goods at the expense of heavy industry, it was natural to assume that there had been an all but fatal conflict in process between the "liberalizing" elements in the collective, headed by Malenkov, and the "reactionary," or Stalinist elements, headed by Khrushchev. And it looked as though the "reaction" had won. For myself I was never attracted to this conclusion, and I think there is still less reason to be attracted to it now. For a start, nobody in a high position to my knowledge had ever suggested that heavy industry should cease to be a first priority—certainly not Malenkov. There was nothing in any of his speeches to indicate that he really believed that the time had come to drop heavy industry to second place; all he said was that the discrepancy between heavy industry and light industry was too great, and that the second should be expanded. I have no doubt that there were many people in the Soviet Union, and in the Party too (though not, I imagine, people who counted for anything), who seized on Malenkov's words as a promise of immediate material bliss and misinterpreted them to the extent of believing that the whole of Stalin's industrial drive was to be modified out of all recognition. Some people will believe anything! And I have no doubt that the leadership thought it a desirable thing to bring wild speculation on this count to an abrupt and brutal end with a restatement of the self-evident truth couched in Leninist jargon. It may well have been, too, that certain elements in the leadership welcomed an opportunity to associate Malenkov by implication with a heretical position—which, in fact, he had never publicly assumed. The fantastic episode of Molotov's formal recantation of something he had never meaningly said was a product of the same mentality.

Be that as it may, the draft of the current Five-Year Plan shows that although heavy industry continues to receive first priority, as one would have expected, as it did even when Malenkov was prime minister, the expansion of light industry and consumer-goods production allowed for is very considerable, and a great deal more than it was under Stalin. Real wages are to go up in industry by 30 per cent in return for an increased productivity of 50 per cent, which is not asking too much, especially as that productivity is to be obtained primarily by better management, better organization, more elaborate mechanization—and side by side with a reduction in the working week. Tremendous efforts are to be made to achieve smooth and rhythmical production, and the old hectic, unbalanced atmosphere produced by shock workers and Stakhanovites earning immense sums, and dislocating the general production flow into the bargain, is on the way out. Kaganovich's commission to enquire into the wage structure is designed primarily to cut down the earnings of the most highly paid and to raise the earnings of their less gifted fellows. All the stress is now to be on arranging a reasonable basic wage structure, which, hand in hand with a more efficient organization of man-power, will cut down the dependence on overtime and special bonuses.

So that what is happening is this: the new Five-Year Plan lays heavy stress, in words, on capital production while providing, in fact, for better living for the masses. It is a reversal of the Stalinist procedure, which perpetually offered immediate prospects of a better life while in fact pressing ever more hard on the masses. And if this Plan is fulfilled, as it should be, not only will the Soviet Union be a great deal better off in 1960 than ever before, but the foundations will have been firmly laid for a further advance in living standards which, during the next period, should utterly transform the country and, for the first time, put the people of the Soviet Union into a condition, morally and physically, from which they will be able to offer a serious challenge to the peoples of the West.

11. REVOLUTION ON THE FARM

IT WILL not be easy. The change of direction in industry will be accompanied by growing-pains of extreme acuteness. One of the great joys of the Soviet technocrats is the idea of automation. One of the first factories to go over to automation was the great ball-bearing works at Chelyabinsk. But at the Party Congress Mr. Malyshev, one of the first half-dozen of the great figures of the Soviet industrial revolution (second phase), who had just been made minister of automation, had sadly to report that it was not going well; since the change-over, production costs had gone up and productivity down, because some of the incidental machinery embodied in the automatic flow-line was simply not up to its work. There will be many more set-backs of this kind. An expanding industry, moreover, will be hampered increasingly not only by the still inadequate transport system but even more by the rampant bureaucracy of the centralized control system, and, above all, by the really hopeless distribution system, which Mikoyan is doing his level best to improve—though always with inferior agents, because the best men go into science, engineering, and all branches of industry. My own view, however, in the light of past successes—which have been remarkable in spite of the patchiness stressed in the previous chapter—is that industry as such has turned the corner and entered the final and triumphant phase of the Russian industrial revolution. There is only one thing that can stop it, and that is something quite outside industry: the backwardness of the Russian peasant.

When Beria was arrested in the summer of 1953, one of the charges against him was that he had been sabotaging agriculture. The world smiled, believing quite rightly that other, more squalid issues were involved. The world was inclined to do the same when, eighteen months later, Malenkov explained his own fall by confessing that he had made a mess of agriculture. Again that was not the real story. Nevertheless it was clear that the Soviet leaders were very worried indeed about agricultural production if they felt the need for the two scapegoats of the highest rank.

Indeed they were, and with reason. They still are. Nothing could have been in sharper contrast than the confident, purposeful, clear-cut directives of the industrial sections of the draft of the Sixth Five-Year Plan and the vague and fumbling generalizations of the agricultural section. It showed that even now, two and a half years after the alarm was first sounded, the Soviet leadership has still not decided how best to tackle the peasants.

The situation Khrushchev announced in the summer of 1953 was a disastrous one. Apart from a continuous rumbling from the Kremlin about the backwardness of livestock-breeding in general, this was the first public acknowledgment that anything was seriously wrong. Nobody in the West who knew anything at all about Soviet agriculture, or had ever set eyes on a Soviet dairy-herd, was in the least surprised. Indeed, Khrushchev's figures for livestock corresponded almost exactly with the laboriously worked out estimates of certain Western specialists, whose findings had been bitterly denounced by Soviet propagandists. Khrushchev said, "The number of cows in the country is still 3.5 million head lower than the prewar level, and in comparison with 1928 [on the eve of the collectivization, that is] has decreased by 8.9 million head. In 1952 alone a reduction in the total number of livestock throughout was permitted to fall by 2.1 million head." These figures were the complete answer to all those Soviet propagandists who insisted that if the Soviet Union had fewer cattle in the early 1950s than before the war, which they denied, it was due entirely to the war. The 1952 fall was due to the general demoralization of the peasants in Stalin's last days. But the figure to remember is that in 1953 there were 9 million cows fewer in the Soviet Union than there had been in 1928 before the collectivization: 24.3 million as against 33.2 million. This in spite of the fact that the population of the Soviet Union had increased by some 50 million and its area had been greatly augmented by the annexation of the three Baltic States, part of Poland, part of Germany, and part of Rumania. And, to leave the war out of it altogether, the country still had not recovered from the damage that the collectivization had inflicted by 1941, ten years later, when there were still over 5 million cattle fewer than there had been in 1928. Khrushchev's general picture was in keeping with this.

Khrushchev demanded great and specific efforts. That was in the late summer of 1953, before his victory over Malenkov; he was speaking then as the senior leader with a special interest in agriculture, the role he had been playing for some years before Stalin died. But eighteen months later, in January 1955, just before the fall of Malenkov, he had to make another gloomy speech. After all the shouting and high resolves things were still going wrong, and by this time it was clear that Khrushchev, and those who thought with him, believed that the very survival of Communism in the Soviet Union depended on the success of the new agricultural policies.

What was it all about?

Primarily it was about food for the hugely expanded urban population of factory workers and technicians. The Soviet leadership had discovered that a modern industrial society cannot be run on a subsistence economy; that it depends on a *regular* supply of food (unlike a peasant society, which can tide itself over periods of famine and semi-famine in a state of more or less suspended animation); that it depends on a *richer* supply, a more balanced and healthy diet, and cannot indefinitely operate precision machines at high speed on a diet of rye bread, pickled cucumber, and buckwheat porridge. The new leadership recognized this and were prepared, as Stalin was not, to pay a price for more and better food. At first the Malenkov government offered various quite important concessions in an attempt to gain the good will of the peasants; but these were not enough. They were only enough to upset the terrible black and white logic of Stalin's economy. At some time, also, in the first six months after Stalin's death, the great inquest into the real condition of the Soviet Union must have revealed that agricultural production was in an even worse case than anyone suspected and that the statistics upon which the planners based their estimates were phoney in the extreme (a fact admitted both by Malenkov and Khrushchev).

Something more urgent had to be done than nursing the peasants back into good heart, and Khrushchev was the man to try. For three years at least Khrushchev had been harbouring plans for what would amount to a new agricultural revolution.

The first agricultural revolution occurred when Lenin let the peasants seize the land for themselves, knowing that in due course he would have to take it back from them. The second occurred when Stalin took it back by means of the collectivization, deporting and shooting the determined resisters and starving the rest into submission. This operation killed off the best farmers in the Soviet Union, the most skilled and energetic peasants, the so-called kulaks, to the tune of several million, and halved the country's livestock population, besides drastically reducing the grain-yield. The third revolution was launched by Khrushchev himself in 1950. Part of his programme, the amalgamation of groups of adjoining collectives to make monster units, succeeded on paper. But when it came to resettling the collective farmers in impersonal "agro-towns" where they would be removed from their familiar fields, deprived of their cherished private plots, uprooted from their villages, and merged into a crowd of strangers under the watchful eye of representatives of the central authorities, the peasants called a halt. The idea had to be postponed.

But the idea lived on. Khrushchev is still aiming at the coordination of industry and agriculture, the removal of the last vestiges of the village economy, and the substitution of an industrialized and depersonalized agriculture run by the state for the state, with the peasants turned into hirelings, or state serfs. This is perfectly logical. There are two alternatives, both inimical to the Communist idea: to undo the collectivization and revert to private enterprise, encouraging a new class of responsible kulaks to rise from the dumb masses and organize them; or to undo the collectivization and let the kolkhozniks organize themselves on the lines of the old Russian *Mir*, with its strip cultivation and common fields.

It is too often forgotten that agriculture in the West was not always what it is today. England, for example, is rightly regarded as the cradle of scientific stock-breeding. But the idea of stock-breeding did not exist until the late eighteenth century, and its

practice was brought into being by the English industrial revolution. Until that revolution there was no question of breeding
animals especially for meat and dairy produce. Cattle were bred
for bone and strength, to make good oxen for ploughing. Sheep
were bred for wool. It was not until halfway through the eighteenth century that stock could be wintered in any numbers. There
were no root crops, and the unimproved pastures provided in-
sufficient hay. So the bulk of the animals were slaughtered at the
approach of winter, and salted down. With the discovery of roots
it became possible to carry stock through the winter. And soon
the demands of the swiftly growing populations of the new industrial towns were stimulating the production of meat and milk
and butter. English agriculture then quickly changed over from
subsistence farming, with the emphasis on grain, to high-value
farming. Then came machines.

The English experience has been shared, with variations, by
every advanced country. Russia stood on the verge of her own
variation in 1917. At that time four-fifths of the Russian population were peasants, feeding themselves in the traditional peasant
way, going hungry in bad times, killing their stock at the approach
of winter, making do with inferior and low-yielding animals, and
exporting grain because it was easy to raise a surplus. But the
normal agricultural revolution, going hand in hand with the
normal industrial revolution, was already beginning to move in
the last years of the Tsars.

Whether in 1928, when the First Five-Year Plan was launched,
the peasant economy would have developed by natural means, by
the law of supply and demand, fast enough to feed the new towns
we shall never know. It was not given the chance to try. The attempt would have meant allowing the able and ambitious, and
often grasping, to set the pace, expand their holdings, and employ
(or exploit) the less able and ambitious as labourers. This, indeed,
the kulaks had already started doing, with the result that by 1928
Soviet agricultural production had recovered from the disasters of
civil war and revolutionary chaos and achieved an all-time record.
The revolutionaries did not like the smell of it. Lenin himself
had said, "Peasant small-scale production breeds capitalism and a
bourgeoisie—every day, every hour—by a natural process and on

a mass scale." The free development of agriculture would have made nonsense of the Soviet system, so it had to be stopped.

There was another reason for state intervention: Stalin's industrial plan called for the concentration of all resources in heavy industry. A free agricultural economy could not work without incentives in the way of goods for money to buy. There were to be no goods for money to buy.

And so to protect the Revolution from the rise of a new class of individualistic landowners, or capitalists, and to squeeze food from the peasants in return for practically nothing at all, the collectivization was pushed through; the peasants were forced to give up their land and their stock, except for small private plots, a cow, a few pigs, and join a co-operative working communal acres, and the state had first claim, at an artificially low rate of remuneration, on the products of their labours. The result of the collectivization was thus not to increase agricultural production but to depress it—and that in spite of the new machines. But Stalin did not care. He was breaking the new class of landowners in the interests of Communist theory, and he was getting his hands on what food there was in return for the smallest possible outlay. The depression was so unimaginably disastrous that, as we have seen, ten years later, on the eve of the war, there was less grain per head than there had been in 1928, and fewer cattle. When the Germans came, the system was still so hated that great numbers of the peasants of the Ukraine and White Russia welcomed them as liberators—until they found that Hitler was worse than Stalin, and a foreigner into the bargain.

The calamity of the war threw everything into confusion. Millions of acres of crops were wasted; millions of animals were killed. On top of this the collective system was breaking down everywhere, not only in the West. All over the Union, when peace came, it was found that the collectives had virtually broken up, and police action was necessary to make the tougher peasants disgorge the land illegally "bought" from the farm managers. It took the government five years to restore some sort of order. The 1946 famine in the Ukraine was a terrible set-back at the beginning of the task. And, at the same time, the new lands in the Baltic State and in the Western Ukraine had to be brought into the collective system. Then, in 1950, Khrushchev's "Third Revolution" was announced.

It did not work. Nor did the grandiose cattle-breeding scheme, which made no proper provision for winter shelter and winter keep; the cattle died in hundreds of thousands on the icy steppes of Kazakhstan. Nor did the Lysenko scheme for temporary pastures: acres of arable land were sown down to grass in arid areas where grass could not thrive. And all the time the towns were clamouring for more and more varied food.

Malenkov's immediate concessions to the peasants—relief from Stalin's punitive taxes, a lessening of the burden of compulsory deliveries, the positive encouragement of private husbandry within the framework of the collective—were sufficient to make life easier for the kolkhozniks, but not to raise their productivity. Khrushchev had fought the principle of every peasant's being allowed his own plot and his own few animals, because he knew that the individual worked harder on his own land than on the collective fields. And he is still fighting it. The frontal assault, the attempt to establish the agro-towns in 1950 and resettle the villages on a gigantic scale, failed. But Khrushchev, and those who think with him, have returned to the attack by devious means. Some of the means are subtle and innocuous seeming; others are spectacular.

The most spectacular of all was the celebrated "virgin land" campaign, launched early in 1954, when Malenkov had still a year to run as prime minister. This campaign, which has passed almost unnoticed outside the Soviet Union, was one of the most fabulous episodes in modern history. Suddenly, and quite unexpectedly (since Malenkov had announced that the grain situation was well in hand), the government came out with a decree calling for the immediate ploughing up and sowing down to grain of 32 million acres of waste and virgin land in Kazakhstan and southern Siberia —an area rather more than the total acreage under crops in England, Wales, and Scotland. Before the scheme had got fully into its stride the acreage was increased to a total which was more than half the cultivated area of Germany, France, Italy, and Spain combined. And it was done. By the autumn of 1955 that vast acreage had been ploughed up, to be harvested by the autumn of 1956. The first harvest, on a limited acreage in 1954, was successful—and compensated for crop failures in the Ukraine. The second, much larger harvest, in 1955, was a failure—but was compensated by an exceptional harvest in the Ukraine. It was a terrible failure, but afterward Khrushchev assured the pioneers that all was well: they must not be cast down. The whole operation would justify itself, he said, if there were one bumper harvest and two indifferent harvests to every two failures. And this he expected to achieve. He admitted that immense mistakes had been made because of precipitate action; huge acreages had been ploughed and sown where no grain could be grown—because of aridity, because of the salinity of the soil. But he waved these mistakes aside; let them go back to grass, he said, let us put sheep on the grass and reap wool instead of wheat. There is an infinity of land to be won deeper in Siberia, he went on—land where the rainfall is good and the soil analysis appropriate for wheat. But he was careful to add (this was in January 1956) that for the time being there would be no more expansion. For the time being they must consolidate existing gains, already colossal, and build their new society where, until now, only nomad Kazakhs had followed their flocks with their black tents.

The actual conduct of this operation passes all imagining. A quarter of a million "volunteers" were picked up by their roots and pitch-forked into the empty steppe. The machinery followed: tractors and combines taken from existing farms, or dispatched straight from the factories, causing fantastic congestion on inadequate railways. New lines were laid. Machinery piled up in the steppe waiting for railheads to advance. It was a Technicolour epic on a truly Russian scale, and the waste, the muddle, and the hardship were frightful. But the land was ploughed up: it was ploughed up by Komsomols who really volunteered, by star tractor drivers drafted or attracted by lavish pay or the spirit of adventure, by soldiers who had served their term and were demobilized as units and sent straight to the steppe to establish new farms named after their own units and often commanded by retired officers from their units. During all the first winter there was nowhere to live. "Pre-fabs" and tents were ordered in vast quantities, but they failed to arrive—or else the walls for a hundred pre-fabs would be sent to one location, and the roofs to another location two hundred miles away. The volunteers got through that winter somehow, living mainly in the traditional Russian dugouts—sunken pits with an earth roof over wood or iron, and a bit of stove-pipe for a chimney. The press reports of the first deployment read like chapters from a Soviet novel in the almost-forgotten days of hope and creative vitality. Akmolinsk, the headquarters of the Kazakhstan operation, was compared to the headquarters of a military concentration area. Everything was urgent confusion. Everything would sooner or later be sorted out. Meanwhile the grand deployment proceeded, regardless, while the steppe lay deep in snow:

> In an overcrowded room in a hotel which serves not only as sleeping quarters but also as an office for many people, a tall figure, pale with fatigue, is bent over a map and briefing the new intake. "Your 60 tractors have been unloaded here," he says, pointing to a cross on the map. "You will find 246 prefabs too. . . . Not enough, you say? I know, I know. But you'll have to wait. You'll get more later. And meanwhile get on with it—dig yourselves dugouts and improvise tents. . . . You're telling me it's not enough! And that's not the half of it! Don't think you'll find water available. The nearest reservoir is a very long way off, and there just aren't any wells. You'll have to make do with melted snow to start with—and then get on with sinking your own wells."

Then the farms did not exist; now they do. Only Khrushchev knows how many people died, or suffered irreparable injury to health, in those first two winters when there was nowhere to live. But the steppe is opened up. And Khruschev has achieved two purposes. He has secured an extra supply of grain, which will make the government partly independent of the soured, hidebound kolkhozniks of the old settled areas. And, even more important, he has moved some way toward his dream of the agro-towns. Because in all this vast new area there is no nonsense about old peasant customs. Khrushchev is building from scratch. The land is organized into gigantic state farms, and the workers are paid hands, living in brand new settlements, which, when they are finished, will resemble very closely the agro-towns of the original project. They are intended as a pattern for all Russia.

But already these new settlements are succumbing to the disease of all Soviet industrial towns. The hard core of volunteers can be relied on; but the draftees, and the demobilized service-men, are causing problems. The new settlements are too raw to produce their stilyagi, but they have produced a formidable crop of "hooligans." Once again, in contrast to the quiet efficiency of the political police, the civil police have proved themselves to be not up to their job; and the settlements which Khrushchev envisaged as impersonal and easily policed have in some cases become a national scandal. There is nothing to do after work but drink. Theatres are lacking, cinemas are lacking, clubs are lacking, even Party pep-talkers are lacking (it takes a devoted agitator to leave his family and settle down in the desert wastes of Kazakhstan). And so the young men drink and gamble and generally carry on as anyone but Mr. Khrushchev would expect them to carry on in such conditions. One intrepid Soviet author, Pogodin, wrote a play about it; his purpose was to show the size of the problems facing those responsible for developing law and order and culture in this barbaric pioneer land. But the authorities did not like the picture that he drew; the play was suppressed and Pogodin criticized for his defeatist attitude.

The emphasis of the new Five-Year Plan is away from the spectacular and toward the gradual taming of the peasants in the old farming lands. Khrushchev's maize campaign is very much to the fore—the planting of maize over huge areas where it was never grown before to provide a fodder base for a big rise in milk and butter and meat production (the Soviet Union is the biggest importer of frozen meat after Britain, and it imports the cheaper and more inedible carcasses: ewe mutton and cow beef). For the rest it is clear from the recommendations of the Plan that Khrushchev's colleagues have put pressure on him to go slow. The drive against the private plot continues. But the main emphasis for the time being is on increasing productivity by various means. Efficiency is to be stepped up by cost accounting; the payment system is to be revised and at the same time pay is to be increased; the peasant is to be more dependent on his remuneration in cash and kind from the collective; and the authority of farm managers is to be augmented. In 1955, because of the crying shortage of peasants

and farm managers competent to run the large collectives efficiently, the somewhat radical expedient was tried of drafting
thirty thousand new farm managers from the cities into the villages: good Party men who had made names for themselves as
efficient organizers in every walk of life. It is still too early to say
how that will work out, but it is an indication of the government's
desperation.

Not all our sympathy should be withheld from the present
leadership, including Mr. Khrushchev. The Russian peasant has his
primitive aspects. There are model farms with model peasants who
take pride in their work and seek to improve; you see their representatives, proudly showing their achievements, at the admirable
agricultural exhibition in Moscow, which is supposed to be, in
effect, a university for not-so-model peasants. But the mass of
peasants, at any rate in Great Russia as distinct from the Ukraine,
are a slovenly and idle lot. The differences between productivity
on the model farms and the general run of collectives shows the
amount of leeway that could be made up even in existing conditions. For example, the average milk yield in 1953 for the whole
of Kostroma Province, a district famous for its cattle, was just over
900 litres; but one collective in that province was averaging 5000
litres from each cow. In Vologda Province the average is just over
800 litres, but "advanced Vologda milk-maids," to quote *Pravda,*
have been getting between four and five thousand litres per cow.
In terms of gallons, the model collective of Kostroma was getting
1100 gallons per cow, which is exceptionally good by any standards
—though often surpassed in Britain. But the Kostroma average
was less than 200 gallons, the Vologda average even less; while the
average yield for the whole of Britain is 620 gallons. Even this is
regarded as a national disgrace by many British farmers, thousands of whom obtain more than 1000 gallons per cow.

Nobody expects Soviet yields, whether of milk or wheat, to
compare with British or American yields. Even when Soviet agriculture is at last fully mechanized and fertilizers are abundant and
intelligently applied, the climate, with its scarce summer rainfall, is against high yields. But yields should be very much higher
than they are. There is only one way to increase them, and that
is to induce the Russian peasant to work harder and take a

pride in his craft. This will not be done through any of Khrushchev's grandiose schemes. It will be done when the state can bring itself to provide adequate incentives. The idea, expressed in some quarters, that Soviet agriculture is going through a normal stage in the transition from low-value to high-value farming simply will not hold water. The transition is in being, as I have tried to show. But there is nothing "normal" about the highly artificial situation, persisting for so long, that arose from Stalin's determination to feed the towns for nothing—because he was not going to allow the towns to pay the countryside in terms of goods and services. The situation will become normal only when the government pays appropriate prices for the food it takes from the peasants and allows the production of consumer goods to rise to the point which will ensure that there are goods in the shops for the peasants to buy with their money. To judge by the provisions of the new Five-Year Plan this simple truth is at last beginning to dawn on the new leadership. And if in fact the peasants are given what they are now promised and the goods are made available in the shops and the village co-operatives it will be found that Khrushchev's bull-dozing tactics and grandiose schemes were so much wasted sound and fury. Self-interest will save the day, and the peasants, whether in collectives or in state farms, will learn for themselves how to produce the most for the least effort.

If, on the other hand, Khrushchev with his doctrinaire notions cannot be restrained, if the rational and comparatively gentle effort to combine new incentives with intelligent organization is dropped impatiently before it has had time to take effect—then yet another head-on collision between the Soviet state and the dark peasant can hardly be avoided. And the state cannot win.

12. PERSONALITIES

THE main worry of Stalin's heirs was the paralysis of initiative and intellect, the cynicism and the apathy that, passing all bounds in the last five years of Stalin's reign, threatened the Soviet Union with disaster. This paralysis had to be overcome rapidly and at all costs. It was affecting every sphere of Soviet progress: industry, agriculture, science, medicine. It was rendering null and void the potential influence of the great new classes of managers and intelligentsia. Fear had to go—the fear of the political police, which made initiative and openness impossible. The blinkers had to go—the blinkers imposed on science and invention and ideas in general by Stalin's chauvinism and pathological suspicion, which led to such things as the canonization of Lysenko and the prohibition of all intellectual contact with the outside world. Stalin had performed a remarkable surgical operation: he had cut the Soviet Union, an organic part of the world as a whole, out of the circulatory system of the world. Something, very quickly, had to be done about it. The danger was that in restoring the circulation of ideas apathy would awaken not into creative zeal but into active discontent, which could be suppressed, if at all, only by a reversion to the Stalinist Terror—without a Stalin to run it.

Individually Stalin's henchmen had another worry. It is perfectly clear from what has since happened (indeed, to any student of human nature it was self-evident from the beginning) that each was filled with a deadly and understandable determination never again to be the slave of an absolute tyrant. There may have been some among them who dreamed and planned and plotted to step into Stalin's shoes: three men above all—Beria, Malenkov, and Khrushchev. But there were others, senior to all these in years and experience, who knew that they could never aspire to the ultimate summit, even if they so desired: Kaganovich, because he was a

Jew; Mikoyan, because he was an Armenian. The Great Russians would not, it was generally understood, take kindly to another "foreign" master; the Georgian had been enough. And these, to say nothing of Molotov and others, would put all their weight into blocking the personal bid for supreme power of any one among their colleagues.

So, it may be believed, would the Army. The return of Marshal Zhukov, a national hero, from rustication in the provinces, whither Stalin in his jealousy (perhaps also in his wisdom) had long banished him, was the first sign that the professional soldiers of a non-political cast of mind were considered to represent a power worth courting by the Party—or else had offered an ultimatum to the Party. There were others, too, who, although powerless in themselves, had an interest in preventing the installation of a new autocrat: the strong new class of gifted administrators and industrial managers, who could be relied on to support those who fought most determinedly against a return to tyranny.

Indeed, at that time, there was only one man in a position to set himself up as Stalin's successor: Lavrenti Pavlovitch Beria, the head of all the security services, and, with Malenkov, one of the first two men in the land. Malenkov had the Party apparatus. But Beria had the secret police—and not only the secret police but the whole apparatus of the Ministry of State Security, under Abakumov and the Ministry of Internal Affairs under Kruglov. He had his men at every key-point in the Union; and he had over half a million of the best-fed, best-paid, best-armed troops. He had, in short, the advantage in every way. He was the only one among the pretenders who disposed of an army of his own.

It was an army, of course, hated and loathed with a deep and devouring passion by the regular soldiers.

I don't propose to speculate about what happened. It is enough to know that Beria aspired to supremacy and his colleagues prevented him and killed him. But the real nature of the tortuous plots and subplots that must have convulsed the closest colleagues of Stalin in the months after his death is beyond speculation. It is possible to argue that Malenkov, modelling himself on his master, allied himself with Beria with an eye on a more distant future—and lost his throw when Beria was arrested. It is possible to argue precisely the opposite. Conspiracies there certainly were; and con-spiracies there no doubt still are. To expect anything else is to ignore the very nature of the ambitious politician on his journey toward the top—not only in the Soviet Union, but in every other country in the world. But it is impossible to unravel the detail of the conspiracies. It is enough to establish that Malenkov, before the arrest of Beria, had his wings clipped; after becoming prime minister in succession to Stalin he was forced by his colleagues to relinquish his office as first secretary of the Party, which in due course went to Khrushchev. And soon after that Malenkov had to resign the premiership too. It is enough to establish that the one man who possessed the physical means to make himself the new autocrat was arrested and shot. It is enough to establish that the fall of Malenkov and the rise of Khrushchev were contrived behind the scenes by their silent colleagues. Khrushchev is now the domi-nant figure in the Soviet Union; but he did not impose himself: he was placed in that position by his fellow-members of the Presidium of the Party. And although he may himself be intrigu-ing and plotting to win absolute authority, by packing the Party organs with his supporters, he still has a long way to go. The Central Committee formed at the Twentieth Party Congress con-tains far more Khrushchev supporters than its predecessor. There are more of Khrushchev's men, too, in the Party Secretariat (Khrushchev's own office) and among the candidate members of the Presidium. But the Presidium itself remains as it was—remains the precise body of men which until now has decided that Krush-chev may go thus far and no farther. Malenkov, also, has held his position and is no doubt looking forward to the day when his powerful and garrulous rival will lay himself open to attack.

Meanwhile, in spite of evident acute disagreements, the Party Presidium is in fact conducting itself as a genuine collective—as, that is to say, a dictatorial committee. Sooner or later, over the years, it will have to move either in the direction of one-man dictatorship or in the direction of a greater democracy; the present uneasy balance can hardly last forever. But the important fact is that, in spite of Western scepticism in this matter, the collective leadership exists, and must exist. It may be that each and every one of the eleven members of the Presidium believes individually in the principle of the collective and has no desire to stand above his fellows. But, judging from the pattern, it is more likely that what keeps the collective together is mutual suspicion; it is a defensive alliance of Stalin's heirs, and the alliance is directed not only against all the forces of disintegration inside and outside the Soviet Union, but also against the individual pretensions of its own members. In the simplest terms, it represents a balance of power, and any individual or combination of individuals showing signs of accumulating too much power would be promptly set upon by the rest.

What sort of men are they—Bulganin, Kaganovich, Khrushchev, Kirichenko, Malenkov, Molotov, Mikoyan, Pervukhin, Saburov, Suslov, Voroshilov? And the candidate members, without voting powers—Marshal Zhukov, Madame Furtseva, Brezhnev, Mukhtidinov, Shvernik, Shepilov?

Nothing is harder than to assess their calibre and their individual standing. There is for me an endless fascination in watching these mysterious beings and listening to their speeches. It is very much like watching fish in an aquarium, and their words do not tell you much more than their eyes. Even when one applies to the living image everything one knows about his past actions there is all too little to be learned.

I have been particularly fascinated, for example, by Malenkov, ever since I first set eyes on him in the middle of the war, in 1942. He was already, at forty, very much in the running as Stalin's successor. In his photographs he appears fat to the point of grossness, with a face like a slab of lard, a sulky mouth above the double chins, a forelock and a stare not unlike a caricature of Hitler's; the first encounter kills that impression for ever. There is no grossness, simply a glandular unbalance; the eyes are questing; the mouth is sensitive; the new impression is of extreme toughness, physical and mental, combined with a lightness of touch and an agility amounting almost to positive grace, and an almost sleep-walking quality of abstraction. The voice is good and well-spoken; there are flickers of wit. It does not come as a surprise to hear that he reads Horace in the original and can bandy Latin quotations with the few Western diplomats who know any Latin. And then you remember his past: the student from Orenburg, the ancient frontier fortress of the steppe, too young to take part in the Revolution, who spent his whole adult life at the very heart of the Party apparatus and at Stalin's side—as Stalin's private secretary, as the personnel chief of the Party, from 1939 as a member of the Politburo itself. He owes everything to Stalin, his life and his career. And during the great purge of the thirties and all through the treason trials, before he became a public figure, it was he who sat in the middle of the spider's web of terror and decided who was to die, piling dossier on dossier, working in interminable sessions, all round the clock, with Yezhov, the degenerate chief of police (Beria's predecessor), and Vishinsky, the perjured public prosecutor, who was later considered a suitable spokesman for his country to the outer world.

Malenkov is an extreme and complex example of a common phenomenon in the Soviet Union: the man of culture and charm and wit who has committed abominable crimes—and then turned round on the men who raised him to power and on whose behalf he committed those crimes. What are we to make of him?

Bulganin is another man with some pretensions to culture. When he was younger he had a striking dark elegance, and knew how to talk to foreigners. He was a man of great administrative ability, though not, on his record, a creator. He organized and built up the great industries of Moscow, at a time when the Bolsheviks had few captains of industry among them. He was mayor of Moscow during the great period of expansion, and then chairman of the State Bank. During the war he distinguished himself as a senior political officer and became a colonel general. The political officers as a caste are loathed and execrated by the regular soldiers, over whom they have the power of life and death. But after the war Bulganin was promoted by Stalin to minister of defence, a politician in charge of soldiers. And now he is prime minister, as well as a member of the Politburo, with Zhukov, the chief of all the professional soldiers, as his minister of defence. His hair and beard are white now, and he is soft and bland, and still well turned out. He is the "sugar-daddy" of the Communist empire—and in more ways than one. For while he charms visiting statesmen and makes elaborate speeches, nicely turned, and oozing sweet reason, the perfect host, the polished patron, with all the power of the Soviet Union behind him, he is also human. I have seen him gaily drunk, ceremoniously kissing a red rose and tossing it across the dinner table into the lap of a handsome ballerina. On public occasions his eyes will wander until they light on a pretty girl, who is thereupon transfixed. When there are no pretty girls, and when he does not have to make a speech because Mr. Khrushchev is doing all the talking, he has the quietly purring air of a cat that has been at the cream. The imposing white head (he is only sixty-one), the trim white beard, nod in grave approval, either of Mr. Khrushchev or of himself. "Well, well, well," one can almost hear him thinking, "so they've made me prime minister. . . . I wonder why. Though, of course, I should be the last person to object. They tell me it's a dangerous job, being prime minister here. Maybe, maybe. . . . But, when all is said, there are plenty of dangerous jobs, and only one prime minister. . . ."

What is one to make of him?

Then Khrushchev himself, who has no pretensions to any culture whatsoever. Direct and down-to-earth, cheerfully direct or brutally direct, according to the exigencies of the occasion as appraised by him, this one-time shepherd-boy and coal-miner got his education in a night school. There is no doubt at all that he is the truly dynamic force in the higher leadership. And all the signs are that by temperament he is a natural autocrat. Immensely confident—perhaps over-confident—brash and contemptuous in his approach to delicate problems, ebulliently vital, he is the man who rushes in when the more circumspect think twice. You see the quality of the man most clearly when he is in repose. I have watched him clowning; I have watched him positively crawling in an effort to convey an impression of deference and respect; I have watched him bringing out his startling interjections in the middle of other people's speeches (for example, throwing Dr. Adenauer completely out of his stride and then, all smiles, apologizing afterward); I have watched him committing indiscretions because his tongue really had carried him away; and I have watched him delivering quite calculated indiscretions and insults, deliberately pretending that his tongue had carried him away; I have seen him apparently drunk and playing the genial buffoon at one moment, and in the next breath deadly sober, bullying with cold brutality the ambassador of a minor power—so that one shuddered to think what it must be like to be bullied by Khrushchev if one is a Russian and completely in his power. I have watched him, in Belgrade, making mistake after mistake in his determination to charm Marshal Tito and the Yugoslavs; and I have seen him each time registering the fact that, without knowing why, he had said or done the wrong thing—and never after that making the same mistake again. It is all a bewildering mixture of clown and bully, blunt self-made tycoon and ingratiating flatterer, cold calculation and irrepressible vitality. You can make what you like of it when the man is in motion. But when he is completely relaxed you are aware of enormous natural authority and power. He sits, and his chair is the seat of power. He withdraws himself naturally and absolutely, creating by some magic a physical gulf between himself and those around him. Sir Winston Churchill and Mr. Ernest Bevin, among English statesmen, had this trick.

He is the natural leader. Stalin built himself up by turning himself into a mystery, an all-seeing monster, dwelling in darkness and obscurity. Khrushchev, I should say, lacks the cunning and the patience to go about things this way. If he aspires, as I imagine he does, to the role of autocrat, he must effect his design by, as it were, taking the people into his confidence and making them believe in him as a man and a friend—a stern friend, but a kindly one. He must work more in the open than Stalin ever did. He must accumulate power visibly, item by item, inevitably and naturally, by presenting himself as the inevitable and natural leader—at the same time working, like Stalin, behind the scenes so to pack the Party that when he has gained an inch it will be hard for anyone to take it away. The Twentieth Party Congress strengthened his position considerably. There are now Khrushchev men in key-posts all over the country. He carries the Party Secretariat entirely. He has subordinated the police and the security services to the   Party—which in this context means the Secretariat. Three of the four new members of the Party Presidium are his nominees, and all three occupy commanding positions: Brezhnev as the uncrowned king of Kazakhstan, the vast scene of the most rapid development in the USSR; Mukhtidinov controlling Uzbekistan; and Madame Furtseva, the first woman to occupy such a position since the Revolution, the Party chief of Moscow city. Malenkov, on the other hand, has lost as much ground as Khrushchev has gained. Yet Khrushchev at the time of writing is still not in a position to bid for absolute supremacy. The Central Committee of 255 members is a more important body than it has been since Lenin died; and the Central Committee is by no means in Khrushchev's pocket. The military, too, have a stronger representation than ever before, and Marshal Zhukov himself has moved up to be a candidate member of the Presidium: the first professional soldier ever to be admitted to that supreme council.

Yet immediately after the Congress Khrushchev was appointed chairman of a special bureau of the Central Committee to supervise the activities of the Party in the Russian Federal Republic, Great Russia, which accounts for more than half the area and weight of the whole USSR. So that this Ukrainian, leaving his own stamping-ground to his nominee, Kirichenko, in Kiev, now lords it over Great Russia. It is a position of unrivalled potency. Stalin would never have publicly accumulated so much power on his upward journey: his technique was to work underground and not declare himself until, in one stroke, he could lay claim to all power. It may be, it cannot be excluded, that Khrushchev, against all appearances, is content to be first among equals, and has assumed this great new office for no other reason than to get certain things done. Or it may be that jealous colleagues are encouraging him to ride too high, so that the fall shall be the greater.

Meanwhile, what are we to make of Khrushchev—Nikita Sergeyevich?

The elders, now in the background, are Kaganovich, Mikoyan, Molotov, and Voroshilov.

Voroshilov, the old sergeant-major of the civil war, Stalin's last remaining contemporary and boon companion, was supposed not to exist apart from his friend and master. But when Stalin died he served as an invaluable figure-head in the presidency, and perhaps as a rallying point for the Army. He counted for a great deal in the Army once and stood for a recognized school of strategy and tactics. He was Stalin's right hand when it came to the purge of the officer corps; and many of the men who stepped into the shoes of the dead chiefs must owe him a great deal. Since Stalin's death he has taken on a new lease of life, has travelled widely in Eastern Europe, has made of the presidency more than any of his predecessors. He is now seventy-five; but it is clear that his voice carries more weight than most people imagined.

For years Stalin's chief of staff, deputy, and butt, Molotov steadily declined after 1953. The prestige of his office was weakened by the admissions of his colleagues of mistakes in international affairs committed under Stalin. His own standing was undermined quite deliberately by the failure of the Party to defend him against Marshal Tito's outspoken attack in 1955 and, again, later in the year, by the extraordinary episode which involved his public apologia for holding false doctrine. He was expendable.

Kaganovich occupies a strange position. This heavily built and taciturn Jew stood very close to Stalin; and to him more directly than to anybody else after Stalin the Soviet people owe the successes, and the rigours, of their industrial revolution. Watching that sluggish and impassive countenance, heavily moustached, the high, strong forehead bald, one perceives nothing at all of the man. He believes in salvation through heavy industry. He believes that all who stand in the way of its progress must be crushed. He has frequently been called in to carry out, to all appearances coolly and phlegmatically, a major crushing operation which had proved too much for others. In 1930 he crushed the peasant resistance to collectivization, deporting and starving millions. After the last war he crushed the nationalist resistance in the Ukraine—moving in where Khrushchev, of all people, had failed. It was he who lifted up Khrushchev and groomed him for high rank. Now, seeing them together, one finds nothing to tell what Kaganovich thinks or feels. Does he resent being outdistanced by his protégé? Or does he still feel the stronger man—though debarred by his race, and perhaps by his temperament, from bidding for absolute power? And what does he think of Malenkov, who caused his brother to be broken and liquidated? At sixty-five Kaganovich is still a powerful man with immense experience behind him, with the great industrialists (whose blackmailing power is great) beholden to him. He is a crucial force. But how will he use that force?

Mikoyan is also a force, and he showed it for the first time at the Twentieth Party Congress, where he not only spoke more openly in denunciation of Stalin's policies than any of his colleagues, but also attacked specific utterances and actions of the late dictator, mentioning him and his works by name. His speech had a freedom and originality entirely foreign to the rest of the proceedings. Instead of echoing the phrases of Khrushchev's mammoth report on the state of the nation, or elaborating particular aspects of it, he gave the impression of a man thinking aloud—a man, however, who, having listened to Khrushchev's speech, considered it quite a good effort, but was concerned to make certain points clearer. It was, in a word, a patronizing speech; and it was Khrushchev he was patronizing.

Mikoyan has had a remarkable past. Alone among the great leaders he himself fought at the barricades in the Revolution, and was wounded. That was in Baku, where the young Armenian, a theological student, destined for the priesthood in the Nestorian Church, suddenly turned revolutionary and became an impassioned Bolshevik. When the British occupied Baku he was captured with the rest of the Bolshevik committee by the Whites, and escaped being murdered out of hand with the famous Twenty-six Commissars, his colleagues, only because of a combination of outstanding bravery on his part and a clerical error on the part of the Whites. He had a first-class revolutionary record, and yet he is far and away the most civilized of the Stalinist revolutionaries. Molotov comes from a more respectable background (the Tsarist intelligentsia: the composer Scriabin was his uncle); Malenkov knows Latin; but Mikoyan is gay and civilized by nature, eager for elegance, a little pathetic in his pursuit of it. He is very much the Armenian, and, as such, for decades has stood for Soviet trade. Because of this, because of his capacity for getting on with foreigners (he is incomparably the Soviet Union's best negotiator), because, too, he fell in love with American technology and did his level best to introduce its graces to the Soviet Union, because finally he fell in love with British Army rations and made a vow to raise the standard of eating in the Soviet Union—because of all this, people have regarded him as something of a lightweight, as being not one of the iron men, as simply a useful and accomplished contact man and go-between.

But Stalin had no use for anything but iron men. The very fact of Mikoyan's survival is a proof of his constitution. He was certainly useful to Stalin because he knew how to talk to foreign businessmen and diplomats—in the war, also, to Western admirals and generals. He alone among his colleagues knew what American industry looked like from the inside. But his task, the task of feeding the Soviet people through all the years when Stalin grudged the diversion of any resources and man-power whatsoever from the great build-up of heavy industry, has been arduous in the extreme; and to build up an extremely efficient food-processing and canning industry at this time was little short of a miracle. Mikoyan must have had to fight for every factory, for every machine, for every can. If there can be said to have been a balance between the demands of capital expansion and the demands of the consumer during the black years, it was Mikoyan's tenacity that made it possible. It may well be shown one day that while Stalin, aided above all by Kaganovich, ensured the survival of the Soviet Union as a power, Mikoyan ensured its survival as a people—and this in face of the almost total neglect, through decades, of the claims of agriculture.

Through it all he retained his imperturbability—not the blank-faced imperturbability of so many of his colleagues, but an air of sardonic, devil-may-care aloofness. At a time when his colleagues, following Stalin's example, were going about looking like coolies, Mikoyan dressed by Soviet standards well and smartly. Gay, alert, immensely quick in the uptake, but when angry having a gaze of hot steel, he mingled with his clumsy Russians without ever seeming to belong to them, for decades the only member of the Politburo who seemed to have any consciousness of the great world outside Russia, the great world from which it was necessary to learn so much before it could be crushed, surpassed, consigned to limbo. Now, with Stalin dead, I have no doubt at all that Mikoyan has played a decisive part in launching the great campaign to learn from the West and profit by its experience and inventiveness, its efficiency, and its manners. I am not suggesting that Mikoyan would be immediately at home in the West; he would not. He believes in the virtues and delights of advertising; he believes in the convenience and efficiency of the retail distribution system of Britain and America; he broods about cafeterias and self-service shops; he is a pioneer for decent cooking and a lighter and more stimulating diet than the Russians normally concoct for themselves; he revels in social occasions, from dances to garden parties; he likes making people around him happy; he has faith in the solvent of good manners. But his specimen advertisements are trite in the extreme; his approach to the diet and cooking question is to issue a cookery-book with a long introduction by himself in which standard dishes are prescribed, in rigid detail and down to the last pinch of salt, with no departure whatever allowed, for all the hotel and catering establishments in the Soviet Union; his idea of making people happy is to press into their pockets at state receptions selected dainties, often unsuitable for pockets, so that they won't be hungry on the way home. Perhaps the power and stature of the man is shown above all in his loyalty to his own native Armenia. He has never deserted it. He has always, in the teeth of heaven knows what grudging opposition, seen to it that the Armenians have been, by Soviet standards, well looked after. Terrible things have happened there—but fewer terrible things than anywhere else in the Soviet Union. And Anastas Mikoyan, helped by the natural vitality and efficiency of his own people—poles apart from the slovenly fecklessness of their Russian neighbours—has succeeded in turning Erevan into far and away the most civilized city in the Union. He is the only member of the higher leadership who has ever done a thing to make life easier for the people nearest to him—to say nothing of the people of the Soviet Union as a whole.

He has survived. It is not improbable that his feelings toward his Russian and Ukrainian colleagues carry a strong vein of contempt. Watching him on the occasion of the fantastic pilgrimage to Belgrade in the summer of 1955, one found it impossible not to feel that he was in a measure disassociating himself from the whole sycophantic performance of his Party secretary, Khrushchev, and his prime minister, Bulganin. Standing always a little behind these two, he showed frequent impatience at their posturings, and on occasion his eyes looked daggers. It was the same aloofness and independence which inspired his challenging speech at the Twentieth Party Congress, eight months later. Mikoyan can never become dictator. But it would surprise me a great deal to find Khrushchev, or anybody else, assuming the role of a new Stalin while Mikoyan is still alive. He is the only man in the higher reaches of the leadership of whom one can say with certainty that he owes his position not to political manœuvring and the manipulation of the Party machine, but to his own character and ability. He is sixty-one. He is indispensable.

So much for the elders—except for Mr. Shvernik. I have no impressions to offer of Nikolai Mikhailovich Shvernik. I must have seen him, probably quite often, possibly quite close to. But I have never consciously seen him; and his whole career, which has had its ups and downs, is shadowy and vague. He fought in the civil war, like Mikoyan, and then for years he worked in the Party machine. But he had a trade-union background, and when the time came to force Tomsky out of his job as chairman of the All-Union Central Council of Trade Unions (Tomsky was not tried, or shot, with the rest of the Bukharinites; he committed suicide), Shvernik took his place. Under him the trade unions were steadily transformed from protectors of the interests of the workers in face of the state to protectors of the interests of the state in face of the workers—a definition which would be objected to by most, if not all, of my Soviet Communist friends, who would insist, like Mr. Shvernik, that since the state belongs to the workers their interests must be identical. Shvernik did well for Stalin and was rewarded by being made president when dear old President Kalinin, with his spectacles and white goatee, expired. He is evidently not without charm, for he seems to have carried on the Kalinin tradition of being the little friend of all the world, receiving endless deputations and individual petitioners—chiefly from among the very workers whom, until that moment, it had been his duty to harrass and oppress—and sending them away comforted and assuaged by personal contact with the titular head of state. When Stalin died he fell, and Marshal Voroshilov, a more imposing figure, took his place. Shvernik went back to the trade unions. He is still on the Party Presidium. But it is Kaganovich who is undertaking the rad-

ical investigation into the wage structure of the Soviet Union,
which has got out of balance, to say the least. And at the Twentieth Party Congress Khrushchev made a point of reproaching
the trade unions for not standing up for the workers in face of
the state machine. So it is a little difficult to see where Shvernik
fits in.

So much for the elders. It is clear that these impressions do not
take us very far. What, indeed, are we to make of them? We see
a group of assorted revolutionary politicians, exhibiting the same
variety of character, the same rivalries, the same relative abilities,
that one would expect to discover in any group of leading politicians anywhere. We see their public faces, but little of their
private lives. We know the private lives exist. We know that
under Stalin the habit of luxury villas in the very pretty country
on the outskirts of Moscow was indulged in by all. We know that
there is a Kremlin smart set led by Madame Voroshilov, who is
now getting on, a countess rescued from the firing squad by her
revolutionary husband, who all her life has acted as a connecting
link between the faded splendours of the Tsars and the waxing
splendours of the new regime. We know that Mikoyan has lively
and spirited interests outside his work; we know that Malenkov,
try as he may, has never been able to tear himself away from his
files for long enough at a time to build the foundations of a
private life. We know that Bulganin can do with any amount of
private life and on occasion gives pain to his colleagues for allowing this proclivity to intrude on his public life. We know that the
abominable General Serov, the heir to Beria's dwindled empire,
owes his present position in the first instance to his skill, under
Stalin, in organizing private lives of the more scandalous sort for
overworked Communist executives (that was when he was in
charge of the Kremlin body-guards, before he rose to fame in 1940
as the gifted organizer of mass deportations). We know that even
in Soviet high society, as in other lands, the line has to be drawn
somewhere and that at least one senior minister (never a member
of the Party Presidium) now languishes in a northern provincial
town, as a "minus six," not for political heresy but because he
repeated his remarkable orgies in a villa outside Moscow once too
often and unwisely allowed photographs to be taken. ("Minus six"

is the term used to describe Soviet citizens who are free to live anywhere in the country except in one or another of the six major cities.) I say we know these things. But how does one know anything at all? These, and many other things, are the subject of Moscow gossip; and, failing documentary evidence, we cannot really do better than Moscow gossip, which at least shows the kind of thing the Russians like to believe about their rulers. This may frequently be as much to the point as what the rulers would like us to believe about them.

All this, of course, is not to say that a prime minister of Russia who has an eye for a pretty girl may not also be a convinced Communist. Indeed, for want of evidence, we are compelled to abandon the attempt to discover what sort of men the rulers are by looking at them and glancing at their careers and return instead to the task of trying to assess their meaning by contemplating the problems they have to face, and how they face them, and the words they give to the world, and how these compare with their deeds. This is a task, it seems to me, best approached with some appreciation, however sketchy, of life in the Soviet Union as it is lived (which I have done my best to supply), and without reverence or even more respect than we normally accord the leading statesmen of America, France, Britain, and elsewhere. We used to blame the Russians for putting Stalin on a pedestal and considering him as an infallible demi-god, but who were we to talk like that? And so, while having every respect for Marshal Bulganin as an administrator and a diplomat, while not in the least underestimating his powers for good or ill as a convinced exponent of what he takes to be Marxism, it seems to me that our perspective is improved if we think of him also as an inveterate pincher of bottoms.

What does he think? What do any and all of them think? How does what they think bear on our own lives?

We have come to the higher leadership through the Soviet people whom they govern. To consider the leaders apart from the people is dangerous and misleading. They grew out of the people and out of the land that they rule. They are quite unconsciously but none the less decisively conditioned by their native characteristics and traditions. In offering my impressions of the Soviet people at this moment in time I have stressed the element of change

and confusion. I have done this partly to offset the popular Western impression of a people regimented out of their souls, partly
to show the shabby side of a regime which in its propaganda will
not admit to shabbiness, partly to show various contradictory
trends at work in that changing society. But there are more positive aspects which are no less relevant, and which bear no less
sharply on the true nature of the regime.

If I had to sum up the fundamental difference between the
average believing Soviet Communist and the average Englishman
with a social conscience I should say something like this: The
Englishman is inclined to think that the better is the enemy of
the good; the Russian is quite certain that the good and the
better are both enemies of the best. The Englishman is inclined
to let well enough alone lest worse should befall; the Russian
would regard this attitude as a betrayal of all aspiration.

> We needs must love the highest when we see it,
> Not Lancelot, nor another.

Nothing but the best is good enough for him; and to me it does
not seem an exaggeration to say that when the highest is unat-
tainable immediately the Russian, uneasy and unsure between
two poles, feels happier and safer consorting with the lowest.
Russian, or Soviet Communist, it is all one, except that the Soviet
Communist through Marx and Lenin has seen the highest and,
with his eye fixed on the celestial city, stumbles toward it through
the mire, steadfastly ignoring the cries of the wretched and the
drowning, secure in the conviction that once paradise is reached
there will be no more misery anywhere—and equally convinced
that to stop now to assuage immediate suffering would be to be-
tray the ultimate ideal.

I am not suggesting that Stalin felt like that, or that Messrs.
Khrushchev and Bulganin feel like it today. But they are borne
up by multitudes who do, and who rationalize their toleration of
infinite cruelty, their toleration of Messrs. Stalin, Khrushchev,
and Bulganin, in very much this way.

On a late September evening in Moscow I was walking along
the inner boulevard, under the trees, with a Party official, about

thirty-five. Two cheerful workmen were struggling manfully to get a wild drunk on his feet between them so that they could bundle him home. They had nothing to do with the drunk. They had just taken pity on him, and he was giving them a rough time, which they took with high-spirited toleration. Russians are good at helping drunks and other fellows in misfortune—save in crises of extreme stringency, when the battle for personal survival turns them into animals. I saw that my companion was upset.

"Swine!" he was muttering under his breath. "Treacherous fools!"

Since this was not at all the usual Russian attitude toward drunkenness, which approximates to the eighteenth-century British attitude, I expressed surprise.

"They don't know what they're doing. It makes one despair!"

What they were doing was going out of their way at the cost of considerable personal inconvenience and with great good nature to help a fellow creature in distress. I said so, adding, a little maliciously (guessing what was coming), "Model comrades!"

"Model comrades!" he positively hissed. "Traitors to the Revolution!" And then: "Don't you really see that it's precisely these warm-hearted careless fools that are throwing everything away? We work ourselves silly for them. Lenin sacrificed his life for them. To put them on the upward path. And the moment we turn our backs, there they are, squandering their energies on helping good-for-nothings who deserve only to die in the gutter."

"I've seen good Party members drunk," I said.

"More shame to us!"

"You don't believe in pity any more?"

"Pity? Pity, yes! What do you know about pity? The pity Lenin felt was a burning pity for the whole of mankind, and it filled him with a cold determination to cauterize all the evils, all the squalors and the cancers, that add to the suffering of mankind. That wretch you're pitying now is a cancer. What else? He was a man once. He has had his chance and thrown it away. We can't afford to stop and pick him up. If I so far forgot myself as to go to his help I should be a criminal in the eyes of the Party."

"As bad as that?"

"As stern as that. We have to harden our hearts. How else can we ever reach the goal?"

And so hearts are hardened, and thousands, hundreds of thousands, millions, tens of millions, are abandoned, their lives destroyed, in the march to the ultimate goal.

I am not suggesting that all members of the Soviet Communist Party would share the emotions of my companion of the Moscow boulevard. Far from it—to their shame, as he would insist! He was something of a fanatic. But there are plenty like him.

13. THE PATTERN EMERGES

WHAT is the ultimate goal? I hope I have conveyed enough of Soviet reality in these pages to show that this is no easy matter to decide—if, indeed, it can be decided at all. We are hearing a great deal nowadays about the Leninist revival, led by Mr. Khrushchev. And, indeed, there has been a marked atmosphere of revivalism in the Soviet Union lately, which found its highest expression at the Twentieth Party Congress. The substitution of the dead Lenin for the dead Stalin as the fountain of all inspiration, the insistence on collective rule and the supremacy of the Party, the new emphasis on the transition from Socialism to Communism in the foreseeable future, Mikoyan's declaration at the Congress that for twenty years the Party had been crippled by one-man rule, the weakening of the authority of the political police, Khrushchev's insistence on the need for a shorter working day and the raising of the pay of workers in the lower income groups—these are some of the signs of the revival at home. But it is the new stress on the Leninist revolutionary dynamic on a world-wide scale that has naturally attracted most attention abroad and is leading us, I think, to false conclusions.

After Stalin's death the chief Soviet propaganda theme was peaceful coexistence; and this blossomed into full flower at the "summit" conference at Geneva in July 1955. Peaceful coexistence was a Leninist term, which was also employed a great deal by Stalin. There was a snag attached to the idea, and the snag was this: according to both Lenin and Stalin peaceful coexistence was no more than an interlude, a realistic appreciation of the fact that the two opposed systems must exist side by side until the bourgeois world, or camp, was so weakened and the Soviet system so strengthened that the one would collapse and the other sweep the world. Lenin also believed, and Stalin after him, that this apotheosis could come only through war. It was this thesis that made all Soviet talk of peace completely unreal and false. The men in the Kremlin did not want war, but they did believe that war must come before the final disintegration of the capitalist system which they ardently desired and also believed, dogmatically, to be inevitable, according to the historical law discovered by Marx and elaborated by Lenin. This meant that they must always be preparing for war—war which would take the form either of a direct assault by the West on the Soviet Union, or of a global struggle arising from conflicts between the Western nations for vital markets in a dwindling world.

For a long time I had been personally convinced that sooner or later we should perceive that Stalin, or his successors, had had to revise this dogma in the light first of the atom bomb, then of the hydrogen bomb. It was all very well for Lenin, thinking in terms of Tannenberg, to look forward with enthusiasm to a series of mighty conflicts that would end in revolutionary triumph and the ultimate victory of global Communism. But nuclear fission made nonsense of such ideas. The nearest Stalin got to amending the dogma, however, was in his last published work, *The Economics of Socialism*, when he hazarded that although there would be further major wars, with good luck and good judgment the Soviet Union could keep out of them, leaving the bourgeois nations to tear each other to pieces. When Stalin died I hoped for something more intelligent; and for a moment it looked as though it were coming. In his first speech to the Supreme Soviet, Malenkov went out of his way to say that "at the present time there is no disputed or unsettled question which cannot be resolved in a peaceful manner on the basis of mutual agreement between the interested parties." But this was not followed up, and Malenkov was careful not to prophesy about disputes which might arise in future. A little later, however, he committed himself so far as to say that atomic war would mean the end of civilization everywhere—in Soviet Russia as well as in the capitalist West—a statement that was later contradicted flatly by Khrushchev himself, who said it would mean only the end of capitalism and imperialism.

It was an odd state of affairs. The new Kremlin leaders continued to profess their belief in the inevitability of a war which, they knew as well as anybody else, would annihilate everything they stood for. Quite soon after his speech about "mutual agreements" I myself asked for an interview with Mr. Malenkov, and sent in the questionnaire without which such occasions can never be arranged. One of the questions was, precisely, whether in the light of the nuclear arm he, Mr. Malenkov, still held to the thesis of the inevitability of war; if so, why?—and if not, why was it still preached in every Communist handbook? I did not get that interview, and I did not get an answer. But it was soon clear that a great debate was in progress. In a remarkable article on foreign policy by a writer called Gus (*Zvezda,* November 1953), it was suggested, without contradicting Lenin, that the rising power of the forces of Socialism might mean that the human race had at least a possibility of "limiting or preventing the operation of the law of the inevitability of war." It was not long before word got round in Moscow that poor Mr. Gus—pronounced "goose" and meaning "goose"—was in disgrace.

What is sauce for the goose should be sauce for the gander— but not a bit of it, for what Mr. Gus got into trouble for saying (on whose instigation?) in November 1953 was precisely what Mr. Khrushchev announced to Twentieth Party Congress and the world in February 1956 as the firm opinion of the higher leadership. And Mr. Khrushchev is not in disgrace. The premise that wars are inevitable, he said, "was worked out at a time when, firstly, imperialism was an all-embracing world system, and, secondly, the social and political forces not interested in war were weak and insufficiently organized, and so could not force the imperialists to eschew war." This situation, he went on to say, applied on the eve of both the last two great wars; but now, he went on, the situation had been radically changed by the emergence of a whole group of powerful socialist forces favouring peace. This meant that there was no longer any question of "a fatal inevitability of war" and Lenin's imperialistic thesis was to that extent outdated—though, he concluded, it was still correct in the sense that "so long as imperialism exists, the economic basis for an outbreak of war will continue to exist with it."

This was not a tactical move designed to confuse Western

opinion and lull the suspicions of the world at large. The present Soviet leadership is well versed in the use of deceit, which is an essential and explicit part of Leninism. Generalized peace over-tures, popular fronts, trade agreements, and the rest, may and should be regarded always with suspicion when they come from Moscow. They may be genuine, but they equally well may not be. The formal rewriting of Lenin at a solemn assembly of the Com-munist Party dedicated to his memory is quite another matter. Nobody, not even Mr. Khrushchev, monkeys lightly with the sacred texts. And his announcement, delivered with all the weight and authority of the first secretary of the Communist Party of the Soviet Union, and afterward echoed by other senior orators, was most carefully considered. It was also plainly the outcome of protracted debate on the highest level, a debate which had been in progress through all the previous three years, and in which poor Mr. Gus was a casualty. Let us hope that Mr. Gus will now get a prize.

The argument for the fateful revision of this basic doctrine is interesting and characteristic. It contained no reference to the hydrogen bomb, quite plainly the real cause. It said, in effect, that we, the Socialist camp, peace-loving and just, are now so strong and also so highly thought of by the decent peace-loving masses throughout the capitalist world that we have a strong chance of forcing warlike capitalist elements to keep the peace and thus of nullifying the iron law of history. This argument was not intended to impress the West. It was intended to impress the Communist Party and the Soviet people in general. And to them it means that one of the basic elements of their doctrine, which for decades has distorted and inhibited all constructive thought about international relations—which has indeed made such thought impossible—has been painlessly removed.

The Soviet leadership is now in a position to make a reappraisal of its foreign policy. And it will be helped by another radical re-vision also announced at the Congress by Mr. Khrushchev: namely that although the capitalist system is doomed to decay and destruction—but not yet, by any means—and will one day give place to universal Communism, the world has so developed during past decades that it is no longer necessary to postulate violence and civil war and bloody revolution; the grand apotheosis in some cases may be reached by peaceful means, even by such pedestrian operations as the winning of parliamentary majorities.

There has been a great deal of speculation in the West as to what precisely Mr. Khrushchev meant by this. Which countries, as he saw it, might achieve their transformation peacefully; which, on the other hand, were still condemned to civil war and violence? I can think of nothing more indicative of the positive idiocy of the Western attitude to the Soviet Union than the raising of this sort of question. For it is as clear as daylight that Mr. Khrushchev himself does not know. All he and the higher leadership were doing in making these highly dramatic revisions of the Leninist gospel was casting off their own chains. So long as they believed, dogmatically, in the inevitability of war and the inevitability of violent revolution everywhere, they were held in a grip of iron and had no freedom of either manœuvre or thought. The shackles are now struck off. They can begin to think and to adapt their thoughts and actions to the changing realities of life. They can now express any action and any thought, however unorthodox, in terms of Leninist doctrine, the revised Leninist doctrine. And they need that doctrine absolutely. Without it they are nothing.

My own view, in essence, is that the present Leninist revival has been engineered by the new leaders not because they, in whole or in part, have been seized by a return of Lenin's revolutionary zeal but, very largely, to provide themselves, and the party they lead, with an authority which they lacked after Stalin's death, and without which they cannot rule.

I first put this view forward, tentatively, when Mr. Khrushchev was preparing to take over the leadership from Mr. Malenkov, with a sustained blast of Leninist fanfare. I returned to it less tentatively after the Geneva Conference. When I was at last allowed to revisit the Soviet Union, after an interval of eight years, everything I saw and heard confirmed this view so completely that it no longer seemed worth arguing about. It has, however, been so sharply attacked since then that the only thing to do is summarize the train of thought leading up to it.

The first question, in the late autumn of 1954, was why a man like Mr. Khrushchev, whose whole career had been distinguished by his qualities as a man of action, who was above all an extrovert and a practical leader and commander of men, should suddenly, in late middle age, take to political theory. Was it because he had undergone a sudden conversion, or did he find in the revival of Leninism a necessary weapon for his own purposes? The first made nonsense: Mr. Khrushchev was clearly the same old overbearing Khrushchev of the Ukraine, who enjoyed knocking people's heads together and teaching grandmothers how to suck eggs (a cherished memory of the celebrated Yugoslav tour is the expression on Marshal Bulganin's face when, in a factory somewhere, Mr. Khrushchev insisted on telling him—him, of all people!—all about the properties of reinforced concrete). The second seemed most likely. What, then, were the purposes for which he needed this particular weapon? It was not that Mr. Khrushchev himself was talking Leninism, except incidentally; what was happening was that the Party journals, at the time of Mr. Khrushchev's ascent, were filled with Leninist discussion, very far removed from the bleak "You ask, I'll tell you" technique of Communist journalism under Stalin. At the same time known Leninist ideologues, such as Mr. Suslov, were being given more prominence, and Mr. Khrushchev had beckoned to his side, and considerably exalted, Mr. Shepilov, then editor-in-chief of *Pravda*, noted for the ardour of his faith in Leninist ideals—and, according to Moscow gossip, in danger of spoiling his career because of it.

What was it all about?

It was clear by that time that some sort of collective leadership had come to stay—for as long as the most interested parties could keep it going. But who were these men who formed the highest collective? Where was their authority? How could they justify their claim to govern this vast and productive land—a land, moreover, very much on the upsurge, to use their horrible favourite word, a land that was producing natural leaders of all kinds, in the Party itself, in the Armed Services, in industry, in the professions. There had been a time when the individuals who featured in the previous chapter were the natural pretenders to power, the country was so short of strong men and born leaders. But that time was long past; the Soviet Union was now swarming with men of first-class ability, and for years, as far as the man in the street could gather, the men who took over from Stalin had been nothing more than the satraps and watch-dogs of a universal genius. Why should they take over when the genius had gone? Why should men as good, perhaps better, be kept out? Lenin was Lenin: a great man whether you liked him or not, a great man, moreover, who was prepared to discuss and argue with his colleagues. Stalin was Stalin: a great man whom nobody liked, a great man strong enough to impose his own personal rule, by sheer force of character and skill in management operating over a long period. Now he had gone, and what was left? The Party, of course. But what was the Party? In Lenin's day it had counted for something; but under Stalin it had become the private body-guard of an absolute ruler. Stalin had derived nothing from the Party; the Party derived everything from Stalin, and owed its existence to him. The only authority Stalin's successors could claim was a Communist Party that owed the whole of its own authority to a dead dictator and was meaningless apart from him. No single individual, neither Malenkov nor Khrushchev nor Bulganin, was strong enough and great enough to impose his will *immediately* upon his colleagues and the country at large (even Stalin had not been strong enough to do that). Where, then, was authority to come from?

There were a number of possible answers. Beria, as we have seen, had physical authority. He had the police, who formed a state within a state. Given a free hand he could have imposed a new terror, reposing his authority in his detested cohorts. Zhukov, the popular war leader, given a free hand, could have imposed a military dictatorship, reposing his authority in the armed might of the Soviet Union. But for very good reasons neither of these was given a free hand, and even if either aspired to a *coup d'état*, they cancelled each other out. The new collective remained, the circle of Stalin's closest colleagues, who, quite evidently, were glad to see the great man gone and were determined, for good reasons and bad, to maintain their commanding positions.

What were they to do?

The first thing they did, in the excitement of the moment, was regularize their position by making a great parade of the constitutional government. For there is a constitutional government in the Soviet Union, which existed like a shadow all through the Stalin era: the Supreme Soviet of the USSR with its Presidium and its Council of Ministers; the chairman of the Presidium of the Supreme Soviet is sometimes known as the president of the Soviet Union, the chairman of the Council of Ministers as the prime minister. In those first days the Supreme Soviet was made much of. The nondescript Mr. Shvernik was removed from the presidency and replaced by the more glamorous and commanding figure of Marshal Voroshilov, while Mr. Malenkov was elevated to the premiership—Malenkov, who had spent his whole career in the Party apparatus, scorning the Supreme Soviet for what it was, an empty sham, suddenly found it desirable to abandon the Party and hoist his flag as head of the constitutional government. There was only one possible explanation for this manœuvre. Stalin's heirs, Malenkov foremost among them, needed a constitutional base if they were to continue as before; and the Council of Ministers was the answer.

But only for a time, for the Supreme Soviet with its Council of Ministers enshrined no idea. It was a revered institution, but it was not an authority. It had been created and lent authority by the Communist Party under Lenin. It stood for nothing in its own right. It had either to continue as the administrative arm of the highest organs of the Party or transform itself into a truly constitutional authority, open through honest elections to all comers.

And so, if the leaders wanted to retain their power, the only source of authority had to be the Communist Party which had had its authority drained from it by the late dictator. That authority had to be restored, and quickly. There was only one way of doing that, and that was to go to its original source, to Lenin. But Lenin was more than a name; he was also a body of doctrine. He was a church. The doctrine had to be revitalized, and it was.

When I got back from Moscow in the autumn of 1955, which was after Mr. Khrushchev had started booming away about the doom of capitalism, I wrote these words, which seemed to me quite incontrovertible:

The new collective is reverting much more to the Leninist pattern. The Party is the spearhead and the guide; the Council of Ministers is the administration; the Army is the sword and shield of the administration; the security forces and the police are its servants.

Where there is no God, no Tsar, no dictator, how can a society find its strength and its focus except through institutions? Stalin made hay of all Soviet institutions. His successors, not one of them able (or, if able, permitted) to emulate Stalin, must revive them and strengthen them because they have nowhere else to turn for support. . . . It is this urgent need to revive and reshape institutions which, I think, is responsible for the revitalization of the Party under Khrushchev, rather than the revival of militant Communism as a belligerent force.

That argument, which seemed, and seems, to me self-evident, was violently contested, to my surprise. And that is why I have given at such length the train of thought that lay behind it.

It was not, as I see it, invalidated by Mr. Khrushchev's booming away all over India and Burma about the inevitable collapse of capitalism and the iniquities of the colonists. He had started doing that even while I was in Moscow. In the course of a banquet to Dr. Adenauer he announced in my hearing and in a perfectly off-hand way that of course the Western system was heading for the rocks, though it had some life in it yet. A week later he formalized that view in a speech at a reception for the East German premier, Herr Grotewohl. And after that came India and Burma and Afghanistan, where he harped away at the same old theme for weeks on end.

What else could he do? How else was he to justify his existence, not only to the people of the Soviet Union but also to Communists everywhere, and particularly in China? For China is ever in the minds of the present rulers of the Soviet Union. It will be shown one day, I believe, that the celebrated Indian tour was addressed far more directly to China than to the West. I have no doubt at all that Mr. Khrushchev and Marshal Bulganin derived a great deal of simple enjoyment from prancing about all over the late possessions of the British, from being cheered by immense and reverential crowds, lately the subjects of the imperial crown, from generally thumbing their noses at the expired pretensions of the British Raj with nobody to say them nay. Who, in their position, would not have experienced a certain mild delight? But the real and serious purpose of that whole operation had to do with China. Communist China has pretensions to the leadership of Asia, and any idea that the Soviet leadership regards these pretensions with favour is absurd. The Indian jamboree showed the world in general that Russia was very much on the move and could not be kept out of any part of the uncommitted world; but, even more to the point, it showed Mao Tse-tung that the Kremlin had no intention of regarding Asia, outside the Soviet Union, as his exclusive province. There is no record of what the Chinese Communists think when they hear the Soviet leaders freely offering to Indians and Egyptians steel and plant and machines which they so desperately need for themselves.

This is not a study of Soviet foreign policy, least of all of Sino-Russian relations. But in any attempt to expose those facts of life which condition the general attitude and conduct of the Soviet leadership it would be absurd to leave out China, which is one of the largest of those facts, and the existence of which, I believe, is one of the main reasons for the Leninist revival in the Soviet Union. The Soviet Union is a vast and under-populated country facing, across a long frontier, a China which is already over-populated, which already contains six hundred million-odd compared with the Soviet Union's two hundred million-odd, and which is expanding at a very fast rate. The Soviet Union does not control China, and when Stalin died Mao Tse-tung had many claims to be the senior leader of the Communist world. China depends on the Soviet Union to carry out her own industrial revolution, and in many ways it is in the interest of the Kremlin to help her in this, at least on the short view. But in many other ways it is not. The idea of an independent and strong China was for decades an occupational nightmare of Tsarist foreign ministers, who went to remarkable and ingenious pains to prevent its becoming reality. The new leadership has inherited that nightmare in a far more complicated version, and one has only to start talking to Russians of the more intelligent and forthcoming kind about the state of their country's relations with China, and to see how they shy away from that subject, to understand that it is not only the countries of the decadent West that have their worries and fatal contradictions, and that success, too, has its thorns.

One way, perhaps the only way, in which Mr. Khrushchev and his colleagues can keep their end up *vis-à-vis* the Chinese leaders is to reassert their seniority as the standard-bearers of Leninism— to say nothing of their unique position as the first country actually to achieve Socialism. It was no doubt with this last in mind that poor Mr. Molotov was made to recant a speech which, viewed through jealous eyes, might have been taken to mean that the Soviet Union had not yet got that far.

The Leninist revival, then, cannot be seen as a proof that the new leadership has suddenly acquired a revolutionary afflatus. It cannot be seen as a proof of anything at all—except that they stood in dire need of an authority beyond themselves in the shelter of which they could stand and maintain their own positions. To discover what the new leadership really believes, if it is discoverable at all, we have to look elsewhere, and far beyond Mr. Khrushchev's prophecies of doom. Western statesmen are always asking the Soviet leaders for deeds and not words; but when they get the deeds they don't like them, and they persist in paying exaggerated attention to the words when they are inimical and discounting them when they are kind. The Communists have themselves to blame for this, double-talk has for so long been their chosen and Lenin-consecrated weapon. But that does not absolve us from the duty of employing rather more discrimination than we do. For example: Stalin was perpetually in the doghouse because he was tough and uncompromising and rude, because his policies were rigid and offensive, because he denied all possibility of communication between East and West. So long as he kept up that sort of attitude, it was said, there was no hope for the world. He kept it up until he died. His successors, warming up slowly, reversed this attitude. They spoke gentle words, they showed a desire to accommodate, they smiled, and they went as far as deeds: they evacuated Austria, which, for so long, the West had begged them to do as an earnest of good intentions; they apologized to Marshal Tito; they came to Geneva. And what was the reaction? It was one of simple horror—and they too were put in the dog-house, not for being tough and rigid and impolite, but for being gentle and flexible and comparatively well-mannered. This is called trying to have things both ways, which really cannot be done with any lasting benefit to anyone. And then, to complicate matters further, after all the shouting about the false benevolence at Geneva, the moment Mr. Khrushchev started speaking of the West in terms that nobody could call benevolent, there came more shouts of outrage and dismay. Could anything be more tedious? Could anything be farther from a serious attempt to discover what is really going on inside the Soviet Union?

What is going on, or some of it, is what I have tried to describe in this book. And if the effect is one of confusion, then I have done what I set out to do. Because Russia is in ferment, and nobody in the world can tell what shape her society or her policies will gradually assume as the ferment subsides. The new leadership is not operating in a vacuum. It is bound up inextricably with the vast and polyglot land, now on the threshold of the final and transforming stage of its industrial revolution, which it is trying to govern.

If they knewe their strength no man were able to make match with them, nor they that dwel neare them should have any rest of them. But I think it is not God's will: For I may compare them to a young horse that knoweth not his strengthe, whom a little child ruleth and guideth with a bridle, for all his great strength: for if he did, neither child nor man could rule him.

Thus Richard Chancellor, the English merchant adventurer, who opened English trade with Russia, by way of Archangel, in the days of Ivan the Terrible, in 1563. He was writing of Russia as a power, and his words have come true. But there is another side to it, one which now, I think, must be ever in the minds of the Soviet leaders: the strength that Russia has found has come from the people of the Soviet Union. Lenin and Stalin were the first to see that strength and to exploit it. But there are many signs that now the people are discovering it for themselves.

The Polish expatriate Joseph Conrad was another prophet who foresaw great changes. Writing before the Revolution, he had this to say:

> . . . the coming events of her internal changes, however appalling they may be in their magnitude, will be nothing more impressive than the convulsions of a colossal body. Her soul, kept benumbed by her temporal and spiritual master with the passion of tyranny and superstition, will find itself on awakening possessing no language, a monstrous full-grown child having first to learn the ways of living and articulate speech. It is safe to say that tyranny, assuming a thousand protean shapes, will remain clinging to her struggles for a long time before her blind multitudes succeed at last in trampling it out of existence under their millions of bare feet.

Conrad was right, and at the same time I think he was wrong. He was right about the persistence of tyranny once the Tsar was overthrown; but I think he was wrong in his implication that there would have to be further revolutions against further tyrannies. He hated the Russians, who had exiled his father to the forests of Vologda and caused his mother's death. Or perhaps he meant only that it would be a long time before the growing consciousness and education of the inarticulate masses would be strong enough to impose decisive limitations on the traditional arbitrariness of their rulers. If he meant that, then I think he was right all along the line. Because that, it seems to me, is what is beginning to happen now.

Increasingly as I approach the end of this book I am aware of a sense of dissatisfaction when I write of the leaders—of Khrushchev, of Bulganin, of Malenkov, of Molotov, of Kaganovich, of Mikoyan, of Voroshilov, of all the old stale names. They begin to smell old-fashioned. They have held the stage too long. And I find myself thinking more and more of the phalanxes of younger men, with names unknown in the West, who stand behind them: the highly capable Party chieftains, virtual governors of areas the size of Germany; the great industrialists, who control the huge trusts and are individually responsible for turning out each year more steel, more coal, more oil, more this and more that than the combined tycoons of Western Europe; the great soldiers who command the largest standing army in the history

of the world; and behind them, rank on rank of brilliantly accomplished assistants—administrators, engineers, scientists, professional men of all kinds, artists of all kinds. And I reflect on the
tremendous, the irresistible pressures generated by these men,
who think in terms not of world revolution but of making the
Soviet Union into a prosperous and worthy country—pressures
bearing from every direction on the supreme leadership, not only
from outside the Party but also from within. And behind them
the other two hundred million, whose moods, preoccupations,
attitudes, and activities I have tried in something of their multifarious confusion to convey: the dark, resisting peasant side by
side with the enthusiastic young kolkhoznik, grooming cows to
take to Moscow for the great and wonderful exhibition; the old
women with their spells, their primitive religion, their hatred
of all things new, side by side with their dedicated daughters,
sacrificing themselves to bring drains and serum and light to
medieval villages; the hooligans and the speculators side by side
with steady-going workmen who take a pride in their skills; the
stilyagi in their flashy and inarticulate gestures of protest side by
side with the solemn young Komsomols and Komsomolkas dedicated, without knowing it, to clearing up in the name of Communism the mess that Stalin made—in the name of Communism;
the factory managers, honest and corrupt, killing themselves to
fulfil their plans, for the greater glory of the Soviet Union, or
scheming away to fake their plans, for the greater glory of themselves; the lucky scientists, who find the world laid out for their
pleasure and glory in their opportunities, and the unlucky scientists, who find themselves thwarted by obscurantism in the guise
of progress. All these people, and many more besides, are beginning to count for something, and the higher leadership knows it.

Let there be no mistake. Khrushchev means what he says when
he declares that the capitalist system is doomed. And of course he
is right. One does not have to be a Russian Marxist to know that:
there is nothing original about it. "There is nothing sacred or
final about the Joint Stock Company system," wrote Lord Milner,
to go no farther afield. "It has its place, no doubt, and performs
a useful function in our present state of economic development.
But no extraordinary power of imagination is required to picture

a future in which we could get on without it." Lord Milner knew all about Marx before Khrushchev was born, and after careful thought rejected him. He also wrote at some length about the idea of labour hiring capital, instead of vice versa. "The idea is neither novel nor revolutionary. It is as old as the hills. What is new, or at least modern, a product of the Industrial Revolution, is the divorce of those actually engaged in productive work from the ownership and control of the materials and instruments of production. At a certain stage of industrial development that divorce becomes inevitable, but it does not follow that we should necessarily regard it as permanent. It is surely conceivable, as it is in every respect to be desired, that the people actually engaged in any industry should themselves be its capitalists, or, in so far as they should need the assistance of external capital, should pay for the use of it, without becoming subject to the control of its possessors."

So much for the "arch-imperialist." Mr. Khrushchev has nothing on Lord Milner, but that is not quite what he means. After all, he is a Marxist, and he expects the rejection of capitalism to be carried out in proper Marxist order. Or does he?

The rejection of the Leninist thesis of the inevitability of war, though plainly carried out under pressure from the hydrogen bomb, and the rejection of the thesis of the inevitability of violent revolution leave the Soviet leadership with a very wide field for manoeuvre and adaptation. For the time being we must assume that the Kremlin is eager and anxious for the destruction of existing Western systems in the preordained manner, and takes precautions accordingly. But we should also keep an open mind.

Russia will always be Socialist in some shape or form, but not necessarily in the Marxist form; communal effort, the subordination of the individual to society, is in the Russians' blood; but the Marxist interpretation of history is something added. Russia will always be messianic, seeking to convert the world to its own way of thought by whatever means come to hand. And the Russians, as people, will continue to combine bleak and shameless cynicism with boundless freedom of mind and imagination. Russia, as far as anyone can see ahead, will always be a problem. The celerity and the virtuosity with which its leaders, having assured themselves at Geneva that they need not fear atomic aggression from the West, turned to the exploitation in their own immediate interests of a dangerous situation in the Middle East gives the measure of that. But Russia will not always be the same problem, and we shall have to show more alertness than hitherto if we want to keep abreast of the problem of the moment.

14. SUNSHINE IN KIEV

SCHOOL was finished for the day, and the broad pavements under the trees were alive with children. Groups of serious little girls, groups of giggling little girls, all very neat at the end of the day's work, chattered their way home quite purposefully. Nearly everyone had her hair drawn back from the forehead and secured and ornamented with a black bow, worn rather high; and all wore black uniform cross-over aprons with cape-like shoulders of an almost frivolously elegant cut, so different from anything else in the Soviet Union. They had bare legs and sound shoes, and they were happy and well. The very small children, clutching the hands of mothers or grandmothers fetching them from nursery school, wide-eyed and toddling, were chubby to the bursting point. A number of these were rather marvellously dressed in little overcoats of magenta plush; at some time, a year or two ago, the clothing shops of the town had evidently been flooded with a job lot of this unpromising material, and a number of mothers had had the same idea. But only infants were dressed like this.

As for the small boys, as everywhere they moved about in gangs, all neatly dressed, some in the uniforms of special schools. About their home-going there was no purposefulness. They were, in fact, in the seventh heaven of delight, because the spiked horse-chestnuts were almost ready—though not quite—to split open and fall, spilling from cradles of white velvet the visions of transcendent glossiness which in England are called conkers. The little boys could not wait for them to fall; and to the constant peril of passers-by they competed, hurling treasured bits of wood (remarkably heavy) into the tree-tops to bring the conkers prematurely down; what they got was mostly leaves. Nobody took much notice. There were no policemen about. And only once in a while an irate citizen, after a narrow escape from being stunned, would call out angrily or make threatening gestures, waiting for a moment to see if the offenders would desist—which they did, until the grown-up turned his back and plodded on. In the smoking late September sunlight, with the damp air of the river holding the odour of decaying leaves, and the shouts of delight sounding sharp and small and without an echo, it was a street scene from any town in the world where horse-chestnuts grow. In fact it was Korolenko Street in the city of Kiev, until four years ago a forbidden city. The river, far below at the foot of the dizzy cliff, was the Dnieper.

Korolenko Street leads to the very edge of the cliff. There, on a terrace cut into the rock, stands the flaunting baroque church of St. Andrew, one of the masterpieces of the Italian Rastrelli, who, with his palaces and belfries, brought the exuberance of the South to Catherine's Russia. (The belfry at Zagorsk, with its wild, barbaric racket, is by Rastrelli.) On the steps leading up to the church old women with white head-scarves rested in the last of the sunlight. From the terrace itself the view was open to all Russia; but already the night was advancing from the East, so that the monstrous plain merged darkly with the sky, like the sea on a day when there is no clear-cut horizon. But the great river below was in full light, the extraordinary waterway that took the Vikings from the Baltic to the Black Sea, and by which, against the current, Christianity travelled from Constantinople back to Kiev, whence it spread like a shallow sea over the plain.

Kiev stands on a high bluff of heavily wooded rock; but, as with all the great rivers of Russia, which run north and south, while the west bank is steep, the east bank is low. And across the river from the sheds and wharves and factories built at the foot of the cliff there is nothing but an expanse of sand, flooded in winter, dotted now with bright blue kiosks and bathing-huts, reaching back into flats which are a tangle of lost channels and reed beds and water meadows, swelling imperceptibly, becoming imperceptibly drier, until the world of water has given place to the world of steppe. Closer below, reached by the steep cobbled street called St. Andrew's Descent, lie the port and the working town, the Podol, which was also the Jewish quarter. As one looks away over the tangle of mean streets and factories, less than a mile away, the barren surface of the strange but characteristic sandy hillocks, seamed with innumerable ravines, on the northern outskirts of the city gleamingly suggests a lunar landscape.

It was there, within sound of the city traffic, that on the last two days of September in 1941, 33,771 Jews, who had been rounded up for "resettlement" three days earlier, were massacred by an extermination squad commanded by a disgraced architect from Cologne, then an ornament of the SS, Colonel Paul Blobel. The position of the Babi Yar, the Babi Ravine, can be seen quite clearly from St. Andrew's Church on its terrace in the heart of the city; and in the late afternoon sunlight, with the children dawdling home from school and the old women sunning themselves, it required a violent effort of the imagination to transport oneself fourteen years back to that scene of desolation and horror, when more than 30,000 men, women, and children, rounded up like sheep, were lined up along the edge of pits sixty yards long and eight feet deep, and shot, rank after rank, the still living trampling on the bodies of the dead.

Soon the snows of winter came to cover Babi Yar with its barely conceivable burden. But in March of the following year a Gestapo officer, who had come to inquire into the state of religion in the Ukraine, found himself driving with SS Colonel Blobel out to the country villa of Major General Thomas, the Commander of the German Security Police in Kiev. And as they passed Babi Yar he remarked on a strange phenomenon. There were repeated small explosions, which threw up little columns of earth. "Here my Jews are buried," Blobel proudly explained. What was happening was that the thaw had released the gases from those thousands of decomposing bodies. But even that was not the end, for in June of that same year this remarkable butcher (he had plenty of rivals in White Russia and the Ukraine) was required by Heydrich, who himself had only a few weeks to live, to remove all traces of his mass burials for fear of a German retreat. So the bodies at Babi Yar were dug up and soaked with petrol and burned. It requires, as I have said, a violent effort of the imagination even to believe in these things, looking out over the dreamlike landscape fourteen years later, almost to the day; but it seems to me a desirable effort.

Time and again in these pages I have referred, without dwelling on them, to the cruel and outrageous actions committed by the Russians under Stalin. For more than twenty years, broken only by the German occupation, it was Stalin who was the scourge of the Ukraine, one of his main instruments being none other than Nikita Khrushchev, who is not loved by the Ukrainians. But at no time anywhere have Russians anything to compare with the concentration of calculated villainy practised by the Germans, who have forfeited the right to speak of Russian barbarism. They have, moreover (and this is far more serious), irredeemably betrayed what we like to think of as Western civilization, because they have made it impossible for the West, so long as Germany is considered a part of it, to maintain any just pretension to superiority over a historically backward people.

I shall not dwell on the inhumanity of Russians to Russians—and Ukrainians. There is little chance that anyone in the West will forget that. And everybody knows that Kiev, as the capital of the Ukraine, has known more than its share. Today that inhumanity is muted; and, watching the children so blissful in the autumn sunshine, I found myself thinking for the first time that they had a chance of a better life.

The children of the Soviet Union are always enchanting and gay, quietly and gravely gay and more formal in their attitudes than English or American children. They are always spoiled. During the war when mothers and babushkas were starving in the cities, often to death, and dressed in shapeless rags, the children were invariably bouncing and pink-cheeked, and warm. The young girls and boys are eager and full of curiosity and hope. It used to be the saddest sight in the world to see these graceful, irrepressible youngsters with their belief that heaven lay round the corner, their passionate faith in Soviet glory, and to know that in a very few years' time they would be reduced to apathy and constant wariness and near-exhaustion by the dreary and degrading battle for survival. That much used to be certain. But on this afternoon in Kiev I no longer felt this certainty. I felt hope: more hope, indeed, than most of the fathers and mothers of these children, who had already known too much of disillusionment, would, I think, permit themselves to indulge in.

I had come to Kiev from Moscow, and I was glad to be away, for Moscow is too big, and at the same time too uncharacteristic, to base a firm judgment on. One wouldn't think it to look at it, but Soviet Moscow is the one city in the world whose streets are really paved with gold; the Soviet citizen who can get a foothold in Moscow is all right—so long as he can keep it and stay ablebodied. This is more than can be said of any other city in the Soviet Union. Moscow has everything, food and clothes and television, electric gadgets, theatres, motor cars and bright lights. It is no wonder that it finds itself the most chronically overcrowded city in Europe with, always crammed into it, several million people who have no right to be there. They prefer Moscow—even if it means a sixth share of a room, even if it means making themselves vulnerable to the political police—to anywhere else in the Soviet Union. They know that so long as there is any food and clothing to be had in the Soviet Union they will get it in Moscow.

But this idea is already becoming old-fashioned. The Soviet Union, as I have tried to show, is by no means so hard up as it was; and there are now other cities that can guarantee survival to those fortunate enough to live in them. Kiev is one of them. But only six years ago, when Moscow was already regilded and repainted after the fearful attrition of the war years, when, although life was desperately hard, the people of Moscow somehow managed to eat, when the shops in Petrovka and Gorki Streets were sufficiently well filled to enrapture delegations from the West, Kiev, with the whole of the Ukraine, was deep in famine; and it was not until 1951 that this lovely and most ancient monument was considered fit for foreigners to see. The memory of the hard years is still very much alive in Kiev—which itself to lesser towns, where the hard years are still in being, is as Moscow to Kiev. My own memories of the Soviet Union are almost wholly of the hard years: the dreadful first years of the war, and the cruel years afterward when Stalin elected to mobilize Russia against the world instead of allowing her to lick her wounds in peace—and, on top of that, in 1946 found himself forced to cope with the worst drought and crop failure since 1891, the year of Tolstoy's "Hunger"; worse even than the appalling summer of 1922, which nearly broke the Revolution. In Moscow now it is difficult to remember those hard times, the place is so slicked up, and life, except for the poorer workers, so comparatively easy and rich. In Kiev is it easier to remember.

The city is full of peasants. It is a city of markets. In Moscow you can live on Intourist for a month, perhaps for a year, and never see one of the great kolkhoz markets, where prices find their true level and reflect the realities of life. But in Kiev they form an inescapable part of the urban landscape. I am not thinking of the huge Bessarabian Market, the pre-revolutionary covered market at the end of the Kreshchatok, the most famous market in the old Russian Empire. That still goes strong under state control. I am thinking rather of the kolkhoz markets, those wide, bare spaces enclosed by sagging wooden fences, their green paint faded, where the peasants come to sell their surplus produce. There is one quite close to the Bessarabian Market, another near the railway station. And at any time of day the streets of the city are full of peasant women, mostly old and wrinkled, short-skirted above thick, grey-stockinged legs, bulked out with shawls, doing their shopping, or resting, with their baskets, on the curb. These are not far from the hard years, and their shopping is still not easy.

Just off the main shopping centre there stands the cream-coloured opera house, modest and charmingly proportioned. It was here in 1911, at a gala performance, that the reforming prime minister Stolypin, who tried vainly to save the Romanovs from the deluge, was shot and fatally wounded by the Social Revolutionary, Bagrov. The Opera, which was at one time named after Karl Liebknecht, faces Korolenko Street, set back from the chestnut avenue, and fronted with a formal garden. At night it is a palace of splendour and light. Just behind it is one of Kiev's larger food shops; and one evening, moving round the corner from the flood-lit façade, I found outside the food shop a monstrous queue, stretching into the darkness for many yards, patient and scarcely murmuring. The queue consisted chiefly of peasant women who had sold their produce in the kolkhoz market and had a little money. They were queuing to buy sugar—or, rather, for tickets entitling them to queue to buy sugar. Moscow had plenty of sugar, but in Kiev it was short, as it had been for a long time past. This was September 1955. And Kiev, for those who do not know, is still, as it was before the Revolution, the centre of the sugar-beet industry; and some of those old women who now queued in the darkness under the eyes of the police, while, ten yards off, unheard, Rhadames celebrated his undying love for Aida, had themselves weeded and singled the interminable fields of pallid roots.

Russia is not the only place in the world where this sort of thing happens. But it has to be recorded because Russia is the only place where the government pretends it does not happen: there was no shortage of sugar in the Soviet Union, not in Kiev or anywhere else, I was assured by a bland official the morning after.

But although, as I have said, the hard years are close enough to be more than a nightmare memory, progress has been very great. And although I could not find a Russian or a Ukrainian (officials apart) to admit that life was anything like as easy as it had been in 1940, which was not saying much, Kiev, even more than Moscow, impressed me with the feeling that Soviet society had at last got up steam and was moving now with a considerable momentum behind it, which would carry it through any bad times that lay ahead. I am not one of those who look forward to another Russian revolution. I do not believe that any foreigner who has a genuine affection for the Soviet people can wish them any such thing. They have had enough. At one time, during the last years of Stalin, I did not see how their society could ever be radically changed without violence; and yet it clearly had to be changed. But now, as I have tried to show in these pages, I think that society is settling down into a long spell of more or less steady evolution. I think Soviet society has grown stronger than the men who helped Stalin to fashion it; that these are no longer in absolute control and, to keep their power, are being compelled to move with the times. If Soviet society consisted entirely of town dwellers I should be quite sure of this. But there is still the dark peasant, neglected for too long. It is only the resistance of the peasant that could now force the government to reassert itself intolerably and produce a situation which could be ended only by violence. And for the time being no shadow of this peril has touched the people in the great towns, who are satisfied with the way things seem to be moving, though apt to be jumpy and impatient because the movement is so slow. Nor, I think, are the peasants yet apprehensive. They are still enjoying the benefits of some remarkable concessions, and, in spite of certain warning signs, I do not think it has yet occurred to them that they are simply not producing the food the concessions were designed to secure.

All this is in parentheses. It is to emphasize again the point I tried to make earlier: that if evolution has to give way to revolution once again it will not be because of the secret police or because of discontent in the great towns (discontent in the smaller, neglected towns is another matter, and counts for next to nothing). It will be because the present rulers of the Soviet Union will have proved incapable of fitting the peasants into the Soviet economy and lifting them up from the mud.

In the cities, in Kiev as well as in Moscow, one is not conscious of this. One is conscious only of an immense effort of construction, which seems to be succeeding. A few years ago the Kreshcha-tok, the grand main thoroughfare running in the valley between the cliff and the hills beyond, was totally destroyed. Now it is rebuilt—not in any makeshift manner, but on a monumental scale, designed to last. The effect to my mind is the last word in monumental hideousness; but some foreigners and almost all Ukrainians think it simply splendid. The drive behind this re-building is, however, quite unmistakably, the sort of drive that produced the early sky-scrapers of New York, the Crystal Palace, and the railway-station architecture of Britain. And one reflects a little sadly on the iron law of nature which sees to it that the overweening confidence engendered by the first heady successes of an industrial revolution always coincides with a general col-lapse of taste. The inhabitants of Kiev are hugely proud of their new buildings, as well they may be; but among the children drifting home from school there are some who before they die will wonder what possessed their fathers and wish for those too,

too solid fantasies to melt, and give them the chance to build all over again. For them Mr. Khrushchev's edict, demanding less extravagant nonsense and more decent functionalism in building, came too late.

The follies are there, and with them many new blocks of flats of more sensible construction, and solider too, than the average Moscow blocks for workers. And above the new buildings hangs the spidery mast of Kiev Television. There are also new restaurants, pleasant open-air summer restaurants perched among the brilliantly landscaped cliff-top gardens, looking out across the gleaming river and the breath-taking view; the smart Dynamo Restaurant, deep in its park, with imposing staircases and a less imposing dance-band. These are always full, and the people who frequent them give the outsider a sharp insight into the way the new Soviet society is developing, and particularly into the strength and weight of the increasing numbers who, quite unconcerned with politics and contemptuous of politicians, nevertheless have a positive vested interest in the *status quo*—that is to say, in the Soviet state as it is today, in the Soviet system.

If one goes to a different restaurant each day and keeps one's eyes open one is first struck by the frequency with which one sees the same faces. On the airplane from Moscow to Kiev (which, characteristically, was much smarter and more comfortable than the one from Leningrad to Moscow, used chiefly by foreigners) there were several very prosperous individuals, who had the air of businessmen rather than of Party officials. There were seven or eight of them, and I kept on running into them again and again, singly and in pairs, in the more expensive restaurants of Kiev. I found out who some of them were. And, in fact, although they were officials of a kind, they were much closer in temperament and activity to the Western tycoon, or senior salesman, than to anything out of a Leninist text-book. One, who looked merriest of all, was a well-known tolkach, or fixer, the life and soul of every party, who lived in a perpetual haze of Soviet champagne. He was on the books of an extremely well-known trust, but in fact he worked on commission, and was evidently a notorious and well-liked go-between. All this I got from a friendly waitress in one of the restaurants, who thought of him as a favourite customer, always ready with a joke and a smile. The rest were bona-fide officials of this or that ministry or trust, travelling round on what is known as a *kommandirovka*—sent out from headquarters on tours of inspection, and enjoying life on a liberal expense account. One of these, with a local friend, had got himself into a state of advanced intoxication in one of the smarter restaurants and was making fairly advanced passes at the waitresses, who, while they kept him in his place, were nevertheless a good deal more tolerant than they would have been with other customers. When he had staggered out, guided by his slightly sheepish companion, I asked one of the waitresses who he was. "Oh!" she replied, "he's an old friend. We know all about him! He's high up in the trust that runs this restaurant."

There were plenty like him; and there were plenty of more sober executives, all with very sizable stakes in the regime.

Then, of course, the Army. In every restaurant there are always soldiers in uniform; and, among these, I was struck again and again by the emergence of a new type of subaltern: very smart, consciously elegant; and clearly modelled in hair-cut, carriage, general turn-out, and expression—a kind of languid, moody insolence—on the pictures of subalterns of the Imperial Guards at the turn of the century.

Then the intelligentsia, in Kiev represented mainly by the actors and actresses from the State Theatre, and the children of professional men and university professors, trying very hard, and sometimes succeeding, to look very smart and copy Western dances. The younger generation of this stratum merged imperceptibly into the stilyag.

There are also sober citizens—decent workers, decent small officials, enjoying a rare night out—and dressed like workers and small officials. They enjoy their night out. They too have a stake in society. And into the middle of this interesting public—the types who go to expensive restaurants because they have money to spend and all too little to buy; the types who go as a conscious extravagance and are magnificently oblivious of the incongruity of their horny hands and shabby clothes with these scenes of elegance—there will suddenly erupt something very remarkable indeed: a group of cheerful and healthy youths encased from top to toe in sky-blue siren suits, or rompers, wearing on their feet the sort of boots that boxers wear in the ring. Each has a girl with him, neatly and conventionally dressed. They are cheerful and talkative and gay, settle down with much chaff at a reserved corner table, and proceed to order a colossal meal. "Who," I asked the waitress, accustomed by now to being treated as a sort of perambulating *Who's Who* of Kiev society—"Who on earth are they?" "Oh those," she replied, with a fond look at the young men. "Those are our Physiculturalists. Thursday is their night." They too, these privileged youngsters, athletes and gymnasts, who spend their Thursday evenings in the splendid municipal gymnasium, and then come on, dressed for the horizontal bar, to a smart restaurant for supper with their girls—they too have a stake in the regime.

This is not the whole of Kiev society. But it is an important part. It is certainly not revolutionary, and I do not think it is counter-revolutionary either, though I may be wrong. Discontented often, grumbling always, yes. But there is a deep gulf between discontent and grumbling on the one hand and active revolt on the other.

This is not the whole of Kiev society. The people with the biggest vested interests are not seen. They do not go to restaurants. They do not queue in the big stores. They live in large flats in the most modern block (that means three or four rooms to a family), and they have villas in the country outside, like the one requisitioned by SS Major General Thomas in the days when the spring thaw released the gases from the corpses buried in the Babi Yar ravine. They are the new ruling class, and their relatives. They cluster in the shadow of Mr. Khrushchev's successor as the party secretary of the Ukraine, the young and forceful Kirichenko, already one of the eleven members of the All Union Party Presidium, who lives the life of a potentate (which, as far as Kiev is concerned, he is), with an immense and luxurious establishment and a garage like a royal mews. The ministers of the Ukrainian Government, the Party chieftains, the senior officers of the services, the chiefs of police in their palace among the trees on the hill—all these and their wives and children do not appear in public (nor for that matter do the cream of the intelligentsia).

As in Moscow, they live to themselves in their own society. As in
Moscow, they have had to work hard for their positions, and all
may consider themselves lucky to be where they are, the survivors
of innumerable purges. As in Moscow, they are still vulnerable
as individuals, but no longer, I think, as a group. It is customary
to say that they could be swept away in a night if there were a
sudden turn for the worse, if the men in the Moscow Kremlin,
if Khrushchev, decided to change the line, to assert themselves,
to start filling the labour camps instead of slowly emptying them.
But I do not believe this. I have tried to show why I do not believe that any individual in the Moscow Kremlin is strong enough
to gather round him a wholly single-minded following which
would allow him to revert to the Stalinist rule of terror. Too
many of them, like their inferiors, have vested interests in the
status quo. They are self-made men of great ability, and their
wives (except when they have cast them off, as some have, in
favour of more showy prizes) are very much the sort of wives
who go with self-made men of great ability. Many are unscrupulous and quite ruthless and have done abominable things
in their climb to prominence. But most of them today, I think,
in the absence of a towering personality to cling to, find safety
and security in the idea of collective rule. There are not so
many of them in Kiev as there are in Moscow, only a handful
by comparison. But they are there—and not only in Kiev, but
in many large and growing cities throughout the Union. And,
in a sense, they are already becoming the prisoners of their
environment, which includes their families. This is no doubt an
over-simplified picture; but it is a truer picture, I think, than
the normal image of Soviet high society as a poker-faced phalanx
of coldly scheming revolutionary conspirators.

The other people who never appear in public are at the far
end of the scale: the very poor. But the very poor are found,
increasingly, among the old and helpless. There are very many
of them; but they grow fewer, and they count for less. If the new
pension schemes now proposed by Khrushchev come to anything, and if the promised rise in pay for the lowest ranks of
the unskilled workers is seriously intended, then, in the next five
years, the Soviet Union will be transformed: for the Kremlin

would never sanction more money for the useless and expendable unless it was certain that it could provide sufficient goods to meet the new demand.

And so we come back to our children, all of them born since the war, all growing up into a world in which the collectivization, the great purges, and even Stalin himself, will appear as ugly and meaningless shadows—unless they are repeated. Many of these children come from quite poor families, and some, through lack of ability, are doomed to perpetual poverty—unless the miracle happens, and the transition from "Socialism" to "Communism" is achieved in their lifetime. But more of them will rise above the level of their parents, so imperative is the demand for skilled and educated man-power—and woman-power too. And it seems to me that they have nothing to fear, at least by Russian standards, unless there is some terrible and lethal fight for power in the highest tier of the leadership, or unless the dark peasants scattered over the great plain which stretches away from the city on every side once more come into head-on collision with the central government. So long as neither of these things happens, their lives will not be so bad and will steadily improve.

Kiev is a city of trees and gardens. I have never seen so many leafy avenues and parks. From the air the city is hidden among green trees. In this capital city of the Ukraine, which once gave government to Russia, there is no trace of the untidy, idle, often dirty fecklessness of the Muscovite cousins. The Ukrainians in Kiev are showing now, as the Armenians in Erevan are also showing, what can be done to brighten life and make it less dreary even under the dreariest of regimes. Everywhere there are flowers. And although the shops are sketchy and the goods in them very expensive, there are compensations. Kiev is also a city of books. There are innumerable book-shops, and several great streets are lined in summer with little stalls, scores of them, selling nothing but books, new and second-hand, and always crowded. Sitting on a bench beneath the chestnut trees, ravished by the golden domes of the great cathedral of St. Sophia, I found myself thinking of the amazing frescoes in that church —eleventh-century figures showing a life, a flexibility, an attack, a certainty of execution that have been totally absent in Russia since the Tartar invasion swamped the growing and vigorous new culture which had its roots in Kiev, and then ebbed away, leaving Moscow, nurtured in vassalage, to fill the vacuum. And it occurred to me that history is not finished yet and that the Soviet Union may be standing on the threshold of an era of counter-colonization. After all they have suffered at the hands of Romanovs and Bolsheviks, the Ukrainians with their superior energy, their toughness and dourness, their innate practicality, may very well find themselves dominating increasingly a Soviet Union where these qualities are urgently in demand, bringing order and self-respect into a land which for all its rare qualities of the imagination suffers from the lack of both these qualities. The Ukraine has already exported a Khrushchev and a Kirichenko, to say nothing of a host of Party managers loyal to Khrushchev. The day may come when it will export trees and flowers and neat and sturdy cottages to the dusty wastes of the Great Russian villages—and, with these, a stiffening of fibre to resist the emotional excesses of the tyrant of the hour.

April 1956

APPENDIX

PICTURES AND SERMONS FROM THE SOVIET PRESS

To appreciate the full flavor of the contemporary morality campaign in the Soviet Union it is necessary to experience the style of the contemporary sermon. I include, therefore, a few typical examples.

THE MEANING OF LOVE

Dear Comrades,

In your letters to the editor of *Young Communist* you write about the difficulties you have met with in your personal life.

Every Soviet man will understand your efforts to behave in these circumstances in the way which the rules of socialist communal life and Communist morals require. You write about men who have betrayed your best hopes and expectations, and about women who, having become your wives and the mothers of your children, have broken their marital and maternal obligations.

How has it come about that love which seemed to burn with a bright flame suddenly died down to a faint glimmer and then went out altogether; that the married life of people, which began with a merry and happy marriage has some time later been broken by a severe family quarrel?

The fact is that we sometimes interpret love in a mistaken, simplified way. Some people accept and propagate as love something which it definitely is not. They consider, for instance, that any physically normal person is capable of loving, that "love at first sight" is possible, that a Soviet person is incapable of being jealous, since jealousy is a "bourgeois survival," and so on.

In the article "Love and Marriage in Soviet Society" it was said that people who were self-centred, greedy and petty and hard-hearted egoists, lovers of themselves, were as a rule incapable of such a noble and self-sacrificing emotion as love. The range of their feelings and interest is narrow and limited. It is still possible, unfortunately, to come across such people in our society.

In one of the Leningrad theatres, for instance, they know a certain lyrical tenor S. He has sworn profound devotion to more than one woman. He has been married three times in ten years, and three times has abandoned his family as soon as his wife has borne a child. What did S. seek in a woman? An object for satisfying his passion and sometimes a source for securing material advantages. It is hardly possible that such a man could ever love in the proper sense. He ingratiates himself, puts up a pretence, tries to play the lover and can deceive persons, worm his way into their good graces, as actually happened.

There are also such people among women. This is a moral abnormality and it still occurs in certain Soviet citizens as one of the most persistent survivals of capitalism, as a result of the influence of bourgeois ideology on the unstable psychology of a certain unstable section of our young people, undermined by bad upbringing.

There are specially many such abnormal people in that narrow and pitiful circle of people which is ironically called the "gilded youth" since their striving, and sometimes even their habit (we still have excessively "loving" parents!) towards a parasitical existence cannot be reconciled with the exalted self-sacrifice and nobility of love.

It naturally cannot be asserted that it is impossible to re-educate such people, that they cannot be imbued with a Soviet view on life. Many of them, under the influence of the collective, of the whole of our life, become in time genuine Soviet people. But they may be encountered by any of us in that form and with those æsthetic views which are characteristic of S. and his kind.

At the same time many of them have an attractive appearance, good manners, are outwardly polite, considerate, and sometimes appear with a halo of romance. They dress well and dance well. There is nothing surprising in the fact that even such greedy, bogus people can inspire "love at first sight."

"Love at first sight" is very deceptive. It is a kind of mirage, a result of the fact that a casually met, outwardly attractive person is arbitrarily credited with the qualities of that ideal person who is created in the imagination of a young man or girl. Very often such a mistaken view is relatively firm and lasting.

But this is not love, since it is impossible to love a person without knowing him. A person is known not by conversation or by questionnaires but by the way in which he reacts to life and to the difficulties which have to be faced in it. . . .

Genuine love is rich not only in joy and happiness. It sometimes causes people to suffer, to be jealous. It sometimes itself creates what appear to be insuperable difficulties in people's lives. How often do people have to carry on an intensive struggle for the person they love, for their responsive love, for the purpose that they should become in fact the person that you want, the person desirable to you. . . .

Love does not tolerate self-satisfaction or complacency. It is inconceivable without an effort for the constant improvement of the individual, for his perfection; without that spiritual breadth and generosity which is expressed in a persistent wish to make all the dearest and most cherished emotions and experiences worthy of the loved person. . . .

Many comrades are troubled about the question of jealousy. Do not let us enter into scholastic debates on this subject. Whether jealousy exists in the world or not, whether or not it is a survival of the past, or whether it is a quality which is inherent in one personality or another. It seems to us that love in our people also implies jealousy, but not physiological jealousy, not the jealousy of an owner who regards his wife as a chattel which belongs to him, but human jealousy as a fear, a secret terror of losing one's happiness, of losing the responsive love of the person one loves, of becoming in their eyes worse than others, of losing the right to their love. . . .

You are jealous of your wife now, Comrade Konov, but were you jealous of her when she loved you and was true to you? Did you strive to retain her love? What did you do to achieve that? Apparently you did very little.

It is not a question of long absence, obviously. Neither time nor distance will wipe out true love. Separation is powerless against love, against the feeling of duty which accompanies love, and finally against the feeling of personal dignity of a woman which would prevent her from behaving in the way in which your wife behaved, according to your letter. The fact that at the critical time your wife did not even have a feeling of womanly dignity is not her fault alone. You, her husband, and the collective in which she was brought up and worked are also to blame. . . .

Young Communist, March 1, 1954

BRINGING UP CHILDREN

In our country children are surrounded by universal love. For them, along with schools, there are created houses and palaces for pioneers, libraries, museums, theatres, cinemas, and children's newspapers and periodicals are published.

Special sanatoriums, pioneer camps, forestry schools, convalescent grounds, stadiums, parks and rinks are organized for the children's rest.

In short, all conditions are provided for our children to be happy, and they are really happy. Unfortunately, it is not all parents who have a proper understanding of what constitutes a happy childhood. Some consider that it is the child who lives in luxury and pleasure, and all whose wishes are satisfied who is happy. Others say that they lived in the rotten old days and did not have a childhood, so let their children go everywhere and see everything. Both kinds spoil their children.

What such views lead to we will show from our pedagogical experience.

Here is Vadik, pupil of the ninth class. At the age of sixteen one may say that he has been everywhere and tried everything. He has travelled over the Volga more than once in comfortable steamers. He has managed to visit Leningrad, Kiev, the Crimea, the Caucasus. Vadik has seen all the productions in the Moscow theatres. But nothing useful has settled into his mind and out of an excess of impressions it has been cluttered with much that is unnecessary and harmful. His stories about the shows he has seen, about historical monuments, about what he saw in the towns are empty and often simply vulgar. His parents have obviously tried to provide their son with as many distractions as possible, to satisfy his lively curiosity, and to make Vadik into an educated and cultured modern youth.

This excess of cultural distraction, unsuitable either to his age or to his development; these travels without any educational purpose or guidance have made him superficial, an empty babbler. Vadik has begun to look at everything with contempt. He goes to school as though it were not an educational establishment but a club where one can meet and rag about with one's friends. Lessons bore him, and he not only fails to listen, but sprawls about, hampering the teachers and his school-fellows. He is not used to doing homework and to learn a lesson is torture for him. . . .

The boy who in his childhood surprised his parents by his intelligence, clever beyond his years, knowing everything, having a brilliant memory, now becomes a real hobbledehoy, a slack braggart. He has not a trace of being a cultured youth. He has fallen behind those of his age group who started learning along with him and who are now honestly continuing their schooling.

Undoubtedly the reader will be interested to know also about Vadik's parents. What sort of people are they? The parents of this lad are ordinary Soviet people, sufficiently cultured and materially comfortably off, like the majority of Soviet families. They do not admit that they are responsible for the bad upbringing of their son, and cannot admit it because they have not taught him anything wrong, but on the contrary took him to theatres and other public and cultural places. What is there wrong in that, they ask, if the opportunity was there to allow the child to get to know beautiful Soviet towns with numerous monuments of culture and art? Yes, all this would not be so bad if Vadik's parents had not only shown him the things they were seeing, but had also interested themselves in finding out how all that he saw and

Cartoons from the Russian Press

"We'd better go on with our discussion, comrades. We can't possibly go home until that hooligan goes away." [Notice on the wall says: "Agenda for today's meeting: the fight against hooliganism."]

Militiaman: "Disgraceful! Why does public spirit put up with it?"

The Fixer: "Hey! This money you 'forgot'—it isn't enough!"

"Perhaps our Kolyenka will **manage to pass into** the Institute this year."

"There now! We must organize a fish trust!"

"Mama, I've failed my scholarship. You'll have to increase my allowance
for restaurant expenses."

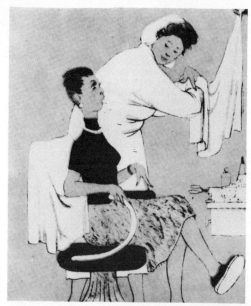

"I want an urchin
   cut, please."

"Give me a permanent."

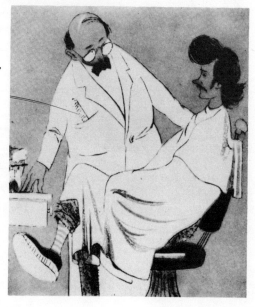

"Mama, I'm engaged."
"Who to, may I ask?"
"He's dark."

The Spares Man. [Notice in the window says: "No spare parts."]

"How is the loading going?"
"By conveyor belt."

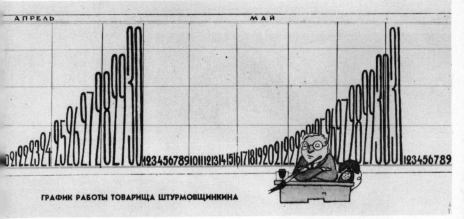

Graph showing the [monthly] productivity of comrade shock workers.

Preparations for the winter—according to methods recommended by the
Ministry of Agriculture.

"Hold it, boys! The inspection committee is coming!"

"But where's the barber shop, the laundry, the shoemaker? They were all
in the Plan!"
"And there they'll stay!"

"You mean to say you've no communal kitchen?"
"Indeed we have, but Anna Ivanovna is busy cooking!"

"We'll have to make do with this until the spring." [The cow is sitting on the architect's drawing of a cow-shed.]

— Ну, вот и вода пошла!

"You turn the tap—and lo! The water flows!"

Village pump—product of the **ornamental school** of architecture.

"Finish up your lecture! It's time to milk the object-lesson!"

Kolkhoz chairman: "Why hasn't your wife been going to work?"
Bookkeeper: "Because yours gets bored without company."

"Hush, children! Daddy's busy again with his political studies!"

"Please read me." [The book is called *Foreign Experience*.]

heard was registering in his mind, and had helped him to grasp what he saw, even if only in a childish way. But this did not happen. Receiving no proper guidance and without the necessary knowledge and experience, Vadik took it all in in his own way, falsely.

The parents are convinced that Vadik has become a difficult pupil, not from an overdose of various kinds of unnecessary pleasures and distractions, but as the result of the bad influence of his school companions, although they are unable to say which of them exactly. We can say that in fact there are none, but that Vadik undoubtedly has a bad influence on a certain section of the pupils.

Such hobbledehoys as Vadik are merely exceptions among our schoolchildren, but they exist and they even have their admirers.

We are bringing this subject into the open court of public opinion because the number of people like Vadik may increase. Each year the material well-being of the Soviet family is growing, and it is growing so fast that sometimes the culture of family relations lags behind material possibilities. This disproportion is the source of all manner of distortions in the family upbringing of children.

Here is a case where a mother came to the director of the school and expressed her annoyance because her daughter in the ninth class had been made to work for an extra hour or so in the school garden plot. What argument did the mother produce in favour of her daughter? Solely that at home she protects her daughter from any kind of physical work.

In many families it has begun to be a custom to give the children wine on the occasion of family festivals. If the child's birthday is being celebrated and its companions are invited, wine and sometimes vodka are given to the children in considerable quantities. This leads to sixteen- and seventeen-year-old lads and girls themselves trying to find various excuses for organizing merry evenings with "drinks for the boys." The harmful nature of this is obvious to everybody. . . .

The family needs the assistance not only of the school, but also the constant assistance of the party, trade-union, and Komsomol organizations. The whole Soviet public must take an active interest in the way in which the education of children is carried on in the family.

Teachers Gazette, February 10, 1954

STILYAGI

Their day usually begins after twelve. For them whistling new dance tunes and banging themselves on the thigh takes the place of morning exercise. Then comes the question—where to get some money? If they find any, they begin telephoning their friends.

"Hello, old chap. This is me, Genka! We've got a place. Now all we need is to gather the clans together. The old folks have gone to the country."

It is difficult to imagine anything more abnormal than the life of the young people called *stilyagi*. You will recognize a *stilyag* by his special "style" of conversation and in his manners—by his flashy suit and his impudent looks. When he meets you the *stilyag* will straighten his dazzling multi-coloured tie with an "elegant" gesture and as if by chance will flaunt an "unusual" signet ring. In order finally to stun you he will pull out of a foreign cigarette packet a very ordinary "Dukat" cigarette and confidentially leaning towards you with a well-greased head of hair will say significantly:

"They're marvellous."

The female of the species wears dresses which reveal her figure to the point of indecency. She wears slit skirts. Her lips are bright with lipstick. In summer, she is shod in "Roman" sandals. Her hair is done in the manner of "fashionable" foreign film actresses.

But the loud motley clothes of the *stilyag* are not only a tribute to "foreign" fashion, nor the sole manifestation of a perverted taste. If we examine the way these young people live and get to know them more closely we shall see that there is a certain consistency in everything which concerns the "style" they have chosen.

Until evening they just "kill" time: some on the beach at Sere-bryanny Bor or at the "Dynamo" boating station (if it is summer), some in billiard saloons or at the race-track, and others in the commission shops. . . . It is in the evenings that they array themselves in their full plumage and begin their "luxurious" life.

The *stilyagi* have their favourite meeting places in the centre of Moscow. From there they spread into the restaurants, clubs, and dance-halls, or stroll for hours on end along Gorki Street. Here you can meet the idle "dandy" . . . whom the *stilyagi* themselves call—evidently with reason—"The Broadway Blockhead." You will meet here a tall, well-fed youth, with an impudent face, nicknamed "Goggles." . . . He neither studies nor works—he leads a "dissipated" life. And there is [one] who has acquired popularity amongst the *stilyagi* by selling faked sanatorium passes. This coxcomb is dressed entirely and pretentiously in things "foreign." It is impossible to look at his coiffure—an unimaginable mop with a parting—without a contemptuous smile. He lives in Kuntsevo and works in Golitsyno, but in the evenings he loafs along Gorki Street. . . .

The most astonishing thing is that some students and young workers copy this worthless group of foppish debauchees and their bohemian way of life. . . .

Then there is . . . a Komsomol member and a fitter from a Moscow factory, who is always dressed up as brightly as a parrot. Unblushingly and without embarrassment, with the most serious expression [he] relates:

"I like all my things to be made according to the latest fashions. I am well up in men's fashions, and choose my clothes myself, on the basis of foreign films. As you see, I wear a long, green jacket with patch pockets and padded shoulders, and I wear narrow trousers. You ask whether my long hair gets in my way. Yes, it does. Especially at work. But I have found a way out and wear a thin strip of wire on my head. The workpeople laugh at my hair-do, but that's because they don't understand! I tried the 'Italian' style, but it didn't suit me. Nikolai Maslov has his hair done that way and has to put it in curlers at night. You think it's funny? I don't see anything funny in it. I dance 'à la mode.' In summer I used to go to the dance-place at Voronok station. You feel more at ease there somehow. The 'style' varies. Earlier it was the 'atomic,' then the 'Hamburg' style, now the 'Canadian' is all the rage."

The *stilyagi* love to discuss wines, the latest scandals they have perpetrated, to show off to each other their knowledge of the fashions. When they visit restaurants they contrive on each occasion to take away a "souvenir"—a knife or a fork or even a wine glass, so that the next day they can boast to their friends. A visit to a restaurant is a subject of special pride.

They lie shamelessly. When he gets to know a girl a *stilyag* will call himself a student of a film institute or of an institute of dramatic art. Perhaps he dreams of entering one of these centres of learning, to attach himself to art? Not at all. Their dreams are confined to the desire to wear "smart" boots, which are unfailingly narrow-footed and two sizes too large so that the toes turn up—a sign of special "chic" this! A foreign tie with a picture of a half-naked woman on it is the object of their envy.

How paltry is the internal life of these people, how worthless their interests, how mean their desires! Heaven knows where they get the low literature they read, the blood-and-thunders and other literary junk from the times of the Navrotskys and Bebutovs—this is what they read. The shrill cacophony of jazz, monotonous "boogie-woogie," convulsive "be-bop," recorded by amateurs and sold on the sly somewhere; post cards of sugar-sweet "beauties" in vulgar taste, and foreign "film stars"— this is the "art" they revel in.

When they organize a sort of "fashionable society" the *stilyagi* spend huge sums of money on collective entertainment, competing amongst themselves as to which "society" disposes of the most "currency" and how many cars it can "show off."

What sort of amusements do they go in for? Firstly, film shows at home —for which one pays admission—where, instead of films from the hiring agency, they show foreign rubbish, which again they acquire by mysterious ways. Secondly, dances.

Here is a picture from life. A group of *stilyagi* come into the dance hall. With studied laziness they look around at those present. Here one can "pick up" a girl you don't know and after the dance entice her into a restaurant. Here, ignoring the manager's protests, you can show the "grey" masses what it means to dance "à la mode."

. . . A student of the Lomonosov Institute of Chemical Technology slouches up to one of the flashily over-dressed young women.

"Let's do a Krakovyak with style."

"Only one dance. I'm already engaged."

"Merci."

As they dance they hardly move their feet. Their eyes are half-closed. On their faces is an expression of assumed indifference. They are dancing, you understand! . . .

An incorrect upbringing at home, an upbringing of irresponsibility and contempt for work, servility to anything "foreign"—i.e., to the tastes and morals of the bourgeois "jeunesse dorée"—these are the things which engender "style" and the *stilyagi*. . . . Ernst S. struck a fellow student with a knife while he was drunk. He counted on his father to fix it all, and in fact his father, an employee of the Ministry of Education of the RSFSR, instead of censuring his son's action, tried to protect him. . . .

There are not many *stilyagi*. They are few, a small handful of people standing alone against the background of the varied, seething life, filled with labour and romance, the genuinely beautiful life of our Soviet youth. But does this mean that we can overlook this ugly phenomenon, however petty and private it might be? Our public and our Komsomol organizations have answered this question by starting an uncompromising struggle with these parasites who imitate worthless foreign "fashions." Not long ago, for example, the students of the Moscow Mining Institute, the Historical Archives Institute, and the Potyomkin Pedagogical Institute refused to allow *stilyagi* at their club evenings and made fun of them. In many student-hall and factory newspapers the *stilyagi* have become the subject of trenchant satire, and their tastes and manners are debunked; they are shown to our youth in all their squalidness. This type of struggle against abnormal phenomena in life has already borne fruit.

We must make the leisure of our young people more interesting and varied. We must continuously, patiently, and allowing no compromise, train the artistic tastes of our youth—instil in them a repugnance to alien deformed "style" and implant a love of all that is genuinely beautiful, healthy, harmonious. . . .

Soviet Culture, January 18, 1955

SMALL TOWN LIFE

Let us say straight out that we do not intend to talk about sporting events, about boating parties, about the young people's evenings in the beautiful palace of the machine constructors, about readers' conferences. All this exists in Zlatoust and all this deserves due praise. Here we are going to talk about that inconsiderable section of the young people, about those young people who are incapable of spending their leisure properly, and who interfere with the leisure of their comrades, of the citizens of their town, and in some cases ruin their own lives.

Let us take a walk on a Saturday evening along the central street of the town, which by unwritten tradition has become the favourite place for evening walks. At first glance it seems that complete order reigns. But this is not quite true. Here comes a drunken party. The young people are excited and are laughing loudly. One of them jostles passers-by, pesters girls, and reinforces his "jokes" with coarse swear-words. Here come two young men, staggering along arm in arm. They are roaring a rollicking indecent song and push everybody out of their way right and left. What is that sound? Crash! You shudder involuntarily as an empty bottle splinters at your feet. Two youths who have emptied a half-litre bottle here in the street have hurled it under the feet of the passers-by. A Militiaman hurries up and leads off the disturbers of the peace.

Let us take a look at the sports ground, or the "Dynamo Garden" as it is sometimes called. In the evenings, dancing replaces sporting events. Most of the visitors to the garden, surrounding the veranda in a closely packed semi-circle, watch the dancers with a vacant air. There is nothing else to do here. On the stage and beyond the railing the crowd is packed like sardines. Some of the young men are dancing, each with one arm around his partner, holding a lighted cigarette in the other hand. They obviously consider this to be the height of smartness. By day the garden is peaceful, but in the evenings you may become the unwilling spectator of some outbreak of hooliganism. . . .

However, let us move on. We will go down the central street. . . . Here is the shady garden of the Lenin factory. It is pleasant to sit here in the evening in the shade. But suddenly your peaceful meditations are interrupted by loud banging like the sound of a roll of drums. Some youths of about fifteen or sixteen are hitting every seat they pass with their sticks. You also see this kind of sorry picture. A youth is sprawling on the grass. He cannot be more than about sixteen years old. He is very drunk. He tries to get up, takes two or three uncertain steps, and again falls flat on the ground. A few minutes later he makes another equally unsuccessful effort. Tomorrow, when the fumes have evaporated, this lad will probably be thoroughly ashamed of himself. How important it is that the moment should be used to warn him against repeating the performance, to convince him that drink will do him no good!

But enough of sketches from nature. In Zlatoust there are many cases of drunkenness, hooliganism, and other breaches of public order by young people. Most of these unpleasant scenes and outbursts of hooliganism take place in the evenings. This is no coincidence, since hooligans do not like broad daylight. They reserve their cowardly actions for the evening, so that in case of trouble they can slip down some dark alleyway or hide themselves in the crowds of strollers. The psychology of a hooligan is simple and primitive. "I can do as I like. The devil take your regulations." Such an "anarchist" considers it "smart" to trip up a woman, throw a cigarette end into somebody's face, drive his elbow into somebody's face, or pour a flood of foul language into the face of some girl. There are no limits to the impudence of a hooligan. He is capable of forcing his way into the ten-o'clock showing in a cinema with a ticket for the six-o'clock one, and hundreds of people will wait patiently for a good quarter of an hour while the noisy hooligan is brought to order. He is capable of picking a quarrel with some innocent passer-by and beating him up.

It must be said that the Militia cannot always recognize and restrain a hooligan in good time. It is here that the public organizations, and particularly the Komsomol, must come to its aid. . . .

It is not only young people who consider it not worth while to pay attention to acts of hooliganism. The Komsomol organizations of Zlatoust have not declared merciless war on hooliganism. They have not been aroused even by the fact that at the beginning of the school year a group of young women workers ceased to attend the school for young workers, because they were afraid to walk back to the hotel late at night. . . .

Among the young people involved in one kind of transgression or another one also finds Komsomols. Last year, thirty-five Komsomols were brought before the court on criminal charges, and twenty in the first four and a half months of this year. These are the facts. One would imagine that this should have shown the red light to the town Komsomol organization. Not a bit of it. The workers in the Gorkom have been slow to react to these facts. . . .

Some of the young people and adolescents who are left on their own, who do not study or work anywhere, are involved in hooliganism. Thus, for instance, in a gang of robbers which operated in the winter of this year in the Stalin Raion there were several young people aged eighteen to twenty who had never worked anywhere. But in the Gorkom, or in the Raikoms of the Komsomol, they cannot tell you how many such young people there are in the town, why they are idle, under whose influence they come. Putting it quite plainly, the Komsomol organizations are not interested in this group of young people. It is a pity. Who can be ignorant of the fact that idleness leads to nothing good, that it is idleness which is mainly responsible for involving people in bad company? . . .

Well-organized work by initiative groups and Komsomol headquarters along with the organs of the Militia is a method of fighting against hooliganism and transgressions against public order which has proved its value. But it is not enough. The decisive front in the fight against hooliganism is daily, meticulous educational work with young people, the influence of a healthy collective on the behaviour of a young person, the prevention of the possibility of bad behaviour right at the start. A hooligan is not born a hooligan, but becomes one. Consequently, at some point in his life—in the family, the school, or at work—the individual has been badly trained, and when he showed signs of kicking over the traces, he was not pulled back, was not given a severe helping hand. . . .

Pay day. The city restaurant. Two young men are sitting at a table, peacefully eating and attracting no attention to themselves. But a bottle and then another one appears on the table (in spite of the fact that drink is forbidden in the restaurant). The vodka acts in the usual way. The behaviour of the young men becomes careless. They light up cigarettes and begin to sing in tuneless voices. The middle-aged waitress tries to restrain them. "Stop it, my lads. It would be better if you went home." The simple, well-meant words become an offence. "Oh you old ——. It is time you were out of this world," comes the reply to the middle-aged woman. Why does a young man, whose hands have the callouses of honest toil on them, allow such words to pass his lips?

Hooliganism and drunkenness must be attacked from all sides, with all forces, and by every means, and an end must be put to this disgusting relic of the past. It cannot be tolerated that a small group of louts and hooligans should tarnish the fame of Zlatoust, the town of hereditary metal workers and engineers, of people who are enhancing the glory of our Fatherland.

Young Communist, July 7, 1955.

ON BEING AN ARTIST

The Soviet actor is a propagandist, an exponent of the highest, brightest, most humanitarian ideas—the ideas of Communism, of Communistic morality. So is it possible for him to disregard the demands made on him by the audience he educates, that he should himself observe most strictly the principles, standards, and rules established by society in all matters which are concerned with good behaviour, morals, and ethics?

How disappointing, how painful it is to hear of cases in which, owing to thoughtlessness, weakness of will, or irresponsibility, certain individuals connected with art transgress against these standards and rules. . . .

Every case of bad behaviour on the part of some particular artist is made worse by the very fact that it casts a slur on all persons connected with the arts. This inevitable generalization cannot be refuted by logical arguments or references to the fact that such disorderly persons and hooligans are only odd units in the mass of Soviet creative workers. All the workers in art have to bear the moral responsibility for these persons. All the more strictly, all the more harshly must it be demanded therefore that the standards of socialistic communal life should be observed by every member of any creative collective.

At the same time there is probably no other section of our society in which there is such a degree of tolerance or even protectiveness for some action or other as there is among workers in the arts. All right, they will reproach the culprit of the latest scandalous "celebration," they will tell him some unpleasant home truths with a kindly intonation in their voices, they will accept his usual "word of honour" that such "mistakes" will not be repeated, and all will be peace and harmony once more. A short time later, in connection with some new outbreak, all this routine of "making it up" will be repeated, ad infinitum.

One usually hears in such cases, "Well, there is nothing to be done about it. He will have to be forgiven. After all, he is a talented artist!" It is on a benevolent attitude toward their gifts that people like Druzhinikov and Rumyantsev and other people with bigger names than theirs base their calculations, when they throw aside, as not being "binding" for them, those rules of conduct which are acknowledged and complied with by "ordinary mortals."

Has not the time arrived, however, when we ought to say "Enough"? Have done with calculations based on talent, because talent is not a merit but a duty. Talent as such is not a gift of nature. It is a gift of society to the individual, since it is only the life of that society, its ideas, its struggles, its builders and members which give content to talent and allow it to form and develop. Talent is communal capital and the individual who possesses it may only multiply it, and certainly must not "squander it in a disorderly way." It is not an idle remark that from him unto whom much is given, much is also required. . . .

Communal exigence in respect to talent is perfectly legitimately extended also to the behaviour of the talented person in ordinary everyday life. Not less, but more must be demanded from such people than from others! Bad examples set by a talented person, who always has numerous "admirers," are particularly infectious, and therefore are particularly dangerous—socially dangerous.

The spirit of Bohemia, disgusting and noisome, has long ago and forever been banished from the sphere of the workers in literature and the arts in the country of socialism. With us there are no causes which so often make talented people go off the rails in a bourgeois society, torn by internal contradictions, humiliated, insulted, hounded at every step. By contrast with bourgeois society, which places actors and artists at the service of capital, in an extremely difficult and degrading situation, in our country workers of the arts enjoy particular esteem and honour. That is completely understandable. With us art does not serve a handful of the over-fed "elect," it serves the people.

But high standing carries its obligations. Having placed an artist on a high position worthy of his gifts, the Soviet people have the right to demand, and do demand, that the artist should set an example and act as a model in all matters concerned with morality.

The artist remains under the eye of his audience, not only when he is on the stage, but even when he is walking in the street, eating in a restaurant, travelling in a bus, or resting at a health resort. Yes, even within the walls of his own house he is really in a glass case. He must never forget that.

Nobody, of course, is going to demand of Soviet artists that they should live like saints. Nobody is going to demand that they should deny themselves the things which are permitted to everybody. An artist is a human being, with all the characteristics of a human being, and it is unnecessary to try to argue the fact.

But, dear comrade artists, whatever you may be doing, remember that people are watching you! Watching you attentively and affectionately. Watching you in order to learn and to imitate. It was not without reason that Konstantin Sergeevich Stanislavski, addressing the great Ermolova, wrote that her inimitable ennobling influence had "educated a whole generation."

This ennobling influence of an artist emanates not only from his creation, but also from his life.

When talent is properly used it is capable of arousing, and does arouse, the enthusiasm of the audience. But woe to the talent when its bearer arouses the disgust of the people around him by his unworthy, amoral behaviour.

Talent and vice are "two things which cannot be reconciled."

Soviet Culture, December 10, 1955

A MOST EVIL VICE

When I wrote about the hard-drinking littérateurs, I considered it necessary to call attention firstly to those "engineers of human souls," the immoral behaviour of whom is incompatible with their role as educators and teachers of life. Such people discredit all the honest and respected writers. I did not concern myself with the indecent behaviour of drunken actors and composers, the names of whom have become synonymous with tavern boozers and hooligans. I supposed that the theatre-going public would become agitated and would demonstrate its attitude towards a Bohemian way of life alien to us. But many people probably see nothing humiliating or shameful in this intoxicated style of living. And now working Soviet people write with anger and indignation regarding the behaviour of certain eminent leaders of art while on tour.

Drunkenness is a terrible and destructive vice. This vice, like a hideous disease, used to spread like an epidemic before and affected fresh generations, not sparing adolescence even. This vestige of capitalism has still not been removed by far. It embraces even certain circles of the town and village intelligentsia. A strange and, in my view, disgusting attitude towards this primitive vice has arisen—not only complacent tolerance, but also amused sympathy. Drunken people totter about the streets, insult the passers-by, use filthy language, get into fights, and lie on the pavement, and people have become used to these outrages as to an inevitable evil; even the Militia pays no attention to them. An intoxicated person is in the power of his lowest instincts. He is beyond society and beyond moral norms. . . .

One need not have raised the alarm if it had not been the case that drunkenness among many of our people is an everyday occurrence. The destiny of those given to this vice is the same everywhere: first a drink, at one's own wish or through the compulsion of friends, then a daily yearning for intoxication, then—drunkenness, debauchery, madness, hooliganism, the loss of ability to work, the disintegration of the family, crime, and then the dock.

A group of women from Yaroslavl points out woefully: "Everyone knows, and particularly women, what unhappiness and dishonour a husband or son who drinks can bring to a family." And they are indignant that the Party and Komsomol organizations are not carrying on there a struggle against drunkenness. The head of the chemical laboratory of a Siberian factory reports that the heads of the workshops at the factory get drunk. One of them arranged a spree with his subordinates in the workshop even. A capable worker in the past, he has reached workshop leader. He was an inventor and has designed several automatic machine-tools. But he began drinking and has reached a bestial state. He has created hell in his family. His wife and children have left him.

At the same factory the deputy head of a workshop, a good specialist, has also begun drinking, not, perhaps, without the influence of hard-drinking neighbours, and has also ruined his family. Debauchery, hooliganism, and criminality have brought him into the dock.

The author says indignantly: "It is much easier at our factory to buy any quantity of vodka than a paper or a magazine. One 'bistro' is situated directly by the factory gates, another five hundred yards to the right, and a third three hundred yards to the left. And they are situated throughout the town on the same scale. But the nearest Soyuzpechat bookstall is four or five miles from the factory."

Many of the authors of the letters call the "snack-bars" "chapoks," that is to say, pubs. "You go inside the chapok; all around there is dirt and drunken people rolling on the floor in their disgusting vomit." And then from here there is spoilage, machinery breaking down, and violation of labour discipline.

A worker from a Minsk factory writes with chagrin that drunkenness there has overcome many of the workers, including good workers. They cause scenes in public places and play the hooligan. Certain well-known actors and artists do not lag behind them. Youths—children of these workers and employees—get drunk, play the hooligan and indulge in theft. In trams, in suburban trains, and not always only in suburban ones, drunken people say filthy things, threaten the passengers, and extort money. The passengers do not dare to muzzle the hooligans, and if anybody is brave enough to reason with them, they are inevitably subjected to insults. . . .

In many places so-called religious festivals are celebrated, people—whole collective farms at a time—drinking for weeks on end. Of course, work on the collective farms drops off with tremendous loss both for the state and the collective farm and for the collective farmers, and after this sort of spree people do not come to their senses for some time.

Instead of untiringly struggling against religious prejudices and superstition, instead of educational work among the masses, certain leaders and administrators are remaining aloof and regard all these outrages "apathetic towards either good or evil," and themselves are not even averse to taking part occasionally in these "festivities."

There are people who are used to this. But this "getting used" to disgusting sights and the immoral behaviour of not only people of little culture, but even so-called observers of culture, is not to the merit of the Soviet citizen. For some reason many people still regard this ominous vice in a passive way. But is not the creation of strong public opinion against drunkenness our affair?

Though in the dark times of Tsarist despotism they used to say, using Dostoevski's words, that a rascal gets used to anything, in our great Socialist age it is shameful and dishonourable to repeat that. Our people is creating amazing historic things and it showed wonders of heroism in the Great Patriotic War and on the working home-front. It can and must exterminate and burn out this alcoholic leprosy which is disfiguring the body and soul of man.

The problem of upbringing in its widest sense is the first problem in this respect. Upbringing is frequently talked about at meetings, sessions, and at all sorts of conferences. The same thing is repeated like a formula known for a long time. But, after all, a formula will not solve the question. The problems of upbringing, however, are burning, extremely pressing and alarming questions which demand an immediate and effective solution. I put forward this problem as one of self-education for our Soviet citizens, as a public matter and as one of the important obligations of our Party, Komsomol, and trade-union organizations. The personal behaviour of a Soviet person is not a private matter, it is inextricably and directly connected with the collective and the milieu in which he lives. At the home, the hostel, the workshop, the institution and the school—everywhere, a person finds himself in very close relations with people and fully dependent on a system of collective living. A new generation has matured which does not know capitalist oppression. But individualistic passions and low proclivities are influencing this generation, too, like a congenital disease.

What is it that furthers the persistence and stormy manifestations of these vile vestiges? In my opinion it is the defects in the system of education, lack of culture in everyday life, and bureaucratism in certain public organizations, where there is no living person behind the instruction and the letter. The problem of socialist culture does not only include school and cultural organizations, but the family and street as well. This subject requires special analysis.

The authors of some of the letters point out that in books, the theatre, and the cinema, drunkenness is frequently depicted and drunken scenes are shown with relish. The actors act these scenes with particular pleasure and temptingly for the sympathetic audience. And the authors of the letters ask with reason—What educational importance can such acting have?

What, then, are the practical measures for the struggle against drunkenness? I think that this burning question demands general discussion at enterprises, in organizations, educational establishments, and at collective farms. There is need for all public organizations to pay serious heed to the struggle against drunkenness. It is essential to select carefully for trade academies and factory schools sober and cultured skilled workers, and not to tolerate drunken and foul-mouthed workers.

Cases of drunkenness and uncalled-for behaviour by workers and employees should be branded in wall newspapers and those with wide circulation. It is essential to forbid categorically the sale of vodka to adolescents and to deny them access to restaurants where there is blaring jazz. After all, we have the most talented and most wonderful music, which has educated great numbers of our advanced people. Control should be established over radio broadcasts and recordings, and the dissemination of vulgarity should not be allowed.

The work of the Society for the Dissemination of Political and Scientific Knowledge should be stepped up and activized. All measures should be used to develop amateur cultural activity and to make it interesting and recreative. The City Soviets should allot ground-floor premises in new buildings for open reading rooms and libraries.

Advertisements such as "Drink Soviet Champagne" and "Smoke Such-and-Such Cigarettes," of which there are a wealth, should be taken away. They are harmful and expensive. I am not a purist, but trade enterprises advertise drink too zealously, and, after all, our trade is also policy, quite different from the policy of capitalist hucksters. This policy of ours needs to be carried out wisely without violating or disturbing the most important business of our Party and our society—the upbringing of the genuine, worthy Soviet person—a creator, thinker and fighter for the new things of Communism.

F. Gladkov, Literary Gazette, July 29, 1954

BEGGARS

I frequently travel between Moscow and the suburbs, and more than once I have had to observe this kind of incident. The electric train is on the point of leaving the station when a man in ragged clothing enters the carriage and in a drunken voice drones some old music-hall song or a "sob-stuff" ditty, telling of an aged mother, a son who dies from his wounds, and orphan children. Then he addresses the passengers: "Brothers and sisters, fathers and mothers, spare a kopeck for a man disabled in the war." Another one, not wasting his voice on any solo singing, begins immediately to go from passenger to passenger; giving out the smell of vodka, he demands insistently: "Brother, give an ex-serviceman something for a drink!"

The memory of fallen comrades is immeasurably dear to us Soviet people; we know the price of a mother's tears and a soldier's blood. To me, who served at the front, it is especially offensive to see idlers and extortioners making use of words which are sacred to each one of us. Even though there be few of these beggars, even though there be literally isolated individuals, nevertheless it is time to ask who they are who stretch out their hands for alms? To whom do Soviet people give their hard-earned roubles and kopecks?

Some of the beggars represent themselves as men who served at the front, men disabled in the Great Patriotic War. Formally this may be so, but only formally. The genuine disabled men from the front are those who cannot imagine life without work, if that is possible, if they have the strength. . . . They shed their blood for the right to labour in a free land. Not all, unhappily, are able to do full-time work; we know disabled men who are deprived of this possibility by the state of their health. But these too try to find some occupation suited to their strength, not to lose contact with public life, and, most important of all, they endeavour to live as people who retain the dignity of Soviet man.

But those who slouch through the railway carriages are drunkards, who have lost their human countenance, who speculate on the sympathy of Soviet people for the disabled, on their memories of the fallen. They want money in order to spend it right away on drink at the next station beer-shop. Sometimes these beggars pretend to have diseases or deformities. Moving through the carriage, such a one will sigh and groan, but you should see how nimbly he leaps from carriage to carriage if the communicating doors are shut. . . .

State expenditure on social insurance is increasing year by year in our country. The network of kindergartens, hostels, children's homes, is being extended. The word "waif" has fallen out of use. The State shows great concern for those disabled by the war or by labour. Industrial training, the supply of invalid carriages to ex-servicemen, special homes for those disabled in the war, allowances for their children in trade and technical institutes—there is no end to it. Provided there is the wish to work, employment will always be found to suit their desires and their strength. Of course, sometimes it is not easy for a large family and for a widow who brings up the children alone. In difficult periods they come to the mutual aid office for a loan, they ask for a free travel-pass for a child, and count up their money more than once before making a purchase. But a self-respecting person will not go with outstretched hand, he will not exchange an honourable life of toil for the life of a drone. Most important of all—in our country a person is not alone. Whatever misfortune may have befallen him, whatever the distress into which he may have come, he will always find friends, he will find help and protection. He will not have to live like a beggar, as thousands of people in capitalist countries are forced to do, where unemployment, hunger, and deprivation drive a man on to the street, where no one will help, though he may die of exhaustion. . . .

Why, nevertheless, do drones, who make a profession of "beggary," appear in our streets and railway carriages?

I think that here a share of the blame lies with the Militia, who sometimes are lenient to these people. One can hear some Militia officials say something of this sort: "He has committed no crime, I have not the right to detain him." Perhaps that is correct, perhaps this is not a crime according to the Criminal Code. But, in my opinion, a Militiaman not only has the right, but is duty bound to remove from a railway carriage or clear off the street a tipsy beggar, who is disturbing public order and dishonouring the high calling of a Soviet citizen. . . .

ATHEISM FOR THE YOUNG

The Soviet school as a means of the Communistic education of the growing generation cannot on principle take up any attitude towards religion other than the attitude of an implacable fight against it. The general theoretical foundation of Communistic education is Marxism, and that is irreconcilably hostile to religion. . . .

In what practical way then is this implacable attitude of the Soviet school towards religion to be expressed? What tasks does it set to the school?

Very many people consider that these tasks consist solely in rooting out of the minds of certain of the pupils those religious superstitions and prejudices which have been implanted in them by their home surroundings or their surroundings generally.

This is not entirely true. Such a view about the tasks of the Soviet school in respect to religion is too simplified. If we root out one set of superstitions and prejudices, we have no guarantee against the appearance of another set under the influence of the same surroundings. . . .

Naturally the uprooting out of the minds of the pupils of those superstitions and prejudices with which they may arrive in school is an essential and important duty for the school, but it is still only one of the duties of the Soviet school. As a whole, however, its tasks are far broader. It is obviously necessary to carry on the work of educating and training children in school in such a way as not only to eradicate from the minds of some of them those superstitions and prejudices which already exist, but also to make all the pupils immune against any religious views whatsoever with which they may come into contact in the sphere which surrounds them.

But even that is not all.

Having in mind that religion is one of those ideological survivals of former exploiting social relationships, and that the sooner it is overcome the better for the success of our building of Communism, the Soviet school must inculcate in its pupils an implacable attitude towards religion, a consciousness of the need to fight against it, and a desire to take an active part in that fight. Formulating all this briefly, one may say that the task of the Soviet school in this sphere of ideological-educational work consists in educating the pupils, the future builders of Communism, to be conscious and convinced atheists, active fighters against all manner of superstitions and religious views. . . .

In order to accomplish successfully the complicated tasks of bringing up active atheists, it is necessary not to confine ourselves merely to the implanting of scientific knowledge in the pupils, but to link that knowledge into a scientific-materialistic system and to lead the pupils on undeviatingly to a formation of the foundations of a materialistic world outlook. It is necessary also in connection with this to carry on a direct and open criticism of the religious views about the world and of the moral attitude and feelings which are based on such views. In other words, it is necessary to give the whole of the educational work of the school a clearly expressed anti-religious direction and to make it aggressive against religious views. . . .

In certain cases the whole exposition of a new subject by the teacher can be given an anti-religious character. This happens when a particular subject on the curriculum is entirely devoted to a particular religion, to the activities of a particular religious organization, to individual religious teachings, and so on. Such, for instance, are subjects out of the course on the history of the ancient world and the middle ages: the origin of religion, the religion of ancient Egypt, the origin of Islam, the power of the Roman popes, the Inquisition, etc. Such also is the question of the reactionary nature of the religious teaching about the soul (course of human anatomy and physiology) and others.

All this together, amplified in out-of-school hours by certain special exercises of an atheistic character in the form of out-of-school readings, talks, lectures, etc., makes up what might best be called the anti-religious educational work of the school. Such work is a specific and important means of Communistic education. It is only in this way that we can instil in the pupil a profound appreciation of all the evil of religion, a conviction of the need to fight against it, and a striving to take an active part in that fight. . . .

Finally it is necessary to warn the pupils against any tactless actions in relation to the clergy, since every action of this kind is regarded by believers as an insult to their religious feelings and therefore will only strengthen such feelings among believers. Pupils must understand that the question is one of religion and not of the servants of the cult. When religion dies out, there will be no clergy.

E. I. Perovski, *Soviet Pedagogics,* May 1955

INDEX